# Seven Candles for my Life

## by

## Peggy Frampton

The Pentland Press Limited
Edinburgh · Cambridge · Durham

First published in 1990 by
Englang Press
This edition published in 1994 by
The Pentland Press Ltd.
1 Hutton Close
South Church
Bishop Auckland
Durham

ISBN 1 85821 162 X

Typeset by Elite Typesetting Techniques, Southampton.
Printed and bound by Antony Rowe Ltd., Chippenham.

Dedicated to my grand-daughter, Joanna

With thanks to my late husband,
Col. George Frampton, for his constant
support and to Mrs Jacqueline Wadsworth
for her assistance and encouragement

# Contents

# Prologue

*July 21st 1909 Bahia, Brazil*

The Portuguese lady rose from her knees, walked to the altar and lit a candle. She had done this every day for a week. Today, July 21st, she had heard that the English lady was in labour, and the baby for whom she had said the Novena was expected at any moment.

Graças.

I was that baby.

P.F.

# Early Days in England

I arrived in this world when the household was in double mourning. A fortnight earlier my maternal grandfather had died of yellow fever. One week later, my grandmother also died – of shock, the Portuguese doctor said. My mother dearly loved her father and wanted a son. She was disappointed when she did not get what she had ordered and would have returned the goods had it been possible. But there I was, the second daughter with little to recommend me in looks.

A few months later my parents, with their two very small daughters, old Nana and Gladys, the nurserymaid, sailed for England. They rented a large farmhouse in Crawley, Surrey for six months, where my brother Jack was born on September 3rd 1910. My father was then working for Lamphort and Holt Shipping Line in Bahia, Brazil, as their visiting agent to large coffee estates. There he met the managers to acquire estimates of the size of their crops. He would then go back to Bahia, meet the captains of the cargo ships and inform them how much space in their holds would be required for the coffee. A pleasant and versatile job which he enjoyed. My mother, however, had decided that they must live in England. She had suffered so much sorrow and ill health in Brazil and did not think it was a suitable climate in which to bring up a family.

## Salcombe 1912-1916

1912 saw us established in Salcombe, South Devon. Our house was situated on a hill overlooking the bay and estuary and out to sea – on one side of the entrance to the bay stood Gara Rock and on the other Prawl Point. There were only three houses on the hill – the Farquharsons', ours and the Brittons'.

A few memories of that period: my father playing on the piano in the evening after we'd been tucked up in bed – we could hear him playing while we went to sleep; my father taking us sailing on his friend Lionel Clayton's yacht – mackerel fishing with two old fishermen brothers in a small boat whose engine seemed frequently to stop working. We got very excited when the mackerel jerked on our lines and quickly became entangled as we hauled in hand over hand. Then there was the day we went to a birthday party at the Brittons next door. Suddenly we heard a tremendous boom out at sea. We saw a small ship break in two and sink in a matter of minutes. That was in 1914. All the maids and nannies and children and anyone with a pair of hands rushed down to the beach to help haul out the lifeboat and pull it with ropes over the sand into the sea.

Another day we were being taken by paddle steamer up the estuary to Kingsbridge on our weekly visit to the dentist. The previous night the ocean liner *Asturias* had foundered on Prawl Point after being torpedoed. She was carrying hundreds of Blue Coat wounded soldiers. Some of the survivors were on our paddle steamer and I shall never forget the horror of seeing men with no legs or arms, or blindfolded or on stretchers, although I could only have been five years old at the time.

Among happier memories were all three of us children going to church on the back of a donkey led by our governess who walked the one mile. We always fought and shoved for position on the poor creature who had a small patch of mange on his back which we did *not* like sitting on. Also, in summer, the milk invariably tasted of garlic which the cows ate on their way to be milked. We played rounders on the beach and ran about naked like small sea sprites over the empty sands.

We three children made up a rhyme which we thought hilariously funny. It went thus:

*Jackie, wackie*
*Perry, werry wackie*
*Perry werry winkle, Tinkle, Tackie.*

Everybody's names could be altered to rhyme this way, e.g.

*Joanie Woanie,*
*Perry werry Woanie,*
*Perry werry winkle, Tinkle, Toanie.*

Our favourite word was Mummy as it inevitably ended in Tummy. Why this should cause such merriment or where and how we thought of this jingle I know not.

While still very young Mother took us to all the museums in London as well as the art galleries. The only one we really

*Joan and Peggy – First game of croquet.*

enjoyed was the Natural History Museum. We loved the dinosaurs and huge octopuses and dragons.

On one occasion the Farquharsons, our neighbours, left their nine children in charge of their nannies and forbade them to take out a boat until their return. The two eldest boys on holiday from school procured a large wine barrel, cut off the top and put out to sea. Mercifully it sank quite quickly and they were rescued by some astonished fishermen. When scolded they said they had not disobeyed their parents as they had gone out in a barrel and not a boat. We thought they were heroes!

## *Eastbourne 1917*

A temporary house in Meads near Beachy Head. My mother had sold our beloved Furse Hill, the house at Salcombe, while my father was in the 1914-18 war. We moved to Eastbourne where she felt she could do more Red Cross war work. I loathed it: the shingle beaches – schools everywhere and always so cold – the grown-ups called it 'bracing'. We still had our sweet Scots nanny, Jeannie Macpherson from Aberdeen (who dosed us with castor oil every Saturday night!), and also a series of Ma'm'selles: Belgian, French and finally Swiss.

Every summer we entrained for Ballater to stay with my Great Aunt Isabella and Uncle Fred Yarrow. They took a large shooting lodge, Monaltrie House, on the river Dee, which had three miles of fishing. We adored these holidays. There were lots of cousins and relations and dozens of guns and fishing tackle, a pony trap and picnics. One of the ghillies helped me to catch my first salmon on the Dee. I'm told it weighed 9 lbs and when a family friend called to announce the birth of her grandchild saying it weighed 8 lbs I remarked scornfully that I had caught a salmon weighing far more than that.

On one of our train journeys to Scotland while crossing the Firth of Forth my mother burst into our carriage and commanded us to get up and look through the windows. Below us lay the British Fleet at anchor – a wonderful splendid sight in those days.

The only uncomfortable things about those train journeys were the handkerchiefs we were forced to wear on our heads by Jeannie. She knotted them at the four corners and enclosed our hair under them 'so that ye willna catch the ringworm'.

## *Forest Row and Pixton Hill Farm 1919-1922*

After World War I my father bought some land with a small house on it at the top of Pixton Hill above Forest Row, there to breed and sell thousands of free ranging chickens. The birds lived comfortably in converted army huts, while we lived uncomfortably in too small a house while it was enlarged to accommodate us all.

The big house and property below us belonged to Admiral Sir Stanley Colville and the Lady Adelaide Colville. He and my father got on well together. They had three sons – John, Richard and Freddy. For a short time Freddy and I shared lessons with my Ma'm'selle and the village schoolmaster. Freddy was always telling me marvellously exciting stories in which the Germans had invaded England and there had been a pitched battle in their park. That there was not a word of truth in this, was part of the fun.

Apart from an unaccountable desire to make a miniature Chinese garden in a copse below the fields, the short time I spent at Pixton Farm is not memorable.

What became of the Colville boys? My brother Jack was at prep school in Eastbourne and my elder sister at boarding school there also. I was sent off to Vevey in Switzerland (with our Ma'm'selle) to learn French. After a few weeks of acute homesickness I went to a small English finishing school called La Peraille.

During the Christmas holidays the family came out and we all went up to the mountains to ski. They had taken a large chalet in a village called La Comballas. Snow began to fall a week before Christmas and continued unceasingly until after New Year. There was solid snow up to the balcony and my father, with the help of some peasants, had to saw off great blocks of frozen snow from the roof lest it should collapse. On New Year's Eve we heard a tremendous roaring and crashing sound followed by silence. Next morning some one hundred yards along the hillside we found the scars of a large avalanche which had taken away everything in its path, including a farmstead, all the livestock and the farmer and his wife who owned it.

Ski clothes in the 1920's: the garments we wore then were heavy woollen objects, balaclava helmets, very thick ski boots, khaki puttees wound round our legs to our knees and joined with our breeches. A jacket or heavy pullover and a pair of woolly gloves completed the outfit. There were no ski-lifts then and we carried small rucksacks on our backs containing our lunch, i.e. raisins and bars of chocolate. In each of our sacks was a waxing iron with its fuel and a matchbox, this in order to wax our skis after removing, from under the skis, the strips of skin which helped us to climb up the mountains. There were *pistes* near our village and we had wonderful skiing on thick virgin snow wherever we wished to go; also where we did *not* wish to go – as when my brother told me to follow him straight down the mountain and I took a slightly diagonal line and unintentionally went over an enormous snow-covered ski jump.

By the time I came home from Vevey Pixton Hill Farm had been sold and my parents had moved to London, to 55 Avenue Road which led off Regents Park. It was a delightful house with a fair-sized garden. Our neighbours were mostly famous actors: the Du Mauriers, the Forbes Robertsons and further up on Hampstead Heath, Pavlova and her husband.

My brother went to Harrow and I to the Francis Holland School at Princes Gate in London. It had an inscription carved into the stone lintel above the entrance: 'The Francis Holland School for the daughters of Gentlemen. May they ever be a comfort to their mothers and a pride to their fathers'!

While there I also attended the Royal Academy of Music, my teacher being Lady McEwan, wife of Sir John McEwan, Principal of the Academy. After I passed my LRAM exam, at the age

*Peggy – age 13.*

of 17, my great aunt gave me the choice of a) being presented at court or b) going out to Burma for six months where my mother's cousin, Edward Musson, commanded the Manchester Regiment. I chose the latter.

Here it is necessary to back-track. During all those years the person we loved most was our great aunt Madrina (god-mother). On arrival in England from Brazil we spent our first days with her in her very large and luxurious flat, 6 North Gate, Regents Park. I remember all three of us sitting in our dressing gowns drinking hot milk on a red Morocco-covered tall fender in front of the nursery fire. Shy-Shy, Madrina's Pekingese dog, used to run up and down the long corridors with us, making the Chinese scrolls fly out from the walls.

In the morning before being dressed our first visit was to Madrina's bedroom. We would sit in a row at the foot of her huge brass double bed, eiderdown drawn up to our small armpits, while she sat opposite us amongst piles of frills and lace-edged pillows. She would make pale gold tea, an elaborate ritual, with water boiled in a silver kettle on a stand and burner beside her bed. The eggshell-thin china cups and saucers and teapot were flower patterned and so pretty. We would each be handed a saucer with a little pool of yellow tea in the centre and in the middle of that a square sugar lump. We used to hold our saucers very carefully so that nothing was spilt, and drink sips of tea, after (I regret to say) blowing on it to cool it. She would ask us if we liked it and invariably all three would reply: ' 'licious tea, 'Drina, 'licious tea'.

Taking Shy-Shy for walks in Regents Park was a daily exercise. He did not like it and would sit down and refuse to budge. My mother was accompanying us one day when a squirrel jumped from a branch on to her hat, ran round the brim and leapt back into the tree again. We always hoped it would do it again but it never did. As the years passed Madrina became the focus of all family gatherings – all ages adored her – she was full of humour, fun and endless 'ideas'. She had her own 'girl' in Masquelin and Cooks who always procured seats in the stalls for First Nights at the theatre, also for Gala Nights and Royal Command performances. Madrina also enjoyed taking us to the circus and to pantomimes.

She went with us and all the maids up to Ballater every summer and had a passion for white heather and the Royal Family. When at the age of nine years I had to have my appendix out, Sir Sydney Beecham the physician called in Sir Crisp English, the famous surgeon who operated on King Edward the Seventh. He agreed to operate on me in Madrina's flat, one end of which had been converted into a private hospital ward! Could that possibly happen today – 1989? I think not.

*Great Aunt Madrina.*

Visits to the zoo were special. Our Great Uncle Fred Yarrow was a member of the Royal Zoological Society, and we were privileged to go behind the scenes and visit some of the animals in their 'houses'. One memorable afternoon Madrina took us there with a bag of buns for the elephants and nuts for the monkeys. Unfortunately when we got to the last elephant in the row there were no buns left. Each elephant was in a separate stall and held out his trunk for us to give him a bun. We fed them one by one until we got to the last elephant. Unfortunately by then all the buns were finished. Although Madrina said a few soothing words when the trunk came out expectantly, this manoeuvre did not amuse the elephant who promptly put his trunk into his water trough and raising it aloft sprayed water all over us – to our huge delight.

The first musical comedy we went to, when I must have been eight years old, was *The Maid of the Mountains* – was Ivor Novello in it? I don't remember, but we loved it and continued singing the songs for years.

*

# Burma

The excitement of packing up large trunks, hat boxes and shoe boxes; having a riding habit made by Simpsons and taking riding lessons with Miss Cadogan-Smith in the park! Oh! Topping!

The voyage out on a Bibbie liner came up to all my romantic dreams – dances every night, very mild flirtations, flying fish skimming over the deck – Port Said and the big shop, Simon Artz. The Gully Gully men who came on board and produced live fluffy yellow chickens from behind one's ears. The Fuzzy Wuzzies who did the coaling at night in the canal, illuminated by lamps and looking like Devils! Throwing pennies overboard for little boys who dived for them like fish. Dolphins racing alongside the ship. Crossing the line and the fun on board. At last, sad farewells and our arrival in Rangoon.

I was taken off in a private launch belonging to the Manager of the Bank of India. The first night was spent with him and his family in Rangoon. I lay awake for hours, smelling the wonderful smell of the East, and hearing cicadas for the first time. It was strange to be woken up in the morning by a turbaned Burmese servant bringing me tea and a small fat banana on a tray. A visit to the gleaming Gold Shwedagon Pagoda and finally setting off by train at sundown for Mandalay.

*Mandalay!* To this day it spells romance. As darkness fell over the paddy fields on either side of the railway, women

11

were still working ankle deep in the waters of the Irawaddy rice fields. All the insects in the world seemed to be humming, women called to their children and splashed out of the rice fields. The smell of frangipani mixing with unknown scents and enveloping me and the world in sleep.

## Mandalay

I remember leaning out of the window a little apprehensively and seeing dear Laura and Edward Musson waving to me over the heads of swarms of Burmese families and a few Europeans who had come to meet relations and friends. To my disappointment, we were not able to linger in Mandalay as Edward had to get back to his regiment up in the Hill Station, Maymyo, above Mandalay. The road to Maymyo had 27 hairpin bends in it, as it wound up the hills. Frequently we swerved into the sides when suddenly confronted by ox-driven carts. The beauty of the country, all green and fresh, with the sun sparkling and vividly coloured birds darting about. In those days the Burmese still wore beautiful silk or cotton sarongs and the men tied brightly coloured cloth on their heads, knotted at one side like pirates. The women also wore gorgeous tight long silk sarongs with short white cotton jackets which turned up at the edges – their hair was piled up very neatly and held in place with large pieces of jade, silver or carved wood.

## Maymyo

What a heavenly place! Cold enough at night to have a fire occasionally – fresh mornings and sunshine all day. Most days began with a ride before breakfast, except on Sundays. Every Sunday we went on a long paper chase, followed by a long breakfast at the club – then bathing, tennis, riding and dancing! Yes, we enjoyed a carefree life and were young and feckless and full of joy. How glad I am for those few romantic months. Cousin Edward and Laura (the C.O. of the Manchester Regiment and his wife) gave a dance for me at the mess on my

*Peggy in Burma.*

nineteenth birthday, a few days after I arrived. First there was a dinner party in the bungalow. One of the guests was a Lieutenant George Frampton. While having drinks before dinner I saw a small striped snake wriggling towards me across the carpet. 'Look!' I screamed. Edward saw it at the same time, 'Don't move!' he shouted to me, and swiped it with his sword, killing it. Nobody moved for a few seconds, then Edward said, 'That was a banded Krait – kills in two minutes.' After the dance I was escorted home by George Frampton in what was called a *gharry*, i.e. a small open carriage on two wheels with an old Burmese driver perched up on a bench sitting with his back to us. After that evening George and I spent any spare time we had together. We used to ride through the teak forests in the early mornings or afternoons. A hundred miles of fire breaks (rides) had been cut leading to different vantage points. Some of our favourite rides were to One Tree Hill or Laughing Water.

There were, inevitably, the formal parties at Government House. The Governor was Sir Charles Innes. He and Lady Innes were dear people – much loved.

During my time out there the Viceroy of India, Lord Halifax, came on a state visit to Burma. The 2nd Battalion the Manchester Regiment did the Guard of Honour in Mandalay for the Viceroy's party.

For this event we all went down to Mandalay for a week. The Burmese staged Pwes (native dances) which went on all day and all night in the grounds of the Fort. The dancers performed on small raised platforms and the Burmese audience squatted on their own coloured mats spread out on the ground. They, the audience, were as fascinating to me as the dancers – whole families came, fat roly-poly brown babies, pretty little girls and boys in coloured sarongs with bright flowers behind their ears, women with elaborately piled hair and large pieces of jade, and amber jewels in their ears. Most of the women smoked very fat green cheroots, like cigars, home rolled.

There were ceremonial displays for the Viceroy. The Palace, Club and Fort were all on an island around which the Irawaddy curled. Hidden behind rose-coloured walls which came almost to the water's edge, were the palace, the club and the palace grounds; skirting the walls a bright green grass verge and beds of brilliantly coloured cannas.

Festivals for the Viceroy included leg oarsmen racing each other on the river in long golden painted 'canoes'. They rowed standing, each with one leg round the oar.

I watched from the fort ramparts where one of the Viceroy's ADCs took me as being 'the best viewpoint'. He was probably right. I can see the scene clearly to this day. So many memory 'snapshots'! A visit to an old halfcast's brassware shop in the village of Mandalay – he took us behind a bamboo screen and showed us what looked like the stump of a tree. But it was in fact a block of jade – all colours varying from dark brown on the outside to pastel colours of mauve, green and white in the centre.

*George Frampton in Burma, with elephant tusks, 1928.*

Wherever one looked in the surrounding country there were pagodas, every size but all similarly shaped and covered with hand beaten gold leaf – dazzlingly beautiful.

At the end of six months George and his friend and fellow officer Lloyd Trevor disappeared into the jungle on a shooting trip to North Burma. But not before George had made me a proposal of marriage while escorting me home in a gharry. I could not believe he meant it – everything was unreal there to me – so I suggested he regard me as a sister – this annoyed him. He told me he had four sisters already! Was I in love? Oh yes! But not ready for marriage and neither was he!

All too soon it was time for me to leave. Friends had asked me to stay at Colombo, Ceylon, where I spent a month. I missed George and Maymyo past belief. My father and brother had gone out to Kenya; my mother had moved temporarily into a flat overlooking Hyde Park and our house had been sold to Marie Tempest, a famous French actress in the twenties. Thank God our beloved Madrina was still at 6 North Gate and her sister, another great aunt Methven (Mrs Fred Yarrow), was established in the next door flat.

*

## Back in London

1930 was an uneventful year. Mother and I were living in a service flat high above Marble Arch and making plans to join Jack and Father in Kenya. Mother was going through a trying time known then as 'the change of life'. She had a kind of nervous breakdown. The doctor advised me to take her away for a month or two, so we went to Switzerland, to the Hotel du Lac, on Lake Geneva. We knew that part of the world well and were joined there by dear Berthe Erny. She took me off to Zurich while Mother had another friend staying with her.

At the beginning of the following year, in February, my dearly loved George Frampton turned up at the flat. My heart was torn in two. We were still far too young to marry and I was full of excitement at the thought of going to East Africa. So we agreed to keep in touch and meet again when I returned to England in two years' time, as I thought. We parted, little guessing that it would be 53 years before fate would bring us together again.

*

In 1928, Father had bought 2000 acres of land on the Kinangop, north of Nairobi. He and Jack developed it into a sheep and cattle farm, first trying to fence the boundary against the herds of zebra and kongoni who rushed at will over the plateau. They were in partnership with a well known settler, Mervyn Ray, who lived further along the Kinangop escarpment. They put in a sheep dip and built a stone house under the escarpment, feeding spring water down to the house in a pipeline, by gravity. As most settlers did, they built the house themselves with the help of local Africans and an Indian Fundi.

Their nearest neighbours were quite close, Tiny Kingsford and the Lodges. The latter were in their seventies and had come over from India to settle. Tiny, a bachelor, was in England in 1931 getting married to Cecily Butler who was to become a lifelong friend of mine. The other neighbours were a retired District Commissioner who had arrived in Kenya in the early part of the century. They had one daughter about the same age as me. She played the cello quite dreadfully but was very pretty and sweet. Their name was Pickford, Mother and I had yet to meet them.

# East Africa

In April 1931 my mother and I boarded the steamship the *Edinburgh Castle* bound for Mombasa. The voyage would take three and a half weeks. Once again I passed through the Suez Canal and the Red Sea. Only two events stand out from that voyage. The first was meeting the world famous lady cellist, May Mukle, a fellow passenger. I accompanied her on the piano sometimes during practice hours and we became friends. She told me she was 12 years old when her mother died and her professor father had little money with which to bring up his family of ten children. She earned her living playing the cello from that time onwards.

The second memory I have is when the Captain stopped the ship in the Indian Ocean to lower the coffin of a fellow passenger into the sea. We stood on deck while the Padre said the burial service. To my horror, looking out to sea, I saw the most enormous octopus with great long tentacles rising and sinking on the surface of the water. What happened to that coffin has worried me ever since.

## Mombasa

Sounds and smells seem to remain predominantly in my memory. The first sight of Mombasa Harbour from the *Edinburgh Castle* caused excitement and slight trepidation in my mind. What sort of country was this! Within two years I thought

I would return to England to all my friends sadly left behind there.

Meanwhile, chaos on board. On the quayside milling people of varied colours – black, brown, pale skinned Arabs, Europeans and red-faced Scots – rickshaws, tin lizzies, donkey carts, ancient cabs, fat coal-black mommas balancing great piles of everything on their heads: wooden crates, trunks and hat boxes, wicker baskets with hens sticking their heads out, goats herded by skinny little black boys; Indians in turbans, women in black robes wearing yashmaks; crooked sheds with rusty corrugated iron roofs, a smart white building flying the Union Jack and a rich mix of smells, smells of Africa. People shouting in every language.

Finally an African wearing a red fez and with a badge on his white coat came up to us. He spoke fluent English and took charge of everything efficiently. During the voyage I had tried to learn some basic Swahili. Somebody had lent me a book entitled *The Man Eaters of Tsavo* – about a small station on the single track railway line 'up country' through which we would pass.

Our guide took us to the club where we lunched and rested before proceeding to the station. All our luggage, a very considerable amount, had been piled into a heap on the platform where our guide checked it with us and saw that it was put into the van. We were installed in our stuffy carriage. Mother instantly tried to remove the dark wire mosquito nets from the windows saying 'I must have *air*', but a railway guard very quickly stopped her, saying 'mosquito mem'sahib, malaria bad, mem'sahib'.

We jolted slowly out of the station and began the long crawl on the single track line up to Nairobi. At one stop I heard people calling 'Tsavo – all out for Tsavo'. I thought of the book which described how man-eating lions had taken several people out of their tents at night and gobbled them up while the railway line was being constructed. No sound or sight of a lion through the window netting! Very disappointing.

## Limuru

My father and brother Jack met us on arrival at Nairobi station and drove us up to Limuru, a tea growing district about twenty miles north of the capital. We were wearing the thinnest of tropical clothing, not realising that Nairobi stood at 5,500 feet above sea level and Limura at an altitude of 7,000 feet. We felt chilled and tired, but soon recovered in front of a roaring log fire at Brackenhurst, a small private hotel owned by a Colonel and Mrs Hudson-Cane. They had come out before World War I, when there were no roads, only earth tracks. Transport then was done by ox wagon and on horseback. The Hudson-Canes rode and walked round the vicinity and decided to build a house on the top of a hill where three muna trees grew in an isolated tuft – the bare trunks of these trees reached up to fifty and sixty feet and only branched out near the top.

When their house was ready Mrs Hudson-Cane was driven up there in an ox cart, surrounded by luggage and holding up a parasol (so wise) to shade her from the fierce sun. When we arrived in 1931 they had made a beautiful garden round their delightful house. There was a large main hall and several log guest houses. The Hudson-Canes were friends of my father's and their daughter Margot (later Howard) became a lifelong friend of mine. That first glimpse of the Great Rift Valley stretching to the end of the world is another snapshot in my mind.

We could not dally in this refreshing place as a long drive along an unbelievably rough earth road faced us. At that time the only way up country was via Limuru and through Kikuyu and Kikuyu Reserve. The native women wore beads and short cow hide skirts and the men and children either a goat skin cape or their bear skins.

We had to descend into the Kidong Valley, slithering and sliding down the wall of the Great Rift Valley, dropping 2,000 feet into the oven-like heat of the valley where the earth was brown and red and dust whirled in spirals into the sky. Troops of blue-bottomed baboons jumped about us and threw a few twigs at the car as we passed. At the bottom of the valley we had to cross a small river by the simple means of driving through it.

Our box-body Chevrolet struggled through what was known as The Splash up on to the far bank, and there in the shade of some thorn bushes was a family of lions! My father remarked that they were very friendly animals if unmolested and that they hunted in the evenings mostly, not at noon. The lions did not bother to get up, merely turned their majestic heads in our direction and possibly thought of Mad Dogs and Englishmen. On and on, up and up we climbed, reaching the scruffy little township of Naivasha about mid-afternoon. But the scenery round about the township was beautiful beyond words. A blue lake lapped almost to the edge of the village. Pale yellow thorn trees, their branches spreading out horizontally gave maximum shade. The steep walls of the Great Rift Valley rose to the Kinangop in two escarpments like a giant's staircase. Round Naivasha were plantations – acres and acres, rows and rows of sisal baking in the sun under a cloudless blue sky.

After buying a few necessities at the only duka (general store) we drove on up the precipitous side of the first escarpment. The earth road led us to the Karati Forest which was full of cedar and olive trees and black and white colobus monkeys swinging in the branches. We came out of the forest on to a plateau some five miles wide and finally to the base of the second escarpment. My father pointed to a red roofed house (the only one I'd seen with real tiles so far, the usual roofing being corrugated iron ore thatch). 'Here we are, this is the house.'

There was no garden yet but plentiful clear water coming from a spring in the escarpment wall. The house was built of rough cut stone outside, unplastered stone inside – with a wide verandah overlooking the Karati Forest, and across the valley to the opposite wall of the Rift. It was all so strange and, yes – lovely, vast, silent except for the cries of animals or birds, dazzling sun and dry hot wind.

But I *would* return to England within two years, I thought.

*Arrival of pedigree bull from England – 1931*

## Life in Kenya

Morning sounds and smells of Kenya: tinkling goat bells, clinking cooking pots, laughter: the pungent smell of wood-smoke filtering through grass thatched native huts. The feeling of sun everywhere and the scents rising from warm untilled soil.

Soon after our arrival, Jack and I drove down into the Kidong Valley to the Cresswell-Williams to buy a couple of horses. It was very hot and we were covered in dust when we arrived. I was to learn that that was normal. Our friends were still in their pyjamas and dressing-gowns at midday. They had mentally remained behind in the Happy Valley days, an era now over – we all hoped. We bought a couple of pretty awful horses. Jack's was a large iron-mouthed brute and mine a Somali bred little mare. She turned out to be a reliable little lady and carried me many a mile without faltering or going lame.

My mother bought a number of hens from the Africans and a couple of turkeys from our nearest neighbours who lived about a mile away. She and I tried to make a garden out of most unco-operative soil. There were many hazards. Goats and their diminutive herdsmen pushed through my mother's garden ignoring wire fencing, or my mother's remonstrations, which included shaking her parasol at them – this had no effect at all.

Ten miles away, down in the township, as Naivasha was called, there seemed to be an everlasting wind blowing. The main up country road which passed through it was bordered by wooden shacks with tin roofs. There was a post office, a District Commissioner's office flying the Union Jack, a police post and a delightful colonial pub called The Bell Inn. The rest of Naivasha consisted of a few African or Indian shops and a petrol pump. Across the hippo infested lake a sort of *Arabian Nights* palace gleamed above green lawns and spreading trees. It belonged to Joss Errol (the Earl). His neighbours round the lake all had beautiful stone built houses set in lovely gardens. One of these was owned by an old gentleman who was a retired architect. His young manager, Charles Hillier, and I were friends. Parties of us would sail across the lake to visit him (the old man) on Sundays. We all wore trousers and shirts and tirais – but on landing on his jetty the girls would have to change into skirts or dresses while our escorts looked the other way! The old gentleman would not permit trouser-clad ladies to lunch with him.

In Joss Errol's palace was a vast room with a domed ceiling depicting the firmaments: stars, moon and all that. By that time, 1931, Joss and Idina were divorced and both had remarried, but Joss was still a menace to each and every woman and always would be.

A few months after our arrival on the Kinangop escarpment we were sitting on the verandah after lunch when the sky began to darken as though a huge cloud had unaccountably blotted out the sun. My mother jumped up crying, 'Locusts, locusts!' She was right. Like a vast dust storm the swarm descended upon us, obviously intending to spend the rest of the day and night beneath the escarpment. In seconds everything was covered with these horrible brown/green insects. We all rushed out banging things to shoo them away, my mother flaying at them with her parasol, a useless endeavour. The whole place was covered with the brutes. Next morning no green thing was left: leaves, grass, maize, crops, all vegetation except the gum trees had been eaten. They could not be shifted, but when the morning dew evaporated and they had devoured the last blade of grass, they rose in a huge rustling cloud and flew away, but not very far away. It was the beginning of a seven year plague of locusts and totally devastating. Later they returned, this time pregnant and yellow in colour, to lay their eggs over hundreds of square miles.

The small rains broke in September and everything returned to its former glory – wild jasmine growing in scented profusion up the escarpment, madonna lilies and pink and white striped 'pyjama lilies' appeared amongst a myriad of other glorious flowers. My favourites were the wild green delphiniums.

Visitors came to stay with us from around the world. One Bobby Roberts, another childhood friend of Mother's from the Argentine, and his wife Vere came over from Gilgil. Bobby was one of the relics from the Happy Valley days. At this time he farmed near Clouds where Idina and her current American husband (no. 5), 'Squashy' Haldemann, lived for a few months each year.

### Lion Hunt

Jack and I were invited to stay with the Roberts. Bobby organised a lion hunt as some calves were being taken at night. At dawn the four of us set out, Jack and Bobby with a 202 rifle each. We drove very slowly through waist high grass for some time. Suddenly three enormous heads appeared on our right above the grass. We halted about twenty yards from them, while they watched. The men got out of the open box-body car. Bobby told Jack to aim at the lion in the centre of the group and he would take the lioness on the right. I could hardly bear to think we were going to kill these wonderful animals. Bobby misfired and Jack shot the lion straight through the heart. The two lionesses vanished and the lion, after somersaulting in the air, disappeared from sight. Rightly we followed up to make sure he was killed and not just wounded. Within a few yards we found his dead body. Bobby then did a most stupid thing. He said 'We must skin the lion here as we can't lift it into the car.' During the process Vere and I got out and began to wander off looking for wild flowers. A sound to our left like 'Eee-owgh' petrified me, and I saw one of the lionesses making towards us from an ant hill some fifty yards away – and the other one coming from the opposite direction. Yelling to Jack and Bobby, Vere and I ran for the car. Jack and Bobby turned and shot simultaneously. Neither shot found its mark but went sufficiently close to scare off the lionesses.

Some time later when I told this story to a white hunter he was very angry indeed and said that Bobby must be a suicidal maniac to skin a lion on the spot, knowing two lionesses were nearby. I was upset at killing the magnificent lion. Never again did I go on safari to shoot game except with a camera.

A few years later Bobby was burned to death quite near to this spot. At the height of the dry weather he organised a 'controlled grassfire' so that when the rains came the new grass would spring up and provide good grazing. Unfortunately the wind got up sooner than he had anticipated. It swept across the plains towards the beaters. Bobby's sister-in-law, who was on a visit from England, was overcome by smoke and fell into the fire. Bobby gallantly went to her rescue and both were burnt to death.

Our nearest shopping town from Naivasha was Nakuru. It was the farming capital of Kenya and turned out to be a larger edition of Gilgil, having a hospital, government offices, the Stag's Head Hotel and the Station Hotel. There was also a Rift Valley Club, where many an old settler had ridden on horseback up the steps into the bar. Lord Delamere used to address crowded political meetings there, and many fiery-tempered gentlemen terminated their disputes with revolvers.

Mother's shipboard friend, Mrs Blundell, invited us both to spend a weekend on her son Michael's coffee estate, so we loaded up the Chevrolet box-body and set off. Our destination was only twelve miles north east of Nakuru, so we did not hurry. Mama wrote a letter to Father to tell him we had had an uneventful drive, while I filled up the car with petrol, water and oil and had our shock absorbers seen to. Father received our letter when he went to the post office one week later, after we had returned home.

After a cup of tea at the Stag's Head Hotel we started off again in the glare of the afternoon sun. We were soon amongst the maize and coffee growing areas in one of the loveliest valleys in Kenya – the Solai Valley. We climbed slowly, leaving the township and Lake Nakuru below us, the latter looking like a giant turquoise set in a cluster of coral. Flocks of flamingoes live on this sulphur lake, flying in kaleidoscopic patterns over the evil smelling water.

Mrs Blundell and Michael took us to see as much of the country in the Solai and Subukia districts as could be managed between rainstorms. Michael's charming stone house was near the top of the Menengai Crater, the second largest extinct crater in the world. It resembles a round pie crust with its top sunk in the middle. White hot steam jets coil up into the air like ghosts from the centre cap, providing material for witch doctors' tales.

Michael's senior partners on this coffee and cattle estate were John and Marianne Price, at that time in Europe. All coffee trees were planted in precise rows, 8 feet x 8 feet apart in blocks of 10, 20, 100 acres or more. All cultivation was done with teams of oxen and the hand pruning by Africans, taught by European Bwanas.

Vast areas were under maize which provided food for the employees as well as the market. That year all the maize plantations were stripped bare by locusts and *posho*, ground maize and the staple food up country, was scarce and very dear.

Early in the morning Michael drove us down the valley to a swamp called Lake Solai where we joined Count Carlo de'Cornegliano for a snipe shoot. Carlo lived alone. He had brought out a beautiful Italian wife with him several years before. The Countess had been quite unable to adjust to such an uncivilised existence and had left, never to return. She left her piano behind which Carlo gave to Michael.

The Equator ran through the farm and I was told we had 'crossed the line' after we had driven over a particularly bad bump! The climate there was similar to the Mediterranean in summer.

We dined late and afterwards sat on the covered verandah and watched the moon rise over the crater. Skeins of flamingoes flew overhead on their way to Lake Baringo. As we got up to go to bed I noticed a pyramid shaped heap beside the verandah steps in the shadow of a creeper. It seemed to move. 'What's that?' I asked. 'Look out – don't move,' cried Michael. 'I'll get a shotgun.' In a matter of seconds he had shot 'the pyramid'. It was a yellow puff adder. 'They do sometimes come in but don't attack unless you tread on them,' he told us.

Michael escorted us to our 'guest house', handing each of us a torch and a hurricane lamp. There was a log fire in each of our bedrooms with a central bathroom between. In those days plumbing on farms up-country was almost unknown. Baths were usually oval-shaped galvanised iron tubs set on a stone floor and filled by the servant with scalding water before you changed for dinner. Another can of cold water was left beside the bath. The water was always smoky and slightly muddy, with bits of leaves and boiled blue-bottles floating about on the surface. It was usually river water or from a well, and heated in square four-gallon kerosene tins, known as 'debbies', over a wood fire. More sophisticated houses had a round galvanised drum fixed over a built-up oven with pipes leading from it to the tin bath in the bathroom. The 'loo' was always 'down the garden path'.

They were pretty little rondavals, or square wooden cabins, with thatched roofs and usually covered with creepers. They were coyly hidden down winding paths or amongst flowering shrubs. The 'thrones' were comfortable wooden boxes fixed over pits, not less than thirty feet deep, and well provided with glossy magazines several years old, bowls of sweet smelling geranium and verbena, and a stout stick. This last not to protect oneself from two-legged intruders but against snakes! Constant watch had to be kept to ensure that white ants did not eat away the structure causing the whole thing to collapse at a touch.

On the adjoining estate were a brother and sister, Chas and Olive Cranswick, getting on in years, and known as the Parrot and the Macaw because of their unfortunate noses. Chas managed the estate for a tall Harrovian called Long Eames. He and his brother Short Eames had come out after World War I and bought several thousand acres in the Solai Valley. But they had flaming Irish tempers and used to have blood rows every time

*'Down the Garden Path'.*

they met. The Africans constantly prevented murder being done by tearing them apart and carrying them off in opposite directions. Finally one of the brothers shot at the other. Although he missed his target it was decided that Long Eames should return to his dilapidated castle in Ireland. The land was split up and Chas was installed, with Olive to look after him.

Beyond Long Eames Farm was another farm owned by an absentee landlord called Tom Banks.

After leaving the Blundells Mother and I continued our journey up country in deluges of rain. Our road from Nakuru up to the Highlands of Molo looked like a river. We stuck in holes several times and dug ourselves out, and passed various up-ended lorries and cars, deserted by their drivers. The country resembled the Border country in England and we were glad to be wearing thick pullovers under our mackintoshes. The hills were covered with mauve lavender, grown for oil to make scent, also geraniums for the same purpose, a most beautiful sight. We stayed the night at the Highlands Hotel, Molo, at an altitude of 9,200 feet. It was a large rambling wooden building with clusters of guest cottages all round it, set in a glorious garden. Fires in every room, scalding bathwater in tubs, excellent food and well trained servants. There was to be a meet of the Molo hounds there next day. Gerry Alexander kept a pack of hounds and the local settlers hunted twice a week with African and European hunt servants wearing traditional pink coats and mounted on any four-legged nag that was available. They hunted reed buck officially but many a time found they were hunting lion!

We left the hotel early, to the sound of the horn, and picked our way in and out of the worst looking holes on the one and only road. At the top of a hill we skidded uncontrollably sideways into a three foot ditch. Kamau, our African servant, was quite unperturbed, telling us he'd bring help, and disappeared – so we sat on a bank and discussed the chances of ever reaching the Sotik, which was our objective.

Quite soon a cheerful-looking European farmer appeared on foot with a team of eight oxen and several Africans. 'My name is Veasey,' he said. 'We'll soon get you out of here.' His eyes were very blue. 'I'm sure he is in the Navy,' said Mamma, 'he is so like Uncle Will.' The oxen were hitched on to our Chev. with chains and with a great wrench and to cries of 'harambe' we were pulled on to the road once more and hauled over the rest of the hill.

Before leaving us, Commander Veasey (as he turned out to be) invited us to his house and said his wife Evie would be delighted to give us a meal and keep us there for the next few days. It was a tempting invitation, but we felt our friends in the Sotik would worry, and declined, so he told us to call in on our way back – 'Just send a wire to Commander Veasey, Molo – it won't arrive until after you've been but never mind.'

Many hours later we arrived at Kericho and there found a totally different world. We had dropped down steadily from Molo to Lumbwa in the Kipsigis Reserve. The rain had stopped and the sun shone. The road seemed to be winding through a garden. On all sides were flowers and creepers and flowering trees – morning glory, mauve convolvulus, green delphiniums, crimson gloriosa orchids, black-eyed Susans, flame trees, pink and white pyjama lilies and countless others. We spent a night at a hotel amongst miles of green tea bushes. They looked like three foot high tables and were shaded at regular intervals by tall shade trees which stretched as far as the eye could see.

The Sotik District, which we reached next day, was more open country with a sprinkling of coffee shambas here and there. We passed weird-looking bands of people, presumably women, with whole cow skins thrown over them, their eyes unseen looking through slits. Beside them strode beautiful naked warriors, their hair hanging round their heads in small string fringes plastered with red mud. They carried long spears and were as tall and straight as their weapons.

'Masai,' said Kamau, rather scornfully. He himself was dressed up in hideous European clothes and feeling superior.

Pretty little hump-backed native cattle were grazing beside the road and wandering over it as they pleased. At last we turned off by a group of 'name boards' and drove up an avenue of scarlet flame trees to Ted and Elianne Gunning's house. Ted Gunning was a childhood friend of Mother's from the Argentine. For a week we basked in hot sunshine in a leisurely timeless atmosphere. Neighbours rode over to meet us and I rode back; we played tennis, danced to the gramophone, arranged large bowls of flowers in a house on a neighbouring estate to welcome back a young planter and his English bride. Mama played bridge by lamplight. When we were playing one night there was a sudden disturbance and a young couple burst in clasping their children in their arms. 'There's a mad jackal running about with rabies,' the young man said. 'It's bitten our nanny and baby – can you look after these two children while we take the others to Kericho to be innoculated immediately.' The two sleeping mites were put to bed with Diana Gunning aged 10 while Ted, our host, got out his shotgun. 'I must go to the labour lines and tell the boys. All the dogs and cats will have to be shot now,' he said.

Little sleep was had that night, and in the morning the three beloved house dogs, all the African 'pi-dogs' and Diana's two cats were shot. After breakfast the two small children were taken to Kericho Hospital for innoculations. Ted Gunning said that everyone on his place would have to be done also if any dog or jackal with rabies ran on to the farm.

Mother and I had to leave. Subsequently we heard that a mad dog had jumped through the sitting room window snapping and slobbering – but Ted had his gun beside him and shot it. The whole family and the servants had to have the innoculations – ten days of puncture on the stomach.

# Journey to Zanzibar

A few months later a friend of mine, Colleen Vallings, and I were invited to stay in Zanzibar. The Vallings were old friends of the Resident. I described our journey in a letter to Berthe Erny, our Swiss Ma'm'selle, who had become a great family friend and married a rich banker. Here is the letter I wrote:

*Chère* Berthe,

So much has happened since I last wrote. Where to begin this letter?

The trip to Zanzibar and Tanganyika by ship fully came up to expectations. Zanzibar spells ROMANCE! The harbour not so! It smells dreadfully of dead shark skins. But the Residency with its coloured shutters, pillars and turbaned servants, ebony black, is like a palace straight out of the Arabian Nights. We felt very grand leaving the ship in the Residency Launch!

Then we were driven through the narrow streets swarming with Arabs, past the slave market (there is still a slave trade going on there) and shuttered houses with beautifully carved doors. The women wore black and yashmaks over their faces. How did they not stifle underneath them in this oppressive heat? After lunch we all went to bed and slept – certainly Colleen and I did. When we woke we bathed off the Residency Beach.

What I shall always remember best of my brief visit to Zanzibar is the drive through the clove groves before dusk. There was magic in the scent of the cloves which transported me far away to lands lost in time.

Colleen and I then sailed down the African coast to Dar es Salaam in Tanganyika where we disembarked. The port felt like an overheated greenhouse – steaming. I thought of the Germans and English fighting it out there during World War I and dying in hundreds of malaria and blackwater fever.

Our host and hostess, the Warings at Kilossa (the most unhealthy station in Tanganyika we have been told), met us at the station with four of their six moon pale little children. Their large bungalow with fans turning in the centre of every ceiling was cool and spacious.

We arrived on Christmas Eve – the Warings being R.C.s were going to midnight mass at the Mission and invited us to go with them. 'We'll walk,' said Ted. 'Onyango will go in front with a lamp and a stick to kill any snakes and we'll follow in line behind.'

The night was clear and very dark – far away a hyena coughed, crickets chirped in the grass – fireflies flitted about – across the little valley a procession of lights wound its way up the hill to the Mission Church at the top. 'The church was built by the missionaries by hand by both black and white men,' Ted told us. Already we could hear singing '*Noel Noel*', and by the time we arrived the church was full of Africans. We were the only Europeans apart from the priests. Everything was there: crib, cross, candles, incense, Christianity – and the singing. How beautifully they sang.

We spent a week enjoying parties, picnics, dances etc. before going on a real safari.

Ted Waring was the District Commissioner at Kilossa and was doing a tour of his district on foot. The lorries were sent ahead carrying most of the children, provisions, tents and servants. We walked, and each night we camped in a different heavenly place under canvas. It was so hot that we nearly always slept under the stars with mosquito nets rigged up on bamboo canes over our camp beds and tucked in tightly round our mattresses. In our party was a young A.D.C. and also a very glamorous young Agricultural Officer up from Ngorongoro, Ralf Couchman.

After dinner one evening Ralf turned on Chopin's Waltzes on his portable gramophone, and almost at once we heard lions, 'talking' and roaring or singing not far away. That night we slept inside our tents. We walked for miles through tropical forests of tall trees hung with 'monkey chains' and clusters of orchids; rested beside muddy rivers, visited African peasants in their smoke-filled mud huts and stared at patients in the Mission Hospital, overflowing with sick people. We laughed with the native women and children, caught some marvellous butterflies and wore our tirais from sunrise to sunset! One night was spent on a sisal estate belonging to a sad-looking Polish prince. He seemed lonely and depressed, which was not surprising as he was surrounded by thousands of flat sisal plantations. There was no one for him to talk to, not even a dog, as rabies was rampant all over the country. Why live like that, I thought? He died a few months after our visit.

At the end of the safari the Agricultural Officer asked me to marry him. I really couldn't live in that atmosphere of unreality and sinister foreboding which I felt all about me. Though it was rather fun to be asked! I expect I shall die an old maid – though my horoscope says otherwise – at least two husbands! *Je finis en français pour exercer mon cerveau.*

*Je t'embrasse*
Peggy

At the end of our walking tour in Tanganyika Colleen Vallings left to visit friends in Dar es Salaam. I followed a few days later wondering if I would ever see any of the Waring family again. They all looked so pale and ethereal. I never did, but from time to time I received a Christmas card to say that another little blessing had arrived, or twin blessings, until there were twelve of them. That was the last I heard!

In Dar es Salaam I had arranged to meet a man called Mostert, a friend of Jack's, former World War I 'flying ace', at that time working as a pilot for Wilson Airways, a private African company. He flew me up to Nairobi with a packet of mail and a K.A.R. (King's African Rifles) Officer. The plane was so tiny we could barely squeeze in. I sat beside the pilot and the other passenger squashed himself up behind us. The roof just covered our heads. With a roar and several bumps we took off and wobbled up over waving palm trees into a sizzly sky. It was the most exciting experience of the whole safari. 'Are you airsick?' I was asked. I said 'No', and did not tell them it was my first flight!

We flew along the coast for a while and I was so thrilled to see the land going on and on under the clear water that Mostert kindly went lower so that I could see more – marvellous coloured coral reefs and fishermen in their scooped out tree-trunk canoes, Arab dhows and breaking surf. Then we flew low over the game reserve. Countless herds of buck and zebra and buffalo galloping across the plains – and elephants churning up the dust and flapping their great ears as we flew over them.

The flight ended too quickly. There was never again to be anything quite like that first flight over Africa.

## Brief Sojourn with Idina

Early in 1933 Idina and her fifth husband, Haldman (known as Squashy) came over to lunch, and persuaded me to be companion to her daughter Diana while they went on a safari, the reason being that Diana's governess, Joan Trent, suddenly married Dan Long the famous Boy Long's brother. Boy Long lived by Lake Elmentaita. He wore the most theatrical clothes, brilliant coloured corduroys, a flame coloured Somali shawl and large pirate earrings with a huge sombrero shading his handsome face.

At that time Idina of the notorious Happy Valley days lived in a large square house called Clouds at the foot of the Aberdare Mountains. Diana, aged four years (Joss Errol's daughter), myself and the French maid, Marie, occupied a wing at one end of the house and did more or less what we liked. When Idina was at home she liked me to dine with her other guests and was always charming to me.

One evening while I was dressing for dinner John Ramsden appeared at the door. 'There's a bit of a party going on in here. I think you had better not join us tonight, Peggy.' I took his advice. Marie next morning told me there had been an 'orgy', but I saw no signs of it.

We all rode at weekends. Either I took Diana home across the Kinangop with me or stayed with her at the St. Maur's on Kipipiri Estate. The St. Maur's cousin, John Ramsden, was a neighbour of Idina's. During the week Gemma St. Maur aged four years would come over to join Diana and me at Clouds while Marie fussed over us like an old hen.

We were accompanied on our rides through the forests by an African syce. Fear of animals big or small, or of Africans, was unknown. Often we came upon honey hunters in the forests. Wild bees used to swarm on the top of the trees. When the honey was ready the hunters would light a fire at the bottom of a tree, smoking out the bees. Then they would climb up and steal the honeycombs. These were huge dark brown, dirty-looking balls. The honey was black, sticky and rather bitter. The forest officers were forever at war with the honey hunters, as nearly all the forest fires started in this way, devastating vast areas of trees.

One evening before dinner I helped to bathe and dress a wound on Idina's foot caused by a stirrup rub. The foot was very swollen and obviously painful, but she never flinched when the scalding poultice was put on. I asked if she was afraid of anything. 'Yes, one thing – old age,' she replied. She never grew old, dying in her early sixties.

After six weeks my life as a nursery governess/companion came to an abrupt end. Out riding one day, when Idina was on safari, my horse bolted and I was thrown to the ground, cracking my pelvis. Marie ran about wringing her little fat hands when I was brought back to the house, her high heels tapping on the parquet floor of the nursery and her tight skirt going up and up, rising higher and higher over her fat little bottom as she ran. '*Cet Affreux Afrique! Cet Affreux Afrique!*', she cried. Without telephones and the nearest doctor living some fifty miles away, there was nothing to do but lie in bed until I was able to be moved back home on a mattress in the back of the box-body Chev. Diana wept bitterly at my departure, and so did I. She was a darling little girl, with satin gold hair and huge blue 'bedroom eyes'. Very lovely.

\*

That year, Kenya was suffering from a prolonged drought combined with a plague of locusts. Day after day vast swarms darkened the sky and settled on the ground at dusk, eating every green leaf and blade of grass until the whole country looked like a desert. In the native reserves, hundreds of Africans died of starvation and with them their goats and cattle. The only creatures who thrived were the vultures. Lake Naivasha almost disappeared from sight, shrinking to half its size – rivers dried up and to add to the misery grass and forest fires flared up everywhere. March came and went and no rain fell – then April. My mother told us dreadful tales of locusts in the Argentine when she was a girl and said they would remain with us for seven years.

In the last week of April the rains came, pounding on the roof and hurtling down the escarpment in rivers – quenching the forest fires – leaping up from the hard-packed earth as fast as it crashed down. My brother stood out in it with his Masai cattle man beside him, letting it pour over him, his cows and his sheep. No wonder they speak of the blessed rains and not just rain as we do in Europe.

I remember the day when Jack and I with N'jirango, the second house boy, piled into the box-body, stuffing camp equipment, rifle and fishing tackle and suitcases into the back. 'Can we stop at the duka on the way?' I asked. 'I must get a film for my camera.'

At Gilgil we stopped at Vitalbhai's duka, one of a string of small iron-roofed sheds which made up the township. At the end of the row was the post office, then the station and a signpost, Nakuru – Nairobi – that was Gilgil. A whirlwind spiralling at great speed along the road whisked my tirai off, smothering everything in dust. Vitalbhai produced a sisal brush and removed most of the earth from me while one of his hundred and one brothers ran off to collect my hat.

It was a wonderful shop! Amongst other things were kerosene, spices, tins of stale chocolates, yards of corduroy, and an old 'ancestor' sitting at a treadle sewing machine making up boys' *kanzus*.* We bought a couple of films, a bottle of whisky and some 'butcher' flies before continuing on our way.

A friend of Mama's, Tiny Reeves, in her thirties, came to stay with us. During her visit the old Chev. was again packed full with camping kit and with the faithful N'jirango we set off on a safari 'round the mountain'. Mount Kenya is permanently capped with snow and is the highest peak of the Aberdare range which rises to a height of 18,000 feet. Our earth road wound through forests, we chuffed up hills and wobbled over rivers and often through them until we came to Nyeri. It is on the opposite side of the Aberdares to the Kinangop. We camped twice beside the road on the outward trip. One night we were disturbed by rhino nearby but they did not molest us. Tiny was thrilled to see through field glasses, a herd of elephant, marching one behind the other along an elephant track high up on the mountains. Having circled the mountain we returned via Nanuki. The air was sharp and clear, and we had a frost on our last night under canvas.

---

* Long white robes worn by African servants.

Soon after we returned home, Mama organised a houseparty and fishing weekend. 'I've invited Tom Banks from Solai for Tiny, as you have asked your K.A.R. friends,' she told me. 'I met him last week and he is a keen angler.'

## I Meet and Marry Tom Banks

The day our guests were due I was busy de-ticking my fox terrier on the verandah – a job I detested, hating the swollen ticks full of blood which squashed if you pulled them off too fast. I heard a car pull up, and a tall spare man came up the steps. I looked up, and thought, 'Oh! there you are. But you are much older than I thought you were, and you are not wearing a kilt.' The stranger came towards me, but I knew him without ever having met him before. 'Have I come on the wrong day?' he asked. 'My name is Tom Banks.' He looked about forty and had the most engaging manner and smile.

Three days later, after a fishing picnic in the Aberdares, he proposed to me as we bumped down the escarpment in an old Ford box-body. I was about to go away to visit friends and said I would answer his question when I got back.

We were engaged in November 1933 and nine months later were married in Naivasha on 16th June 1934. Deluges of rain had poured down for days before the wedding, and still continued until 1 p.m. when the sun came out and remained shining all day.

Rebecca and Hugh Ward on the Kinangop had put Tom up the previous night. They nearly failed to 'get to the church on time' owing to the torrential rains causing them to stick in mud holes several times on the way down to Naivasha.

Meanwhile Mama had stormed down to the church at an early hour – found no flowers yet done – then gone on to the St. Maur's farm to ask them the reason why Hope St. Maur had not done them as she had promised. Hope said they would be done and not to worry. Mama returned to the Bell Inn Hotel where the reception was to be held and found much to criticise, which she did loud and clear. Father then told her they

*Tom Banks.*

must go home and change or there would be no wedding. Somehow everything fell into place and all went well.

Until I met Tom I had been corresponding with George Frampton and many other friends. George had invited me to visit him on the Blue Nile where the Manchester Regiment was stationed, but it was too late. I had become engaged to Tom.

### First Days as Mrs Banks

After our honeymoon at Nanuki we returned to Banks Estate, our coffee farm in Solai. On the first morning when I got up for breakfast I saw a row of African women and children on the lawn. Our head boy explained that they were 'sick' and expected me to do whatever was necessary. This was to be a daily event. Tom was away down amongst the coffee so could not be applied to. All I could think of was *Mrs Beeton's Recipe Book*. At the back of this marvellous tome was a chapter on basic medicine and home nursing. We had a stock of cod liver oil, Collosal Agentum for sticky eyes, Epsom salts, also carbolic and Permangamate crystals. Most of these were applied inside and out with a small prayer to *le bon Dieu*, and seemed to cure most ailments.

On our coffee plantation we also grew maize and wheat and had a herd of native cattle crossed with a Guernsey bull. There was a permanent labour force of 120 men plus their families. They lived in a camp below us and two men were employed to keep it clean and tidy. Our water supply to the house came from Crater stream and was no more than a trickle which we shared with a testy-tempered neighbour, Chas Cranswick. In the dry weather the stream shrank to almost zero and often nothing came down the pipe at all because our neighbour had shut off our half of the division tank by stuffing a sack over our pipe hole. The farm itself was supplied with water from our stretch of the river a mile away. It came in forty-gallon diesel drums in an ox cart. Frequently we had to use this water for baths etc. in spite of it being full of leaves, creepy crawlies and heaven knows what other bugs, and was brown with mud. My beautiful coloured linen sheets were soon a brown ochre colour, beaten to death by the African dhobie on stones before being strung up to dry in the equatorial sun.

We lived at an altitude of 6,000 feet right on the Equator at the head of the most beautiful valley. The climate was similar to that of the Mediterranean and we grew both European and tropical fruit and flowers in abundance.

We could not let our dogs sleep on the verandah at night as leopards took them. Which reminds me of an encounter I had with a leopard soon after arriving in Kenya, when riding through the Karati forest to visit the Pickfords. A leopard suddenly leapt out of the bushes and landed directly in front of me. It looked so beautiful with its black spotted golden body and large cats' eyes. After glaring at me and switching its tail a bit, it bounded in one movement over the scrub and out of sight. It was more startled than I was I think, but Janie my little mare was trembling with fright and bolted all the way home.

During my first year as a 'bride' a great many friends came to visit us. Our house was made of mud and wattle *pisé* with very tall thatched roofs, a series of large rondavals really, attached to one another by covered verandahs. The floors were all highly polished olive wood, and the doors and windows of cedar. Our family furniture had come out by ship along with china, glass, silver, pictures etc., but did not seem incongruous.

A great friend, Rebecca Ward, who later when she was a widow married George Fane, was one of our first and most frequent visitors.

After about a year living on the Solai farm we had a letter from my brother-in-law, John Banks, asking if we would care to go down for six months to Rhodesia to look after his 20,000 acre ranch while his manager went on leave to the U.K.

'What about this, sweetheart?' asked Tom. He pushed the letter across to me. 'As you see, all travelling expenses will be paid and I shall have a manager's salary while we are there.' 'Oh!' I exclaimed. 'Do let's go, I'd adore to.' 'Well not a word to your dear mama before everything is settled, tickets bought and agreements signed, or we shall never see Rhodesia,' warned Tom.

In no time we were off, leaving our Scottish manager, Chalmers, to run the coffee Shamba. After a dusty journey by train to Mombasa, we embarked on a B.I. steamship for Beira, the Portuguese port of disembarkation for Rhodesia. The sea was like glass but I felt dreadfully seasick. Tom said he did not know what it was to be seasick – the rougher the sea the better he liked it – adding that a great great uncle of his, Sir Joseph Banks, had sailed the seas with Captain Cook. I could take no interest in his ancestors or Captain Cook.

Beira was suffocatingly hot. After disembarking we went to the station and were told that the trains went up-country on Wednesdays and Fridays only. It was then Monday. We booked in at the only hotel and then went for a walk along the quayside. The mosquitoes were enormous and bumped into us as we walked. 'What a terrible place,' I said, 'even worse outside than in that dismal hotel.' With the aid of whiskies and horse's necks we survived long enough to catch our train up to Salisbury a day later.

The compartment was buzzing with monstrous mosquitoes – in spite of screens fitted over the windows. But once we'd left Beira behind and squirted and swatted these voracious insects we felt happier. Not for long. 'I'm going to be sick,' I said. 'Sick? Hold on a minute, I'll give you a neat brandy,' called down Tom from the upper bunk. That is all I remember until we arrived at Umtali. The sun had just risen and the scene was unlike anything we had seen so far. Tall deep pink cliffs rose all round us, a clear river sparkled on the grass beside the railway track, cheerful Africans came below the windows with tray loads of paw paws, bananas and last week's newspapers, and then an astonishing sight – little rush baskets full of strawberries. The air was cool and refreshing and the strawberries delicious. 'Do they grow near here?' I asked. 'Yes, memsahib, on top of those hills,' the vendor replied. On we lurched to Salisbury where we changed on to another train for Bulawayo.

\*

# Rhodesia

Before leaving for Rhodesia we had read everything about Cecil Rhodes we could borrow from our friends. Bulawayo was impressive – its streets were certainly 'wide enough to turn a span of 16 oxen in them'. The shops were well built and most of them made of stone or brick with tiled roofs. Very different from the tin-roofed dukas in Kenya townships.

The Duffus family met us at Bulawayo station. It was a small township which had grown up round Bulawayo station some ten miles away from the Matopos mountains. They drove us some twenty miles to the township Fig Tree which consisted of a station, a post office and a few shacks, and was situated near the Matopos. Cecil Rhodes was buried on the top of these hills. The ranch called Collaton was like all the surrounding country, flat, dusty and dotted with curious-shaped groups of boulders known as kopjes. The house was large and faced with a portico of white pillars.

Vera Duffus took me on one side. 'Are you feeling all right?' she asked anxiously. 'Well, I seem to be a bit travel-sick,' I replied. 'Better go to bed before dinner,' she said. Next day we drove in to Bulawayo to see her doctor. 'You can expect your baby in seven months' time,' he told me, as though informing me the laundry man would call next week. 'I must go back to Kenya in five and a half months' time,' I told him. 'Oh well, we shall see about that. Come in once a month meanwhile,' he said. We stayed with the Duffus family for a fortnight before they left for the U.K.

44

It was the hot weather season and that year it prolonged itself into a drought. No rain had fallen for six months. We were surrounded by carcases of dead cattle. The Artesian wells having dried up, thousands of cattle died trekking from one dry water hole to another.

One day as we sat at lunch there was a resounding crack. The sideboard surmounted by a large mirror had split from top to bottom because of the intense dry heat. Slowly the glass fell out and smashed on the floor. 'That's because you brought orange blossom into the house, madam,' said Margaret Grant, our nice Scottish housekeeper whom my sister-in-law had insisted I should have to help me. 'Nonsense, Maggie, it is contraction from heat which caused it.'

That evening while changing for dinner I heard a little tapping noise on the parquet floor and thought it was a mouse. When I turned round to look, to my horror I saw it was an enormous oval-shaped spider. I shrieked and jumped up on to my chair while it shot out into the sitting room. Tom instantly grabbed a knobkerrie and killed it. 'Oh sir!' wailed Maggie, 'that's awfa' bad luck to ye.'

Next day we were expecting the Matron of Bulawayo Hospital to come out for the weekend. She arrived in time for lunch in a battered old Chevrolet. We had barely finished eating when the Matabele headman appeared on the verandah. 'Come at once, Bwana – the new young assistant has broken his leg and is lying on the ground dying.' Matron quickly offered her assistance and accompanied Tom to the other farm some six or seven miles from our house.

They returned long after dark, having given first aid and driven the poor young Afrikaner to Bulawayo Hospital 20 miles away.

Sunday came, the heat was intense, worse than ever, and in the evening Matron returned to Bulawayo.

While we were preparing for bed Tom stopped and looked through the window. 'What is it?' I asked. 'By Jove,' he exclaimed, 'I believe that's a grass fire – somewhere over by the Matopos. I must go and investigate. Won't be long.' With that he left, taking the torch with him and a box of matches. Wearily I climbed into bed and was instantly asleep. Some hours later he came back and told me he and the boys had lit a counter fire along our boundary some five miles away and he hoped it would do the trick – but it depended on whether the wind rose before the fire was out.

At breakfast I smelt smoke. Jumping up and calling to Tom I ran to the verandah and looked out. Sure enough, clouds of smoke were blowing across the plain from the Matopos and the wind was rising. 'Tell the syce to saddle my horse and his,' Tom shouted. 'We must round up the cattle and drive them across the main road.'

That seemed an endless day. Dense clouds of smoke blew across the house as the fire came nearer. We could see flames shooting up into the sky when a tree or shrub caught fire. There was no sign of Tom, nor any news, as all the labour was out 'beating' and lighting counter fires. Around 5 p.m. the wind dropped, the smoke lifted and dwindled and we could hear faint cracklings coming from the direction of the fire. At last the household staff returned with dirty faces and cheerful smiles. 'Fire out now, missy – Bwana coming.' When Tom got back he looked as black as they did. 'We only just got the cattle away. The fire circled round us and we had to drive them through a bottleneck.'

Three months later the Duffus family were expected back and we were turning our thoughts to Kenya and the journey home. A cable arrived by a postman riding a bicycle – 'Lyall Duffus killed motor accident Edinburgh, will you please remain on another six months. Writing Jack.' 'But the baby,' I cried, 'it will be born here and not at home!' But we felt it was the only thing to do, so we stayed.

A week later the rains broke. They came with a tremendous clap of thunder and fork lightning. This was followed by a terrific hailstorm. The hailstones were the size of plovers' eggs. I went out and collected a handful as I couldn't believe my eyes. Later we read in the newspaper that in some parts of the country and in Johannesburg hailstones the size of tennis balls had fallen, killing several people as well as many calves and sheep and smashing in the roofs of cars.

Within a few days, from being a desert the landscape was transformed into a sea. 'No driving to Bulawayo this week or next, if it can be avoided,' Tom remarked one day. 'When is the Blessing due?' 'Any moment now,' I replied, 'but I'm told you never can tell.' It rained and it rained, grass grew as fast as mushrooms and trees burst into leaf and blossom.

Every few days Tom went off to inspect the main road. In 1935 the Rhodesian main roads were laid with 18-inch wide strips of asphalt spaced to match the width between the wheels of an average motor vehicle. These strips ran down all the main roads and were a splendid idea until you met an oncoming car – then one or both of you had to get off the strips on to the dusty earth surface. Frequently this caused a skid or a tyre would be cut on the rough edge of the strip. There were dry river beds or spruits which occurred every few miles. You drove in and out of these – an easy performance in the dry weather but often impossible during the rainy season. On New Year's Day Tom returned from a road inspection and said he thought I'd better go into Bulawayo the first time the rain stopped and stay there, as some of the spruits might become un-negotiable. So Maggie helped me pack a few things into a suitcase and we all crossed our fingers before going to bed that night. Cubic tons of rain thundered down all next day but towards sundown the clouds lifted and kopjes were suffused with pink light.

Birds were singing just before dawn when I woke to find the Little Blessing was on the way. When morning tea was brought in I told Tom we had better go to Bulawayo after breakfast. When Maggie brought in the breakfast tray I told her what was going on. She scolded me for not calling her before and was all for leaving immediately, without breakfast. I persuaded her it was not necessary. A few hours later we drove off as a peal of thunder crashed overhead and within minutes we were driving through waves of water. We got through the first two spruits easily enough, but at the third one we pulled up. Tom looked doubtfully at it but I told him we had no choice but to get through, as Little Blessing would certainly not wait all day for the rain to stop. In we dived and mercifully emerged the other side before the car came to a halt. 'Water on the ignition,' Tom informed us. 'We must wait until she dries out.' The Little Blessing tactfully decided to go to sleep.

Three days later in the Truby King Nursing Home, Bulawayo, the Little Blessing was born. A label with her name Christina Rose was firmly stuck round her tiny ankle. As soon as we reached Bulawayo Tom had sent off a telegram to Mama telling her the baby was on the way. The reply came back from Mama 48 hours after Rose's birth reading, 'No further news what *are* you doing?'

Mama's first letter of congratulations to me was full of instructions, particularly that I should put the embroidered linen bonnets she had made on to the baby straightaway to prevent her ears from sticking out. A second letter arrived the following day. The first half was taken up with plans for the christening 'after you get back home,' and the second half was full of complaints about our manager, Chalmers, who, she said, refused to remove the swallows from the verandah roof. By the same mail we received a letter from Chalmers categorically stating that if Mrs Benn went to the farm again he would have to give in his notice.

My elderly sister-in-law Nessie Banks telephoned from Cape Town to say she was coming up to visit us before we left. Before she arrived we had a great reorganisation as I'd moved the heavy furniture around and taken down most of the seascapes and all the religious pictures from the walls. They were all rehung in time to welcome her. While watching me bath the baby one evening she said, 'I would have loved to have had a large family. But you see, dear Jack and I were engaged for 21 years before we married. We met at Biarritz – that is why I have so many seascapes, all of them of Biarritz. He did not consider himself wealthy enough to marry me then so he went to South Africa to make his fortune – which he did. My parents lived outside Cambridge where father owned a bank and kept a string of race horses. I had four brothers, the youngest one died tragically at the age of 18.'

I asked her about him. She told me that one day a dog rushed at him and bit his leg. 'Mother got the doctor to come round and dress it and bandage it up and no one thought any more about it. Three weeks later he complained of a headache and great thirst. In the afternoon he went into the garden with a book and lay down on the hammock. I was in the house when I heard terrible screams coming from the garden. Looking through the window I saw him wildly running round the garden, howling. He had rabies. It is a sound and sight I can never forget. Mercifully he died very quickly.'

We grew to love my sister-in-law Nessie dearly, and were sad to say goodbye. She had asked if we would not sell up our coffee plantation in Solai and come to live at Collaton permanently but Tom and I both agreed that our hearts were in Kenya and that we preferred to struggle on there.

While she was with us Tom and I slipped off to see the Victoria Falls, leaving Rose in the charge of her doting aunt and Maggie. We went by train through endless miles of dried up land until we got to the Zambezi. I had expected to look up at the Falls and was slightly disappointed to see the massive fall of water dashing down below us. We were given oilskins to put on at the hotel and were guided down the cliff path where we did look up at the falls, through rainbow spray. The roar of the water was deafening and we stood there awed by the dramatic scene and drenched with spray.

When we came back Nessie and Maggie were loathe to give Rose back to me. Nessie had to leave for the Cape where Jack was waiting for her. 'Jack rang me up last night, dear,' she told me, 'and we have decided that you all need a good holiday before taking up the reins again on your own farm. So we are giving you ten days at the hotel in Durban at our expense before your ship sails. Miss Grant must go with you to look after baby and we'd love to give her a holiday too.'

We were delighted with this wonderful plan. Quickly packing our belongings, we said a tearful goodbye to Nessie and were soon rumbling along en route to Durban. This time we were accompanied by Rose aged three months and Maggie and a pantechnicon full of baby paraphernalia.

We reached Johannesburg on the evening of the next day. We had to change trains at Johannesburg as our train was going on to Cape Town, and we were bound for Durban. It was 6 p.m. and time for Rose's bottle. We decided to give it to her in the compartment as this was the terminal. There would be three hours to fill in before the next train left. Tom and the porter put all our luggage down on the platform and then Tom said he would go and scout around for a hotel where we could get a good dinner. After he had gone Maggie opened a tin of baby food in the train, she laid out the bottle and the powdered milk tin on the opposite bunk in the compartment and was setting off to get some boiling water from the buffet car attendant when the train slowly began to move off. I jumped up and put my head out of the window. 'Stop, we have to get out here.' Two African porters gaped at me stupidly. 'Stop,' I called again as we slowly passed a European guard. Putting two fingers in his mouth he immediately let out a piercing whistle, at the same time waving his red flag. The whistle and flag waving was taken up by other porters, and at the end of a very long platform we came to a halt. Our carriage stopped beyond the terminal. Several porters and a guard ran up to help us out. Putting Rose with her dining room on top of her into the Moses basket, I passed the whole lot through the window to upstretched arms. Everyone was most sympathetic. Poor Maggie was shocked and I felt foolish, especially when Tom raced up the platform asking 'What's going on? Are you absconding to Cape Town?'

Natal was looking green after the rain. Wild flowers carpeted the hillsides. It all looked very like an English seaside resort, full of hotels, holiday makers and noise. Long white-crested breakers rolled in from the Indian Ocean. Our clothes, hair and skin all felt soft again after being dehydrated in Rhodesia during the brittle dry atmosphere before the rains broke.

At last we had to leave. As our ship sailed away I held Rose up to wave farewell to Maggie who had begged us to take her with us, offering to look after the baby she adored 'just for my keep'. But it was not possible, much as we would have loved to keep her.

*

# Home Again

At Nairobi station the whole family was there to welcome us home and see the baby. Tom pulled down the window and I passed Rose in her Moses basket to Jack. 'What a way to present me with my first grandchild,' Mama objected. We all stayed with friends in Nairobi for two days – the Hamps. They lived in a spacious old-fashioned house on stilts overlooking the Langata Plains. Tom bought a second-hand Chev. box-body, slightly bigger and a more recent model than our first one. We stuffed it full of baby luggage, vegetables from the market, medicines and stores, before driving home to Solai.

Our house was illuminated by oil lamps, attracting 'doodle bugs' and moths if we left the windows open. This mud and wattle house was to have been our temporary home until the coffee came into full bearing and we were able to build a stone house.

Tom had cut off the top of a hill in front of our house so that we commanded a glorious view of the whole of Solai Valley. He made a 20 foot long terrace below the lawn, making a wide platform, with a third, narrower terrace below that. From our windows we looked across the lovely Solai Valley to the distant outline of the Menengai crater. The valley sloped gently down into the blue distance with the hills of the Kamasia Reserve closing it

A group of three 'umbrella' thorn trees stood at the side of our terrace. Rose's pram was put there every morning. During the dry weather a 'dust Devil' whisked past, spiralling higher and higher into the air. It swept up leaves and sticks and narrowly missed the pram which spun round and made off in the direction of the terrace below. Fortunately the garden boy was pottering about close by and flung himself at it just before it reached the edge. After that we always tethered the pram to the tree with an ox-hide thong.

While we had been in Rhodesia drought and locusts had ravaged Kenya. Famine was kept at bay by the Government importing thousands of tons of maize to feed the African population. Coffee crops dwindled to nothing, the trees losing all their leaves and the blossom dying and falling off at the spiking stage (early budding spikes). We were all in the hands of the banks and all labour was reduced to a minimum. Emaciated Africans would turn up on the farm daily, begging to be taken on just for the food. We gave them hot soup but had to send them away.

Soon Chalmers, our Scottish manager, had to go. One day before he left, after paying out the wages, he had supper and retired to bed. (He lived in the manager's house in the centre of the farm about half as mile from us.) We were woken early next morning with the news that Chalmers had been attacked by thieves in the night and had his head cut open. What happened was that he was woken up by a torch (his torch, taken off the beside table) being shone into his face. Instinctively he put up his arm and caught a blow from a panga two-edged knife which glanced off on to his forehead. Being a powerfully built man, he sprang at his assailant who fell down, then took fright, and dived head first through the window, taking the remains of the wages in a bag with him. Chalmers roused the house boys, got them to help him on to his motorbike, and with blood pouring from his face and arms drove himself eleven miles in to the Nakuru hospital. The doctor found that a piece of bone four inches long had been hacked off his forehead and his arm broken. Fortunately he healed quickly and only remained in hospital a few days.

Every morning at 6.15 a.m. we were called with morning tea – not later than 6.45 a.m. work began in the coffee shambas and plantation, and Tom was out on the farm by 7 a.m. All the cultivation on our farm was done by oxen, also the ploughing and carrying of water to and from the river one and a half miles away to the labour lines. When the drought reached its peak, our supply for the house from Crater stream gave out. All our water was carted from the river by oxen in 40-gallon galvanised iron drums set up on a cart. By the time it reached us most of it had spilled out. It was brown with mud and ruined my trousseau and linen sheets. But that was nothing compared to the difficulty of cooking in it and bathing in it and boiling it for drinking water before putting it into the distilling tank.

A year after we returned to Kenya from Rhodesia the short rains failed to arrive in the autumn. Rose got dysentry and had to go into the Nakuru European Hospital and I was asked to stay and help nurse her. The hospital was a long single storey building with a wide verandah all along the front. It stood slightly higher than the main road at the foot of the Menengai crater and facing Lake Nakuru a mile away. The entrance was in the centre of the verandah. The men's wards led off to the right and women's to the left with a new very small wing at one end for maternity cases.

The view from the hospital verandah was very lovely, over wide mown lawns and mauve-flowered jacaranda trees and on to the distant flamingo-covered lake backed by its half circle of mountains. When I took Rose to the hospital the lake had almost disappeared. Due to drought and evaporation the surface of it was covered with white sulphur. Evil-smelling sulphur clouds rose off this when the wind blew towards the Memorial Hospital – it smelt awful.

Except for a ward of four beds at each end, most of the cubicles had only one or two beds in them. All the doors were left open on to the verandah and as most of the patients knew one another, we strolled about in the convalescing stage visiting. One old lady was perpetually ringing the bell and demanding ice for her whisky and sodas – in the mornings she refused to be washed at 6 a.m., complaining loudly that it was unkind and unnecessary. When the doctor came on his rounds later at 10 a.m. she would say 'Doctor, I am quite unfit to be seen, no one has bothered to wash me!'

We were allowed visitors at almost any time of the day or night that was not inconvenient for the doctors, and if one was not too ill, great 'parties' were held up and down the verandah. Lying in bed one could see cars drawing up in front of the gateway across the hospital lawns and watch friends walking up the 200 yards of gravel path bringing flowers, letters, presents etc. There were only two European doctors in those days, who cordially disliked each other, and who would never have anything to do with the other one's patients. Apart from this the Nakuru Memorial Hospital was happy, informal and an excellent hospital and remains so to this day.

Rose was soon well enough to come home again and we got a coal black Seychelles nanny to help us look after her. In Kenya, it was not desirable to leave children in the charge of African girls (ayahs as they called themselves) as far too often they went off to the labour lines and allowed their charges to be tampered with. This was not in *their* eyes wrong – so we never left our children. When we dined out we put them in their cots in the back of the car and then on arrival carried them into the house and put them to bed with the other children until it was time to come home. Children of all ages always accompanied their parents in this fashion when they dined out, unless there were European or Seychelles nannies to look after them. They enjoyed it and used to sleep quite happily, either in the car or in their hostesses' bedrooms.

## A Baby in the House

Life became more interesting with a baby in the house. Owing to the droughts and great scarcity of water we had to economise and save every drop and those drops were brown with mud. We boiled and filtered all drinking water, but even so could not get it absolutely clean. Week by week one's clothes and household linen became browner and browner.

Several friends in the Valley had grass tennis courts, and most afternoons found us piling into the Chevrolet – Tom, Rose and I sitting on the one and only bench seat in front, and ayah, dogs, pram and tennis rackets in the back. When we set off in our freshly laundered 'whites' we tried to protect ourselves from the dust by wearing dust-coats and old Burberries and fastening down the canvas side 'flaps' round the car. But the powdery dust was almost impossible to keep out and by the time we arrived back from the party we were saturated with it.

During this time I suffered from chronic attacks of amoebic dysentry, which added to the complications of life as our 'little house' was forty yards down the garden path. I vowed then that as soon as possible we should install a proper plumbing and drainage system – but the first necessity was water, which we did not have in sufficient supply. Frequently no water would come through to us at all. Sometimes it was because a toad had inserted itself in the end of our pipeline and blocked it, but often it was due to deliberate interference. The Cranswicks never admitted to this and always maintained that the Africans had duplicate keys to the division tank and they were responsible – but we thought otherwise.

Water, boundaries and fencing were so often the cause of blood rows in Kenya – specially in the dry weather season, from December to April. The heat combined with the high altitude at which we lived strained our nerves, and tempers flared over the smallest incidents. Directly the rains broke harmony was usually restored.

There was a single track railway line to Ol'Puniata station at the lower end of the Solai Valley. When the maize was harvested the Solai farmers loaded up their ox wagons with sacks of maize and took them to the station where they themselves put it into trucks. Many months before this was done trucks would be ordered in their names and each farmer had his own trucks allotted to him. It was often a case of first come first served, and if a farmer found an empty truck when he arrived at the station and had more maize than he could fit into his own allocation, he would load his bags on to someone else's truck. This permanently led to glorious battles when neighbours would fly at each other – much to the Africans' delight. Sacks of maize would be hauled out on to the ground and more sacks thrown into the trucks.

But it was not only the neighbours who caused commotions in the valley. Soon after we were married a herd of elephant stampeded through the shambas and took up residence near the Solai swamp where Tom and Michael Blundell used to shoot snipe. The elephants broke down the water banks, churned up the water and rooted up banana plantations and sisal. So the game rangers and a white hunter had to be called in to get rid of them. A young visitor from England, Paul, was visiting us at the time of the elephant invasion, so we took him down to the swamp hoping to see the herd. But we were unlucky and only heard them squeal in the distance. Paul was a charming boy but he had an extraordinary habit of wearing gloves whenever he went outside, whether to the garden, or to ride or help dose the sheep. The Africans were fascinated and seemed to think he had some magic in his gloves. Even when we went out after elephant, the gloves came too. I never discovered why.

The only frightening encounter I had with a snake was when Rose was about a year old. She was in her pram under some thorn trees across the lawn. Pishi (our cook) burst into the room where I was cutting out baby clothes and said, 'Come quickly Memsahib, a bad snake is beside our baby.' I had no gun ready, so told Pishi to give me the knobkerrie he was holding. We went out, Pishi warning me the creature would spit in my eye and blind me. Sure enough, some six feet from the pram was a black cobra, sitting up, hood spread, swaying its head about. I approached carefully to within a few feet of it while it looked at me warily. It was evil and beautiful, I quite understand how rabbits are mesmerised by snakes. Not knowing what to do next, I swished at it with the knobkerrie –

it swayed to one side and back. Again a swish with the stick – again a swaying movement from the cobra. Once more a swipe at it, but this time the knobkerrie flew out of my hand, missed the snake and we were left staring at each other. Suddenly, it slid to the ground and wriggled away! *Mamma mia!*

Christmas fell at the beginning of the hot weather season. An ox was killed and given to the African labour force. They and their families would come up to the house singing and dancing, decorated with garlands of bougainvillaea flowers, geraniums etc. Our head house boy used to stick a geranium flower behind each of his ears. For ourselves we would cut down a small conifer tree and make the decorations out of small fresh oranges cut into baskets and hollowed out. We filled them with homemade sweets or raisins etc. Cake icing was used for snow and gelatine sprinkled over to make frost, and so on.

We only had one guest-house at first and lots of friends. Sometimes when unexpected visitors turned up and the guest-house was already full, Tom and I would move into the dressing room and give our room to them. The African staff were never put out by visitors and enjoyed them as much as we did. How the cook produced meals out of our rickety Dover stove stoked with resinous gum tree logs at any time for any amount of people remains a mystery – just part of the African magic.

After dinner we entertained each other with music, singing songs accompanied by the piano and the accordion which I used to play. Michael Blundell, Tom's best man and now our neighbour, had a very good tenor voice and we enjoyed many musical evenings with him in the days before the war.

On one occasion, after spending a weekend with friends, we arrived home to find guests happily sitting down to dinner. They had arrived from afar the previous day. Our head house-boy had insisted upon them staying. They told us he did all the honours of a host for us – plying them with drinks, meals, clean sheets and fires in their rooms. He told them we would be back 'bado-kidogo' (soon) and that we would wish them to wait.

Fires at night were a delicious luxury as it was always chilly enough to want one, in spite of God letting up the blind and the sun racing up into the sky at 7 a.m. every morning.

\*

The world on the other side of the globe was moving to a crisis.

*George V had died – January 1936.*
*Edward VIII had abdicated December 1936.*
*George VI was crowned.*

*Adolf Hitler was menacing Austria and on 12th March 1938 he invaded Austria.*

### The Coronation Ball – 1937

One day a telegram arrived from Mama: 'Expecting you all next week to join us for Coronation Ball – Government House. Stop. Have arranged baby sitter for Rosebud here.'

As I was expecting my second baby Tom did not think we should go. So we telegraphed, 'Very sorry unable to come as expecting addition to family.' Three days later an infuriated Mama got out of her car on our doorstep. Seeing us sitting peacefully on the verandah she advanced, saying, 'What is all this nonsense about "additions" and what has it go to do with us all going to the ball? Papa and I have set our hearts on this, our last ball, as we shall be too old to want to go later – and my darling Rosebud will have a Seychelles nanny to look after her, and Jack's wool is all bailed and the head man will see to the farm again now that he's been acquitted of the murder of his wife – after all none of these Africans know what they are doing after drinking Nubian gin, so they couldn't say it was premeditated, and I've arranged for you to stay with the X's in Nairobi and we shall stay at the Club and I have still got a second pair of elbow length gloves which came from Paris which you can have. Can my chauffeur sleep in the camp here or will your cook look after him? He is a Kikuyu, so much better than your Laluo boys. You have your wedding dress for the ball? Fortunately I brought out Jack's and Papa's tail coats when we came.'

Tom and I looked at one another. We knew we would go to the ball.

Meanwhile, in England, George Frampton and a fellow officer went to the Coronation Ball at Buckingham Palace. But I only heard that some fifty years later.

Next day my dear mother left, triumphant. 'You know,' warned Tom, 'we shall regret this.' We did.

A week later we rattled off in the Chev. box-body to the Kinangop – Rose was in her Moses basket with a green mosquito net firmly tied over it – the ayah sat beside us in front. Onyango sat amongst the luggage behind with the Moses basket beside him. The dust curled up over the sides of the car and came in under the canvas 'flaps' which were fastened down all round the car by 'press fasteners'.

The earth road was full of enormous 'shell' holes and we meandered from side to side trying to avoid them. It did not matter which side of the road you drove on as there was no traffic in those days, only an occasional vehicle picking its way through the holes and rocks, sometimes an ox-cart, and always game of some kind, mostly buck or giraffe. The car boiled going up the Gilgil escarpment and again up the Kinangop – but we were well equipped with two-gallon cans of water and just waited until the radiator cap was cool enough to touch before removing it and pouring water into the radiator. Time meant nothing at all.

Feeling unwell after the jolting drive, I retired to our guesthouse before supper. Mama was delighted to be in sole charge of the baby and I heard her talking volubly in French to the Seychelles nanny, who busied herself with me and looked ominously sulky.

In the morning Tom still thought we ought not to go on to Nairobi but Mama could see no reason to alter her plans and added that 'no one in my family has had a miscarriage and it

will do Peggy good and cheer her up to have a little gaiety.'
Five hours of terrible roads, heat and dust separated us from
Nairobi – but we eventually arrived.

Before the ball we all met for dinner dressed in our best and
looking tremendously smart. Then we drove to Government
House and got caught up in a long queue of every sort of
conveyance – 1920 cars, a rickshaw or two, an ancient Rolls
Royce limousines, shooting-brakes, a tub cart drawn by a fat
pony, vans, lorries, everything on wheels.

The Coronation Ball was in full swing by the time we had
been presented to H.E. and Her Excellency. Hundreds of old
friends from all parts of the country had come to celebrate. The
band was playing, tiaras glittering, champagne flowing, all was
well.

Just before the supper dance Leonora and Nick Lee from the
Kinangop came up to me. We knew each other before we were
married and used to sail across Lake Naivasha on Sundays to
visit an old gentleman who lived in a palatial house shaded by
tall yellow thorn trees. Leonora had married a year before we
did. I told her Rose was on the Kinangop with Mr and Mrs
Lodge, old neighbours of Mother's, and a Seychelles nanny
provided by Mama. 'Lucky you,' she remarked, 'our two, aged
one year and three months respectively, are in the back of our
car with our Kikuyu cook – guarding them – we hope,' said
Leonora. As we were talking I suddenly felt a fearful spasm
grip my stomach. 'Leonora,' I gasped, 'get me out of here – I
think my next little number is arriving prematurely' – and that
was the end of the Coronation Ball for me and also the end of
little 'might-have-been'.

\*

The drought continued and a new plague arrived in the shape
of hoppers. These were newly hatched locusts who appeared
out of the ground like a moving black carpet. One Sunday
morning not only was the entire garden and farm undulating in
front of our eyes, but the whole of the Solai Valley was covered

with them too. We called out all the labour to sweep them up – burn them – dig trenches for them to fall into and be burned with paraffin – all to no purpose. Every day they grew bigger and every day there were more – gnawing right down into the earth to eat any plant or grass roots. Every day they hopped a bit higher and more and more eggs hatched out. To my horror one day they swept into the house and up the walls. We made a trench all round the house and as they fell into it we burned them with handfuls of lighted newspapers. This was slightly dangerous as our roof was thatched with tinder dry grass. Weeks later they flew away, darkening the sky and fouling the air with their sickly sweet smell. They left a desert behind them, only the droughted coffee trees remaining intact.

In the spring of 1938 Granny and Grandpa went to England for a holiday. While they were away Tom and I took Rose up to Jack's farm on the Kinangop. On the way there, as we were driving through the Karati forest, a lion sprang on to the road straight in front of the car. It ignored us (we had to pull up), and slowly moved off into the bushes. Rose aged three and a half was sitting on my lap in the front seat of the box-body Chev. 'I must get that lion,' she said.

We left Rose and her Seychelles nanny in the charge of Jack while we went down to the coast.

## First Visit to Malindi

There was no main road to speak of between Nairobi and Mombasa, the track being full of pot-holes and impeded by elephant and wild game. Our old car was not up to five hundred miles of this type of road, so we decided to go by Kenya Uganda Railways to Mombasa. There we spent the night at Manor House Hotel. The Manor House was renowned for its ancient tortoise and also its good food. I think it was the first European hotel to be built. We were only there for 24 hours as we were on our way to Malindi, 80 miles north along the coast. Mombasa teemed with Arabs, Africans, Asians and Europeans.

The fruit market under its wide-pillared roof was cool, noisy and smelt wonderful. I bought a *kikapu*, a type of African basket, and filled it with luscious mangoes and paw-paws to take with us, also shiny dark green avocados. 'Feeling hungry?' asked Tom. 'Always for avocados,' I replied.

There was a punkah in our bedroom at the hotel worked by remote control. That is to say an African toe out of sight. That evening we pulled a couple of chairs on to the verandah. Beyond the roof tops we could see the Indian Ocean gleaming in the moonlight.

A thousand smells rose from the garden below: frangipani, sun-drenched flowers, ripe fruit, hot dust, cocoa nuts, smoke from a wood fire, spices, seaweed – so good – so very good.

At 8.30 a.m. the native bus was due to leave from the Manor Hotel. The head waiter told us not to hurry over breakfast as the bus never left on time. At 9.30 a.m. the bus arrived. 'Are we going on that?' I asked. It did not seem possible, but it was either that or not getting to Malindi.

A surge of Swahili and Arabs pressed round the bus while the Indian driver got down and yelled at the African conductor. Both of them climbed halfway up the outside of the bus and then the conductor hauled himself up on to the top – how I do not know. He then handed down crates of chickens, bunches of bananas, bundles and bicycles to upstretched arms, finally jumping down himself. There was much haggling and laughter before more parcels, bundles, bananas, chickens and bicycles were thrown on to the top again and carelessly tied down all round. The passengers embarked including ourselves. We sat in front beside the driver. The bus moved off to the accompaniment of *kwaheris* (farewells) and handshakes, some of the passengers leaning out and hanging on to their friends' hands while they ran alongside. It was then 10.15 a.m., and extremely hot.

We had two rivers to cross in ferry boats. These boats were barges, pulled by hand on ropes stretched across the water. Everything went on board. First we slithered down a ramp which seemed to have minimum contact with the barge so that you splashed into water and up again on to the boat with a jolt – if you did not sink completely, which happened frequently, we were told. Girriama girls, wearing only banana leaf skirts or short kilts made of layers of white cloth strips, boarded the craft with large bundles on their heads and with babies at their breasts or astride their hips.

The bargees, ten or twelve of them, all sang while they pulled on the ropes or played tunes on large conch shells by blowing into them and opening and shutting their hands over them.

It was fortunate that I had brought my *kikapu* of fruit and that the head waiter had provided us with sandwiches. The journey took eight hours.

Several times we skidded off the road and subsided into deep ruts of powdered coral dust. All the passengers then disgorged and helped push. While the driver swore and sweated, the wheels spun helplessly in the dust. Sooner or later a few naked local inhabitants would arrive from nowhere and be bribed reluctantly to assist us.

It was dark when we arrived at Malindi, our destination, and were deposited by the driver at Lawfords Hotel. What a heavenly place! Even in the dim light of oil lamps it was charming. Wide verandahs ran round the building which was single storied, Makuti-thatched and surrounded by lots of little guest huts.

A silent-footed servant led us to one of these huts, showing us our bathroom leading out of the bedroom. He brought us drinks and cans full of hot water and then disappeared. After dinner we went to bed early. We fell asleep to the sounds of gently swishing waves.

Malindi in 1938 was virtually unknown except to a very few. An immense curved bay with warm sands slopes gently to the sea. It is protected from sharks by a coral reef a mile out, which stretches for many miles up and down the coast there.

The beach was bare of trees and had less than a dozen houses on it, which were dotted here and there on the edge of the sandbanks. We had rented one of these for a month and were to be joined by some cousins a few days later.

All day long we bathed and surfed in the long breakers and lived on fruit and brilliantly coloured fish brought round in baskets to the house by local fuzzy-haired fishermen. At night we wore sarongs, lengths of gaudy-coloured cotton cloth, which we wound round ourselves, native style.

Mrs Hervey, aged 80, mother of our friend Venetia Irvine from Solai, had just built a coral house for herself on the Northern end of the bay. She had brought down from up-country her own *fundis*, planned the house herself and super-vised the construction while she camped in a tent on the beach. It was whitewashed inside and out, and thatched with local Makuti dried seaweed on the roof. She had furnished it with Arab and Indian furniture which would stand up to the damp salty atmosphere. Round the sitting room she had painted a frieze of local brilliantly-coloured fish, life-size and accurately portrayed. The fishermen knew her well and brought her differ-ent specimens every day which she popped into a bucket of sea water and then put into a large goldfish bowl where she sketched them.

Her cook ('chef') Queenie had been trained by her to cook quite beautifully and was particularly good at continental dishes. We spent as much time with her as we could spare from surfing and bathing and were highly entertained by her parrot as well as herself. She had many friends of all nation-alities. While we were at Malindi a young French Countess and her son, Louis, aged nine were staying with her. At lunch one day Louis refused his food. 'Mais Louis,' said his mother, 'tu mange pas?' 'Non, Maman.' 'Mais pourquoi pas? Voyons mange donc Zu Zu.' 'Non, Maman,' 'Mais pourquoi Louis?' 'Moi,' said Louis, 'moi je me méfie des mishmaches de Madame Hervey.' He had suffered from a severe tummy upset the day before.

Mrs Hervey painted with her needle as well as her brushes, working large panels of flowers and fruit, seascapes and land-scapes into rugs and cushions with wools and silks. She was fond of telling us how one of her ancestors, the Earl of Bristol, founded the Bristol Hotels right across the continent.

One evening a swarm of live bees came into our kitchen and we were forced to stay outside on the beach for several hours until they were 'collected' by a Girriama honey hunter. At that time Mrs Hervey's daughter, Venetia Irvine, was staying with her. One day Venetia was attacked by a swarm as she came out of the sea after her bathe. She tried to get rid of them by rolling in the waves at the water's edge, but they only attacked her more fiercely. Queenie the cook happened to see her from the verandah of the house and instantly whipped a sheet off a bed, and rushed to her rescue. He threw it over her, covering her from head to toe and beat off the swarm with a wet towel he had brought with him. Venetia was half killed and had 237 stings removed from her – undoubtedly Queenie saved her life.

After a few days Tom said he needed exercise and took himself off to explore the country clad in bathing shorts and shirt hanging loose over the top. Later when we walked along the beach to Lawford's Hotel for sundowners Tom told Major Lawford that he had crossed a river a mile or so inland and asked what it was called. 'You crossed it – waded through it?' Major Lawford enquired. 'Yes, twice, there and back,' replied Tom. 'Well it is full of crocodiles, or supposed to be, and I call it Croc-ford for the want of a better name. I wouldn't make a habit of wading through it if I were you.'

As the days passed we fell more and more in love with Malindi. Tom visited the District Commissioner and enquired whether there were any plots of land for sale. But the Land Commission was having difficulty with the Arabs who had no title deeds but *knew* that their fathers had owned it, therefore it was theirs.

\*

All too soon our holiday came to an end. We got out of the train at N'sa station where Jack and Rose and 'Nanny' met us on the platform.

Mama – 'Gran' as she was now called, had arrived back from England a few days earlier. The afternoon we arrived from

Malindi there was a welcome home party for Gran on the farm. Seventy-two women and children, the families of about a dozen farm labourers on the estate, all turned out in their best cotton dresses and clustered together on the front lawn; much giggling and scuffling took place. 'Gran' had organised this tea party herself from England. Having learned from Jack how many dependants were on the farm she went to Woolworth's and bought seventy-two garments of all sizes and colours, scarves for the girls and the right amount of shirts for the men. A table was put out on the front lawn, and on this were the parcels and Rose in the middle sitting upright, her short legs sticking out in front of her. Gran then told the head boy to call the children, women, and men, in that order. One by one, as they came up Gran put a parcel into Rose's hands and told her to give it to them. This was a great success except for Rose who expected a parcel for herself and kept asking where hers was. After the presents had been given out to everyone on the place (there were some spares in case one or two more babies had been born in her absence) large trays of rock cakes and sponge fingers were handed round and Jerango poured out gallons of tea and milk into their tin mugs and gourds. Finally, after handfuls of paper-wrapped boiled sweets had been thrown into the air for a 'scramble' (in which the men all joined and got most of the sweets) the party broke up and disappeared singing into the distance.

*

Before we left Jack's farm on the Kinangop, we went on a fishing picnic with friends who lived at the foot of the Aberdare Mountains, at an altitude of 8,400 feet. Hugh and Rebecca Ward were building their second house of cedar wood. They built it themselves with the help of their young Scottish manager, Johnnie Nimmo, some African friends and a book of instructions. The approach road to the house was a remarkable feat of engineering. It was surveyed and constructed by Hugh Ward and his Africans. It was cut out of solid rock and wound up and down for three miles through cedar forests covered with lichen and alive with colobus monkeys. These beautiful creatures cavorted through the branches, leaping and swinging in much the same way as squirrels do. There were two bridges across rivers about twenty feet wide, strong enough to take heavy lorry loads of stone. The rarified atmosphere was sharply cold out of the sun and smelt of the giant hypericum bushes which abound all over the Kinangop.

Tom, who was an expert angler, disappeared for the whole day and returned to the picnic rendezvous before sunset with a bag full of rainbow trout. Unfortunately we could not bathe in the rivers as they were supposed to be infested with bilharzia – a dangerous bug which attacks the muscles.

In the shallow pools large flocks of small butterflies fluttered about, pale blue and pale yellow in colour. Rose easily caught them in her tiny hands and referred to them as 'fly-butters'. The birds in the forest were exciting too, flocks of green parrots who live on the wild olives, birds who glided silently through the trees, ruby-coloured wings spread out and the sun glinting on their blue-green bodies. Bullbulls and whydah birds were everywhere, the male bird resembling a flying snake with his long tailfeather three times the length of his body dragging behind him.

Driving home that night we were startled to hear crashing in the forest beside us. But whether it was a buffalo or a rhino our car lights evidently frightened them/it away. Far across the Kinangop plain a light was shining in isolation. 'That is Leonora and Nick's new farmhouse,' Jack told us. 'They still have the farm below us, "Fernside", and another house on the escarpment. They call that one "Occasionally" and the one you are looking at "Sometimes", their permanent residence being Fernside.'

Tom was looking for land at a higher altitude than our coffee estate in Solai (6000 feet) where he could grow a new crop called pyrethrum. Next day we drove up to the Wards again with Jack, having sent on the horses beforehand.

With Rebecca and Hugh we set off in a cavalcade of five carrying our sandwiches and beer in saddle bags. The scenery was very like Scotland except that the sun was much stronger and the vast spaces empty of human beings. We rode along the edge of the forest following a river which wound in and out of the thick tussock grass which reached up to our stirrups. At midday we stopped for lunch and sat down in the shade of a wild fig tree. We unsaddled the ponies and let them crop the grass.

Immense views stretched out on three sides of us. 'This plot is about 1500 acres and is for sale,' Rebecca told us. 'It would make a marvellous site for a house,' Tom said. It was a wonderful place – and yet – I felt my 'fae' instincts warning me. 'There is something I can't explain. Is there any other land for sale in this area?' But there was not. Rebecca and Hugh were extremely disappointed. Tom, however, told them that he had come to the conclusion that the Kinangop was too inaccessible for him to be able to run a second farm there economically. It was sad to have to give up the idea altogether, as we had been looking forward to seeing more of Rebecca and Hugh.

Many years later a family called Ruck bought that plot. Their name was blazed across the world during the Mau Mau rebellion. Mrs Ruck, who was a qualified doctor, her husband and small son of six years were dragged out and most brutally murdered by the 'Sacrificial Tree' – the fig tree where we had picnicked so happily in 1938.

*

## First Rumblings of War

When we got home we were greeted by the head man. 'Is all well?' Tom asked. 'Oh yes, Bwana, all is well, *Mzouri sana.*'

World news grew worse and we bought a Phillips radio set. Sitting by the fire in our pyjamas and dressing gowns with our nearest neighbour, Michael Blundell, we discussed the Anschluss and Neville Chamberlain – the possibility of war. Tom said it could not be avoided and that Neville Chamberlain had merely postponed the evil hour. Michael disagreed and would not contemplate war – he was against wars which have never decided anything and thought that if people would go to war they had no right to bring children into the world just to be cannon-fodder! We turned on the wireless and heard Adolf Hitler screaming hysterically against the Jews.

Earlier that year, on March 12th 1938, Hitler had invaded Austria and was menacing Czechoslovakia. The rumblings of war grew louder and Granny stated that conflict was quite inevitable now that 'Chamberlain had allowed Hitler to invade Austria.' She said that we had obligations to Czechoslovakia and must *not betray our friends*. Being a great partisan and Royalist and Loyalist she had clear-cut boundaries between right and wrong in her own mind and suffered no one to disagree with her. There was no other point of view.

New Year's Day 1939 dawned serenely beautiful in our Solai Valley. Dew glistened on the coffee trees and grass when I took Rose out for a walk before breakfast. Africans sang and called to one another in the valley below. A team of 16 oxen yoked together ploughed up a maize field. White steam jets curled up from the sunken crown of Menengai crater. No breeze rustled the leaves for the hot weather wind would not get up until 10 a.m. Minty the spaniel accompanied us as well as Rose's ghost children, Petsy and Tsin-Tsin.

The sound of running footsteps made me turn round. It was the gardener. 'Memsahib, Memsahib, don't walk along there. Come back,' he urged. 'There is a big snake up in that acacia tree; it has eaten a goat only yesterday and now it will eat you.' The tree was a few yards away beside a water trough and I could partly see a thick black python twisted round an over-hanging branch.

I knew that Tom had ridden through the Jubilee plantation and had not gone by the drive. 'Wait on the road for the Bwana to warn him about the snake,' I said.

'I have already sent word to the Bwana,' he replied.

When Tom came in for breakfast he went for his gun and disappeared outside again. I heard a bang followed by gleeful shouts of 'M'zuri, M'zuri sana Bwana,' and knew that was the end of that python. At breakfast I remarked that he had not mentioned having pythons on the farm. 'Well, it is the only one I have ever seen. There has to be a serpent in every Eden,' he pointed out.

During that dry weather we put all thoughts of war out of our minds. We installed a porcelain bath in the bathroom, a great innovation, and were able to have cold water running direct into the bath from a tap for the first time. It also ran into the nursery basin much to Rose's delight. Galvanised iron tanks were set up on a small hillock behind the house. One pipe led from them to the top of a tank placed over a brazier in the kitchen. This was stoked with large pieces of blue gum branches called 'kuni' by the Africans. A smaller pipe ran from the bottom of this tank to the bathroom – thus, our hot water! Heath Robinson if you like but efficient. We felt that we had taken our first step towards a more civilised way of life!

Mother sent us a telegram. 'Daddy returned from England stop bring Rose stay over my birthday stop War imminent.' She sent her Vauxhall with native chauffeur for us. Tom was preparing for the coffee picking season so was not able to accompany us.

Daddy was looking years younger after his holiday in England, which he had spent mostly with his sister, Aunt Doll, at Crawley. Both parents were full of gloom. Daddy said that Hitler would have to be stopped and that England was totally unprepared for war and that he had come back while he still could.

Jack arrived back from his annual two weeks camp with the Kenya Defence Force. Most young European settlers belonged to the K.D.F. and went twice a year for a fortnight's training.

Mama's birthday went off unusually peacefully. Mother's next door neighbours (only about half a mile along the escarpment), a Mr and Mrs Lodge, came over for a game of bridge, Eton v Harrow. Old Frank Lodge was an O.E. and Jack an O.H. All was peace.

## Call-up for War

Next morning the post boy brought up the post bag from Naivasha with telegrams for Mama's birthday and one for Jack. He was up on the top farm dosing sheep and did not come down until tea time. He opened the telegram and passed it to me without a word while going out to the dairy. It was his call-up telling him to report back to camp immediately.

The rest of the evening was spent collecting blankets, writing materials etc., all the endless things needed for – War! It had happened, or was about to happen. Unbelievable!

By chance I had brought Alfred, our second house-boy, with me to help with Rose's laundry. He was a Jaluo, huge and coal black and had a delightful grin. He was also very intelligent and capable. Jack would need a Batman, so I asked Alfred if he would like to go with Jack to fight the Italians or Germans. He was thrilled at the idea. He said he could darn socks and took off one he was wearing to show me how he had darned it quite beautifully with pink wool. 'The Mission Memsahib taught me,' he said proudly.

My sister Joan who came out to Kenya with me before I married in 1934 was living on the Kinangop in a small house she had built for herself on part of the farm. Jack went up to fetch her and she agreed to manage the farm for him as her War Effort.

At daybreak next morning Jack, Nick Leigh and Johnnie Nimmo set off in Nick's old Ford accompanied by a jubilant Alfred – destination the Northern Frontier bordering Abyssinia. Joan settled down to run the farm, for the next few months and remained there for the next four years.

Rose and I returned immediately to Tom in Solai. As we drove through Nakuru, our local township, a neighbour stopped me. She had two small children in the car and was fighting back tears. 'Geoff left for Mombasa on last night's train to rejoin the Royal Navy. I've been in to get supplies. You better get what you can now as imported goods will run clean out.' So Jerango (mother's chauffeur) drove us to the biggest

Indian store, a tin shack which had an advertisement outside promising to 'supply all housewife desires'. The only things I could think of at that moment were soap and paraffin oil, but we could come into Nakuru again next morning. It was August 18th – already every member of the Kenya Defence Force had been called up as well as all Naval and Air Force Reserves.

Back on the farm, Tom was busy picking the coffee crop. He told me that he would be going to Nakuru first thing in the morning to try to pass the medical test for active service. Did I think that I could run the farm if he should be passed fit? For one second the abyss opened at my feet – and closed again. 'Yes. With Pedro Onyango (our head man) I can manage perfectly well.'

He did not pass his medical. Not only was he over-age but unknown to me he had a dicky heart, the result of typhoid contracted in India some years before we married. This was a bitter blow to him, and a relief to me. Instead he was told to produce 100% food, i.e. maize, coffee, wheat etc. and to assist on three other farms where the owners had enlisted and left their wives to carry on. Still he tried to pull strings to get into some sort of active military service, but was told his War Effort on the farms was just as important, so that was that.

Rumours of war escalated. We put in supplies of wireless batteries, essentials such as medicines, farm implements, spares for the machinery at the coffee factory etc.

# War Breaks Out

The morning sun glistened on the coffee trees, birds sang, the valley looked serenely beautiful. Rose, now three years old, could be heard arguing with her Seychelles nanny while being dressed for her pre-breakfast walk. An African syce brought our one remaining horse round to the front of the house and Tom set off for the shamba. My little mare had died of horse sickness as soon as I brought her to the Solai Farm.

It was the coffee planting season and the Little Rains had begun. All planting was done by hand, usually twenty or so acres at a time. It would not come into full bearing for five years. The labour force worked from 7 a.m. until 2 p.m. unless on a 'pima' (task) which they could do at any time of the day they liked, mostly early in the morning.

As usual my first daily task was to dose the Africans. Sometimes I did not know what they had at all. But bubonic plague was easily diagnosed, even by the Africans, and we all had to be inoculated from time to time. On the morning of 3rd September, a baby was brought up to me with half its skin off its back from burns. Its mother told me unemotionally that it had fallen into the fire which is always set on the floor of their huts in the centre of the room. The baby was a terrible sight. After wrapping it up in a sheet soaked in raw cod liver oil, I drove mother and baby into the Nakuru Native Hospital 12 miles

74

away. The town was in turmoil, preparing for war, should the Italians invade across the Abyssinian frontier. We had not heard the morning news as we never turned it on in those days until the evening.

The District Commissioner's office was close by so I joined a small crowd of settlers to hear the latest official news.

'England is at war with Germany.' The words rang out loud and clear in a tense silence.

Life was never the same again for anybody.

All able-bodied men rushed to the colours and the women took over the farms and the African farm labourers.

We were still cultivating with oxen. The Africans would call each animal by name and the leading pair were led by a M'toto pulling them on a rope.

## The Pyrethrum Farm

At the beginning of 1939 we had bought another farm at a higher altitude to grow pyrethrum. It was virgin land at the edge of the lovely Bahati forest. Tom designed and built a pyrethrum drier and we installed four Jaluo families on the 70 acres of land to look after it and plant the pyrethrum daisies by hand. Tom went up there every two days or so, so our petrol ration was quickly used between the two farms. Before planting anything, the land had to be terraced and cultivated. One day we had hoped to retire up there where the views were glorious and the climate fresh and cold. The forest behind our plantation was inhabited by colobus monkeys and green parrots, and a small river ran through it. Tom and a neighbour, Short Eames, stocked the river with rainbow trout and had many a pleasant day's fishing together.

Green delphiniums, crimson gloriosa lilies, black-eyed Susans and sprays of white orchids grew in profusion, amongst many other wild flowers, in and around the Bahati Forest of olive and cedar trees.

One of the first two people to grow pyrethrum in Kenya was a Swiss called Jacques Richard. He and his young wife lived above the Bahati Forest at an altitude of 9000 feet in a house made of bamboo and mud, while they were building a large wooden bungalow. In 1939 they were picking pyrethrum off a thousand acres and making a fortune. She had three little girls under three years but was quite happy and very efficient. All the Kikuyu women were very envious and thought she was marvellous.

Soon the little white daisies were covering the terraces. Sacks of dried flowers were sent down to Nakuru for processing to be made into the basic ingredient for the insecticide Flit and other disinfectants much in demand during the war. It rapidly grew into an important industry, becoming one of the country's main exports.

Weeks passed and the Phoney War lulled us into a semi state of unreality. We all began to believe that the Maginot Line had really stopped the Germans from invading France and that it might all be over sooner than we had expected. As we all know, that was only a small breathing space given to us.

On the other side of the world, a young officer in the Manchester Regiment called George Frampton had been sent out to France and later was in the retreat to Dunkirk. Forty years would pass before I learnt of his experiences at that time.

## Seaside Holiday at Nyali

Early in 1940 we took Rose down to the coast for a holiday at Nyali. It was essential to go down to sea level once a year to retain one's sanity. We shared a bungalow with the St. Maur's. The weather was stormy but we bathed and ate mangoes and rested. At night we had to tuck the mosquito nets firmly round the end of the beds as large green crabs crawled into the room and clawed their way up the netting. The first time one did this I found it facing me at eye level. Not a pleasant encounter.

Hope St. Maur and Gemma were sitting with us on the verandah one evening after a very hot day, no breeze even to move the palm trees. A new moon climbed up the sky while the Indian Ocean murmured far out beyond the reef. 'It looks a bit murky out there on the horizon,' Tom remarked. 'I wonder if we shall have a storm tonight!' We sat outside until darkness enveloped us, as it does very quickly in the east, talking about the Phoney War, wondering when it would all end and where. Freddie St. Maur was overseas and Hope and Gemma were soon to join him. Jack was in Madagascar with the 4th K.A.R. We never doubted that we would win the war.

During the night the wind got up and rapidly turned into a tornado. My bed shuddered, a noise of shrieking demons filled the room. Tom's figure was moving in a kaleidoscope of wild patterns. He bent down and shouted in my ear to get up while he struggled to light the hurricane lamp. We could see nothing but sand with branches and whole trees hurtling horizontally through the air.

We crawled hand in hand round the back of the bungalow to Hope's room. We were situated in a curve of the beach and relatively sheltered. We all sat in her bedroom hoping the whole hut would not take off and take us with it. After a night of noise and chaos dawn broke and the wind seemed to be dying down although we still could not see much but whirling sand. The whole bungalow was covered in it and so were we. Clothes, bedding, toilet things, furniture, everything moveable seemed to have had a mad ball. Our African servants who had accompanied us from the farm appeared looking scared and wet. 'Mungu has taken everything,' they said (Mungu meaning God). 'Not quite,' Tom assured them. 'Let's have a scout round and get some breakfast,' he said. 'Or lunch' suggested Hope.

The Kasuarina trees were still standing but no huts or palm trees. The natives in the village did not mind very much, it was an Act of God which often happened. They had simply run inland taking their pots and babies with them until the tornado passed. Later we heard that only the fringe of the storm had touched us. Further along the coast damage was considerable, and also loss of life.

*

At home on the farm again after our holiday at sea level, all seemed to be going well, except that our head man had been put in gaol for brewing Nubian gin. He was an hereditary witch doctor. Tom paid his fine for him, telling the police that he could not be spared from the farm.

What does one remember of those war years? One day we turned on the B.B.C. news and heard that the submarine *Spearfish* had been torpedoed and all the crew drowned. A cousin of ours was the Commander, Jock Forbes. A short time before this the *Spearfish* had sunk a pocket battleship. Jock had wirelessed the Admiralty 'Spotted pocket battleship' followed up with 'Have pocketed battleship'. Now he too had gone. The Germans steamrollered over the Netherlands taking a young Musson cousin with them.

The Epic of Dunkirk and the agony of waiting to hear if the B.E.F. had got through the net. The Battle of Britain and the whole world holding its breath. Churchill's famous remark, 'Never have so many owed so much to so few.' The sinking of the *Royal Oak* in Scapa Flow. Uncle Bill Benn was the Captain and we did not know for several months if he had survived. Years after he was to tell me that he could never forget the sound of 800 men rattling down the ship to their deaths. He himself was picked up on the surface of the oil-covered sea and lifted into a boat with a lot of dead men. He heard someone say 'this one ain't dead' before losing consciousness.

In our valley every household lost at least one relative serving overseas. Dauby Baillie, wife of Frank Baillie in our valley had a teenage son in the R.A.F. fighting the Italians. She was told that his plane had been shot down in flames and he was missing. He was her only son by a previous marriage. A few days after she had told us, I was writing in the sitting room when I heard her son say to me quite clearly, 'I am dead but quite all right. I was shot and suffered no pain. Tell Mother . . .' I told Frank who passed on the message.

Subsequently the War Office confirmed this to be true, i.e., that his body had been found and that he had been shot and not burned to death in his plane.

Then there was the day that France capitulated. The little stationer in Nakuru that morning was terribly pessimistic. Once again I knew that we would win and told him that we were far better without the French if we wanted to beat Hitler.

Our old friends and neighbours, John and Marianne Price, were full of stories brought to them by the many soldiers and serving personnel whom they had to stay and convalesce. We all grew lots of vegetables and fruit, and we had about twenty rabbits for eating (soon numbering forty as they enjoyed life and ate huge amounts of fresh food.) An R.A.F. training camp grew up on the planes outside Nakuru and we took in baskets of yellow sugar tomatoes, along with the rabbits, to the mess. We also had soldiers billeted on us on their way to the Northern Frontier, a lot of South Africans amongst them; very uncouth they were too. The Italians always complained that they did not have enough oil in or with their food, but did a lot of useful things while in Kenya. They surveyed and constructed the new main Kenya Uganda road. Another innovation was a glass-making factory near Nairobi.

When we ran out of necessities such as soap and polish we made our own locally. The soap was horrible, being made out of magadi soda and animal fat.

At home we struggled with drought and coffee diseases due to lack of rain. Fortunately for us the pyrethrum flourished and was a profitable crop.

Time passed. We were looking forward to another baby in October 1941. Our old friends John and Marianne Price frequently came to see us, usually to complain about Venetia, their next door neighbour and a much loved friend of ours! Marianne was a great character and believed in speaking her own mind. She fell violently in love at the age of sixty with Count Carlo Cornegliano and dragged John with her to Italy to see Carlo in his own stately surroundings before war broke out. John said that the Contessa was *not* pleased to see them and the whole visit was a disaster. Marianne never saw Carlo again and heard that he had died in Italy early in 1939. Whether he returned her affection nobody knew, but poor Marianne never really got over this sad affair.

*

When the Italians joined forces with Hitler they had massed their troops on the Kenya/Abyssinia border. There was no way we could have stopped them from walking across Kenya and our defences were ludicrous, one man to about every five miles it was said. But they did not invade.

Our local District Commissioner summoned us to a meeting at Lavender's Corner at the end of our valley. The Provincial Commissioner was there to speak about a plan to evacuate us all from Kenya by road.

'Those of you who wish to leave Kenya must do so now,' he said. 'There is, of course, only one way out. You would have to go in convoy through the Masai Reserve, down through Tanganyika and on to South Africa. You would provide your own transport and provisions etc. and the rallying point would be here.'

No one volunteered to leave. Stay we would. Our farms were our livelihood.

There was another occasion after France capitulated when we sank the French fleet. John Price appeared at the window while we were having lunch. 'Can't dismount. I've been on the shamba all morning. Just came round to make sure you know that the French frogs have deserted, and we've sunk the French fleet. Don't think the French were much help to us anyway, do you?' He rode away.

Michael Blundell had been kept in reserve to form the African Pioneer Corps owing to his knowledge of tribal languages which would be necessary in training the many different kinds of African. He was bombarded with white feathers by angry young wives who did not know why he was still there when their husbands were not!

## Dunkirk and the Battle for Britain

Tom had got out an old map of France. 'The British Forces will be caught in a trap now as the Germans will do a pincer movement. Damn those b.... French.' For days there was little news and our wireless went ceaselessly most of the night while Tom paced up and down the room. Then the name Dunkirk came over. 'By Jove we've done it, sweetheart – I do believe we've DONE IT!' Tom was right. We all know about the miraculous evacuation in little and big ships, anything that could float on the water.

Major George Frampton was one of the last to get out from Dunkirk.

Then the Battle for Britain. We felt desperately frustrated at being so far away and longed to help, somehow – do anything.

Much later, after Jenny had arrived and was about two months old, there was the awful news that the *Hood* and the *Prince of Wales* had been sunk. I had put out Jenny's milk feeds in six bottles when Tom came into the nursery to tell me. I jumped up, knocking over the first bottle of milk, then it knocked down all the other five bottles like ninepins, and *all the milk lay on the floor!*

In May 1941, as I was threatened with a second miscarriage, it was decided that Rose should go to kindergarten boarding school at Thomsons Falls forty miles away over an atrocious road. The day she left was the worst day I had ever known. She went off very happily but I wept for days and days. After three weeks Tom took me to see her with the promise that if she was unhappy she would return home with us. But she seemed to be very happy amongst all the other small children there so we returned without her.

## 1941

When the Abyssinia campaign was over, Jack came home on leave and I went up to the Kinangop for a few days to see him. Alfred, his Jaluo batman, greeted me jubilantly. 'Memsahib,' he said, 'we won the battle of Gondar. It was like this: Bwana Jack led his Askaries into battle – we saw Gondar up on the heights – guns were firing – boom, boom, – I dropped to the ground – I looked up – Bwana Jack and lots of Askaries were scaling the cliffs – the Italians fired – boom, boom, boom – I dropped to the ground – boom, boom – I hid my head in the ground – I looked up – the Union Jack was flying over Gondar, Memsahib.'

This account may not quite tally with the official records but will remain in the structure of Alfred's personal history (and the story will be told around the fireside for many generations to come, improving as it goes along). Jack informed me that so far as he knew, Alfred had remained behind with the supplies and had hidden under a lorry during the entire battle. But he was a splendid batman and darned socks beautifully.

*

Before Rose came home for the holidays we bought her a small donkey. It was not a success. It took a dislike to our horse, refused to be caught and bit anyone who approached with a bridle. It looked unhappy and brayed persistently. Each time we succeeded in cornering it and putting on a head collar, it stopped moving altogether. It allowed Rose to sit on its back

*Difficulties with the donkey.*

and thereafter remained rooted to the ground – no amount of shoving or bribing with carrots had any effect. Rose kicked her heels into it while the syce pulled its bridle and I spoke encouraging words. It simply shut its eyes, elongated its neck and dug its hooves more firmly into the ground. After six months we sold it to a Somali.

Meanwhile our pedigree spaniel bitch 'Minty' had given birth to six puppies. We named the boys after the Generals: Alexander, Montgomery, Archibald Wavell and Gott, and the two girls F.A.N.N.Y. and W.R.E.N. They were all sold at six weeks except Archie. Wavell was my great hero then.

On October 8th 1941 our second daughter was born in the new maternity wing of the European hospital. Tom was in one of the men's wards down the other end of the hospital recovering from a severe attack of double pneumonia. In those days the cure for pneumonia was a pill called 693 which nearly killed its patients.

Mama sailed into the hospital, her arms filled with huge bunches of sweet peas to see her latest grandchild. She took one look at the baby, then went along to visit Tom. 'I've just seen your new daughter,' she told him. 'She's so ugly, and why do you call her Jasmine – it should be pronounced 'Hassmeen' as in Spanish – very pretty. I shall call her Hassmeen.' Later Tom sent me a note by one of the nurses on duty. 'For heaven's sake sweetheart call the child Jennifer – will explain later,' which he did. So Jennifer it was and is.

Ten days later Jennifer left hospital and returned to the farm in the expert care of Joy Percival, a great friend of ours, Truby King, and a great nurse. The Percival family lived south of Nairobi near Machakos and Joy's parents were amongst the very first pioneers to take up land there. When Joy herself was born at Potha, a red blanket was hung out of the window so that their nearest neighbours far away across the plains would see it and know that the baby had arrived and was a girl. Had it been a boy, a blue blanket was to have been hung out.

Back on the Solai farm Joy found Mother installed and had to use all her tact to keep the peace. We had a P.O.W. from an

Italian camp helping us then to run the farms. This man was forbidden to use or drive our car. When Joy arrived with the baby Mother was looking rather embarrassed. It transpired that she had commanded the Italian to get the car out and drive her to a neighbour down the valley. The Italian promptly drove it into a culvert and broke the axle. So a van had to be hired, unknown to us, while expensive repairs were made. In addi-

*Rose & Jennifer.*

tion to this, Mother disliked the swallows who built regularly on the inside of our verandah roof. She said they were dirty and must be removed, but the house servants refused to obey the order until the Bwana came back. With them she met her Waterloo.

Rose came back from school full of Red Cross enthusiasm. We made her a Red Cross apron and cap and she spent the holidays organising a dolls hospital, giving everybody injections with a pencil. Baby Jennifer was inoculated too but survived!

When Tom came out of hospital he was not at all fit and had to go down to sea leave for a month, the doctor ordered.

Everywhere in Mombasa were soldiers and airmen and sailors from all over the world. The war with Japan was raging fiercely on the other side of the Indian Ocean and Kenyan boys on leaving school all joined the R.A.F.

Most of the K.A.R. Btns. went to South East Asia, Ceylon and Burma. Imported goods such as cotton and woollen garments had become very scarce so we all took up wool spinning and dyeing. We taught ourselves and tried to teach the African girls as well. Food production became of paramount importance to provide for the thousands of troops now in Kenya and also for the large P.O.W. camps. We also learned how to make macaroni and dry it in the sun. As a result of the Army and P.O.W.s coming to Kenya, our roads and communications were developed and lasting improvements made.

Mombasa, until recently a sleepy, steamy, commercial port, now teemed with people in smart uniforms. Large areas of the docks were cordoned off except for those who had permits. No one spoke of what was going on and no one was supposed to have eyes or ears – but the Bush Telegraph operated as usual with deadly accuracy.

There was a big farewell party in Mombasa given for all the service personnel going overseas, many of them were born and bred in Kenya, one girl in the WRENS, Ann Hook, amongst them. As soon as the ship sailed out into the Indian Ocean she was torpedoed – there were no survivors.

## 1942

January started gloomily with Rommel regaining for Germany all territory in North Africa which the British had won in the Christmas campaign. Simultaneously the Japs were sweeping all before them in Malaya and Burma. Geographically this brought the war even closer to us in Kenya.

The surrender of Singapore, following so quickly upon the fall of Hong Kong, cast a deep gloom over everyone in Kenya which not even the glorious daily sunshine could dispel. There had also been anxiety over Malta and the convoys and our own defence seemed in a parlous state. But out of this welter of disasters came the clear sound of Churchill's repeated clarion calls, one memorable one was 'Provided we all stand together . . . and we throw in the last spasm of our strength, it looks . . . as if we are going to win', and of course his reference to the Norway campaign 'We shall cleanse and purge the territories of the Vikings from the foul pollution of the Nazi hordes,' and many other victorious peals.

Later that year a Danish friend of Mother's came to visit us. She had four sons, three of them serving with the R.A.F. and one a Nazi sympathiser still farming on the Kinangop. She had many tragedies, poor lady, before coming out to Kenya to visit her two eldest sons. She sewed exquisitely and was helping me to mend and turn my double linen sheets one morning on the verandah when an African postman rode up on a bicycle. He saluted and handed me a telegram. It was for Mrs. Kühle. She turned pale when she opened it. 'My son,' she said, handing it to me. 'Killed in action'. I read while she folded her sheet up carefully, put away her needle and thimble and quietly walked into the house. For two days she remained in her room, sending me a little note excusing her presence and asking only for some milk to drink. When she emerged she begged us not to speak of it – life went on as usual.

From us she went on to visit other friends down the valley with whom she stayed on as companion help for a couple of months. At the end of that time, the postman rode up on his bicycle again and handed me a telegram – for Mrs. Kühle. With a dreadful presentiment I told the postman I would take it to her. She was in Frank Baillie's garden when I found her. At the sight of the telegram in my hand she stopped as though turned to stone. 'Read it to me please,' she asked me. It announced the death of her second son in action with the R.A.F. We stood there in silence while the sun shone down on to the lotus-covered pond and a gentle breeze swayed the weeping bottle brush trees. Birds sang joyously and a brilliant humming bird fluttered beside fuchsia bushes. Death and life! What was the meaning of it all?

## *Holiday at Diani*

In early 1943 Tom and I left Jenny and a little friend in the charge of Miss Tirrell on the farm, also Rose and a little friend of hers, and went down to the coast to Diani, twenty miles south of Mombasa. We had a two-roomed cottage at one side of the main building set amongst palm trees on the edge of the beach. The owners were Nellie and Maxwell Trench. She was small, looked a thousand years old and was as round as a tennis ball. Maxie, her husband, was slim and aristocratic-looking with a wicked twinkle in his eyes as he looked up from under a battered banana-leaf hat.

The first evening a bath tub was brought to the shower closet off our bedroom. Tom looked at it and decided he could never get his long legs into it. After such a long journey I deemed a hot bath essential so doubled my legs up and squeezed into the tub. When I tried to get out I found myself stuck fast to the sides. Pulling was in vain. Nellie was sent for – she got a bucket of cold water and soused me with it and then jerked me out.

All meals were taken on a big verandah in the main building and consisted mostly of delicious fish dishes accompanied by native beans, vegetables and rice. Mangoes were in season, also the brown thin-skinned Zanzibar oranges, pale yellow/green, so delicately flavoured and refreshing.

Nellie had friends in every community – Arab, Asian and Girriamas, and was no respector of persons. Full of humour, generosity and kindness, she was tireless and shrewd too and in a few years had made Jardini into a most popular family holiday resort.

Nellie and Maxwell Trench had been in partnership with John Carberry some years before taking up land along the coast.

We discussed Joss Errol's murder and June Carberry's evidence. 'Who killed Cock Robin' was anybody's guess – but was certainly not Delves Broughton who was tried and acquitted of the murder. We all suspected Diana Delves-Broughton.

'You must meet my friends the Fathialidahlas,' Nellie said, 'when they come over for a bathe tomorrow. He owns the biggest general store in M'sa and I'm hundreds of pounds in debt to him'.

The following afternoon an enormous limousine car drove down the sandy track to the beach, followed by another even bigger. Fourteen children got out of the first one, and six women and eight children out of the second. A third car arrived with four very fat Asian passengers and driven by an Arab. The largest of these Asians, wearing a red fez and white Tassau suit, was presented to us by Maxwell as Mr Fathialidahla. 'You have enjoyable holiday, yes?' he enquired, bowing. 'I supply all best foods, Mrs Trench, no?' What with yes and no the conversation became confusingly monotonous – all I wanted to do was watch the beautiful little Indian girls fluttering about in their saris, looking like a lot of sea fairies dancing in the wind.

At full moon the tide was high and swished up almost to the edge of the garden, sucking back bubbles and shells and exposing hundreds of tiny transparent pink crabs which popped out of the sand and raced about until the next wave broke over them.

All too soon our month was up. Tom had regained his health and we had to leave for the farm, promising to bring the children down next year. Before we left an Arab *dhow* sailed in and anchored outside the reef, providing the final touch of romance. It was difficult to realise that only a few miles out in the ocean, ships were being menaced by submarines and the world was in the grip of a most terrible war.

We were relatively fortunate to be living in Kenya during those dreadful years though every one of us felt, quite erroneously, that we could have helped more had we been in England.

Soon after the Italians entered the war, old Mrs Hervey, Venetia's mother at Malindi, was a target for the only aerial attack ever made on Kenya. In the middle of the morning a flight of six bombers zoomed out of a cloudless sky and dropped several sticks of bombs around Malindi before flying back to Mogadishu. No one was hurt and the only recorded damage was to Mrs Harvey's front door, which was slightly chipped.

Up country there was one scare when the wife of a retired general rang up G.H.Q. Nairobi to say she had seen two enemy aircraft flying over the house. Later, when everyone had been organised and disorganised, the two enemy aircraft flew over again – and were discovered to be nothing more than a pair of Kavirondo cranes.

Our worries were of a different kind. Drought followed drought and locusts darkened the skies. Grass fires swept the country and the forests caught fire and blazed for weeks on end. The army often came to the rescue and joined the farmers, everyone beating the flames to try to put them out. The great cedar and olive trees would crash, sending up a fountain of red sparks into the air.

Vast quantities of maize were imported from America to help in famine areas, and amongst the maize came a new weed, Mexican marigold. This rank-smelling plant spread like wild fire and was soon all over the country and causing much damage amongst the arable crops. At that time spraying of crops in Kenya was rarely practised except in the coffee growing districts of Kiambu where the planters had already begun spraying for some of the coffee pests, and that was done by hand, the cans being strapped to their back.

## Artificial Insemination Arrives in Kenya

About this time a new invention arrived in Kenya – Artificial Insemination. As the regular importation of pedigree stock had virtually ceased with the war, A.I. became almost a necessity. Tom was one of the first people to take it up in our valley. We had a meeting at our house of all the old farmers and officials and 'grass widows' to discuss A.I. and its important contribution to modern farming. They began to arrive at 10 a.m. and at 4 p.m. they were still there. Our staff (a cook and Toto and two house-boys) were hugely pleased with what they called the 'Baraza' and as more people arrived they just sent word to the neighbours' servants to come and help and bring more food – which they did, most efficiently, and without reference to the Memsahibs.

While the Baraza was in session on our deep front verandah, Jennifer was in her cot under a pepper tree behind the house. When, rather late, I went to give her some lunch, she was quite happy sitting up in her cot in nothing but a sunbonnet and a pair of pants, eating small green caterpillars as they fell on to her mosquito net.

There was a baby Cranswick next door to us, Chas Cranswick having married. The baby was a few weeks older than Jenny. Our gardener used to talk to Jenny when she was put outside before breakfast and would tell me proudly, 'Our baby beats that baby next door *kapisa* (which means completely)'. No doubt next door the gardener said the same thing about the little Cranswick. Our lives were simple and restricted by the severe petrol rationing. Tom and I read a lot and I made all the clothes for the children as well as myself and began to embroider a Queen Anne quilt. Gardening was the greatest joy as every sort of fruit, flower and vegetable grew prolifically. It took no time to make a garden out of African bush. The Kikuyu boys were natural horticulturalists. The first fruit tree I planted was an avocado pear. There was no shortage of unskilled labour and the Africans learned to plant and weed and water very quickly.

Our old friend Venetia was in process of making her garden and using the stream to make artificial ponds and small waterfalls. She borrowed Tom to help her build a 20-foot high dam wall, 30 feet across, strong enough to withstand the terrific downpours which occurred during the rains. One afternoon while it was being constructed there was a terrific thunderstorm. Six inches of rain fell in one hour. The stream became a torrent and overflowed the dam wall, but thanks to the spillway the dam stood up to it and so far as I know it is there still. Venetia's 'Stream Cottage' was high up on a hillside with a magnificent view on one side of it and a small gorge dropping down to the stream on the other. This gorge was entirely cleared of scrub and cultivated in small terraces down to the water. All the indigenous trees were left undisturbed and other flowering trees and shrubs added to them.

A grass path covered by a pergola of vines wound down to the pools. Tree tomatoes, strawberries, mountain paw-paws, figs, chou-chou pumpkins etc. grew amongst fuchsias, roses, lavender, delphiniums, cannas and lilies and countless other beautiful plants. Venetia used to have her lunch taken down to the pool where she made a little lawn under overhanging trees opposite a miniature waterfall. Children of all ages adored going there, either paddling in the stream or swimming, or punting in the boat, or just hanging a bamboo rod and string over the water with a worm on a pin at the end of it – waiting for a tulapia fish to nibble at it. The tulapia was a delicious white fish, imported from Lake Naivasha. Venetia's husband Sandy had rejoined the Navy at the outbreak of war and their only child Sally was at a local boarding school.

When Sally was a few months old lightning struck their thatched house in Songhor. Venetia just had time to pick up the baby in its cot and carry her out before the whole house went up in flames. All their family furniture and treasures from home had just come out and were lost in the blaze. Venetia just had what she stood up in and nothing else. Sandy was declared bankrupt and like many others went off to the Kakamega gold fields, to remake his fortunes, while Venetia came to Bahati with her mother, old Mrs Hervey. The old lady and her parrot ruled the household. Mrs Hervey designed and embroidered tapestries for the dining room chairs while Venetia ran the pyrethrum plantation and taught African girls how to sew and to make mattresses and stuff pillows, weed the garden, serve at table and do the laundry. She also taught her head men how to work the electric light engine; to mow the lawn, cut hedges into steps and shape them into birds and animals; how to drive a car; how to feed horses; how to 'doctor' the sick if she wasn't there; how to do carpentry and run the pyrethrum drier on which her bread depended. When war broke out she was already making a success out of the few hundred acres of pyrethrum which she had.

The news grew worse, especially in the Middle East and North Africa. Things such as reels of cotton, pins and needles, imported goods of all sorts began to be in short supply or disappear from the dukas. This forced secondary industries to spring up overnight in Kenya. A soap factory was started and we were able to buy bright yellow bars of rather soft soap full of soda, but quite adequate.

Tanning factories worked by Africans with Europeans in charge turned out leather for shoes and bags. Chocolate was made locally. A lot of these enterprises originated with the Jewish refugees from Austria who had poured into Kenya after the Anschluss. They arrived with a couple of suitcases and within a few months had established themselves on farms and in business and were flourishing. The astonishing thing was that although they had 'fled' the country, soon after they came their houses were filled with furniture, china and all manner of precious things, all from their homes in Austria. How they did it has always remained a mystery to me.

# 1943

At last we began to hear better news. A General Montgomery figured largely and was successful in mopping up the Italians in Eritrea. Japs halted by U.S. Navy and Air Force and Chindits' success in Burma. Tom thought things were beginning to look up. On our own front life grew ever more hectic.

In July 1943 excitement grew as we learned that an invasion of Sicily had begun. A gigantic sea, air and land assault was in progress. We held our breath and scarcely ever turned off the wireless. It meant a great deal to us in East Africa that the Italians were being chased out of North Africa and the Germans with them. If the invasion of Sicily was successful the enemy on our doorstep would be eliminated. The operation was successful. There was great jubilation in the valley, and the young grass widows began to allow themselves to think of handing back the farm management to their soldier husbands some day. Not all of them, for some were already widows and others mourned their sons.

The Africans joined in the celebration although not clear as to why or what we were celebrating when the war was still going on. Lorry loads of Italian prisoners depositing their belongings on farms and working in local factories caused much derisive comment among our employees. 'They are not white men,' they said, 'they are like pale Kikuyus.' (Most of our labour force was recruited from the Kavirondo Reserve by Lake Kisumu and were ebony black. They held the pale Kikuyu tribe in contempt.)

Two P.O.W.s were sent for us to employ, but after three months we had to return them. First they complained they did not get enough oil in their food so we were given a ration of edible oil for them, gallons of it. Then one of them had an affair with the head pruner's wife, which caused a near riot in the camp. Then the other one took to his bed and wept and wept and wept and said he was homesick and could not live any longer without his Maria, so we took them back to camp. Other people were more fortunate and had wonderful furniture made and sheds built and even rooms built on to their houses. Some had patios with swimming pools made in their gardens when the prisoners were not working on the farms.

The new main road being built by Italian P.O.W.s slowly crept out of Nairobi, and with luck it might reach to the top of the Limuru escarpment before we grew too old to appreciate it.

The short rains came at the proper time in the autumn, and the country was green and deep in grass. The lake at Nakuru filled up with water and looked like a bright blue saucer with a pink rim of flamingoes. At Naivasha, where the lake had almost disappeared during the prolonged drought, people on the land round the perimeter had extended their cultivation farther and farther into the dried lake bed. Now they had to contract again as the water level rose.

Every Christmas the settlers gave a feast to the labour on their farms. Although ours was a small farm, only 750 acres, it was intensively farmed and we employed a permanent labour force of not less than 80 to 100 men, plus their families, and in the coffee picking season, daily pickers came in by the score. We gave the camp two oxen at Christmas time, which they slaughtered and ate every bit of, including ears and entrails. Then they dried the skins and used them for various things such as sandals, cloaks, thongs and so on.

## End of European War in Sight. Christmas 1943

The Christmas of 1943 was a very happy one for us with the expectation of better times ahead. Jennifer was two years old and Rose would be eight in January. We had cut down a small fir tree on the upper farm. After the children were asleep we collected clusters of gum tree seeds and oranges from the garden. The oranges were hollowed out and made into baskets and filled with home-made caramels. Then, having no cotton wool (which was too scarce to use except in emergencies) or snow, we made some water icing out of our very dirty local sugar and dabbed it all over the tree and soaked the gum tree seeds or fruit in it. After tying on the usual miniature dolls and animals which we had had since we were children, and fixing on the locally made, rather big candles, we sprinkled the whole tree with gelatine powder to make it glisten. The effect was surprisingly good.

A friend of ours, Tootles, who came now and then to help with Jennifer, stayed with us that Christmas. Rose raced about early in the morning emptying her own and Jennifer's stockings and then disappeared. Curious to know why there was no further sound from her, I went to see if she had found the tree. She was standing staring at it in the sitting room, one tiny hand over her heart. 'What is it?' I asked. 'Such a shock,' she said. 'It wasn't there last night.'

Church was held once a month in one or other of our houses in the valley. That Christmas it was to take place at the Watkins' farm, further down the valley. The congregation was mostly female, and over-agers and a few soldiers, sailors and R.A.F. on leave. It was a hot morning and the poor little padre droned on mostly unheard, at the far end of the sitting room. After the service we were pressed to drink home brewed apple cider and dandelion wine and to eat fluffy little cakes made by our hostess.

Then home to our Christmas tree and presents for the staff and ourselves.

After this some friends came in for a drink (South African sherry) before lunch. Marianne and John Price had brought Venetia with them and the Frank Baillies and the Beau Fawcuses were also there. 'Looks more hopeful now of the war coming to an end next year, don't you think?' asked John. 'Well there's still a long way to go before we get to Berlin,' someone replied. 'What are these awful doodle-bugs we hear about?' Venetia enquired. At that point a noise faintly heard before, now swelled to a loud crescendo of singing and shouting. Over the end of the terrace a stream of dancing flower-bedecked Africans came swaying towards us. Our ginger cat, asleep on the verandah, leapt up in fright and disappeared like lightning round the house. Minty the spaniel tore after it, and Jennifer let out a yell from her pram. Quite undeterred, the entire labour force, all dressed in gay bits of cloth and wreaths of bougainvillaea, danced and stamped and sang all over the front lawn. Then they clapped hands, said thank you for the oxen and went away singing. 'Do your boys always do that?' asked Beau Fawcus. 'Ours don't.' 'Ah! but you probably only give them a skinny old beast. This year one of our fattest animals broke its leg, two days ago – so I had to give it to them!' said Tom.

Marianne and John had been having a succession of naval ratings spending their up-country leave with them on the Bahati farm. They found them delightful but full of slightly bewildering ideas on how the world should be run after the war. One of them had told John that all employers should pay their employees according to what the *employees* considered to be 'living wages'. When John asked what should happen if the employer were not in a financial position to comply with the employees' requests, the reply was 'that was no concern of his. It was up to the employer to arrange those things properly.' Marianne went on to say that a great many of these nice naval ratings held these views. On one occasion a young naval rating informed her that at home his wife would be horrified if he carried anything for her, not even a bunch of flowers, or anything like that. But he did not object to carrying Marianne's basket of tomatoes from the house to the car, 'presumably because nobody would see him doing it.' Marianne remarked.

She continued to depress us all by asserting that England would go Labour immediately after the war and that 'the likes of us will disappear'. John, however, threw a gleam of light on the gathering gloom by telling us how two Scottish naval ratings had bought a bottle of port at great expense from the NAAFI and insisted upon giving a drink to their host and hostess before leaving. They particularly asked Marianne to wear her best dress and John to put on a tie for the occasion, then in solemn state after dinner they toasted John and Marianne and thanked them warmly for their hospitality. 'I hope you did wear your best dress, Marianne,' said Venetia, 'as you *will* always wear that ghastly colourless affair you brought out in 1920.'

John said that discussion with the naval ratings made him giddy, in fact he was in a continual state of dizziness from the time they arrived until they left, but thought them 'all damn fine fellows, just the same.'

One of the best Christmas presents I received that year was from my cook, whom Tom called 'the Maker of Heavenly Pancakes'. He had just been on leave to his reserve to buy a second wife and brought me back a Kikapu full of sweet potatoes.

The day ended with a family picnic beside the river near our coffee factory. A large indigenous fig tree grew on the bank, its leafy branches casting a deep shade over the water. We paddled with the children and ate home-made cakes and avocado sandwiches.

That night, having supper on little tables by the fire, we listened to the B.B.C. news and wondered if our food parcels had got through to friends and relations in the U.K. in time for Christmas. The two African servants said 'Kawaheri' to us. 'Bahati M'zuri.' they said, and danced out of the room! 'Bahati M'zuri' said Tootles as she went out, plucking a rose from a vase and sticking it in her hair. It had been a *mzuri sana* Christmas for us all. Little did we guess it would be the last.

# 1944

A few days later Mother turned up in a great state of emotion. 'Granny-pa has had a stroke – and has partly recovered. The doctor says it is arterial sclerosis. Will you have him here to live with you? He is always happier with you than with us.' After talking it over with Tom it was decided that we would have my father to live with us until the end of the war, when he would be sent home to England to a cooler climate and lower altitude. He was then in hospital in Nairobi.

A doctor friend of ours and his hospital trained wife kindly drove my father up to us. After their arrival she took me on one side. 'Do you realise what you've taken on?' she asked. 'Your father will go on having strokes, mild or severe ones, which may or may not kill him, but he will never be the same again.' So began a period of constant anxiety and uncertainty.

The hot weather set in and the wind blew daily from 10 a.m. to 2 p.m. and again every night from 8 p.m. to about midnight.

On the first Sunday in the New Year, 1944, an extra church service was held in our house. Afterwards I asked Tom what he had thought of it and in particular about the sermon on 'How can true Christians be superstitious?' Instead of answering, Tom said 'By Jove, darling, did you see that awful ass?' He was, it seemed, referring to a large man with mutton chop whiskers, brought by some neighbours. 'Which ass?' I asked. 'The one with whiskers – obviously an admirer of Henrietta's – looks like the Prince Consort – ASS!'

Tom went on to say that H's mother informed him that 'The Prince Consort' was a marvellous man – that our King had met him while reviewing South African troops in Libya and told him never to shave off his whiskers. A few years later Whiskers was to take up Kenyan politics. He became a member of Legislative Council – the only white man in an all-black government as Minister for Agriculture. But that was unsuspected then.

Convoys were being sunk on all the high seas and imported goods became more and more scarce. We were filled with anxiety for Britain and whether she would be starved out. Then came the news of a new and deadly weapon – doodle bugs – remote guided missiles – which were fired from across the Channel. 'But we shall win all the same,' Tom assured me.

Jennifer, who was a very good baby, was now walking and talking. She decided to assert herself one day at lunch. She put spoonfuls of vegetables into her drinking water and poured the precious Parish's food on to the nursery floor where the waiting ginger cat lapped it up. It was the last of the Parish's food until the war was over, and she invited me sweetly to look at what she had done. It had been a trying hot-weather day, the grass was burnt brown and the wind scorching and our water supply stopped from a pipe we had laid on to crater stream a mile away. I smacked her hand. She looked at it, then at me, then said 'Kiss it better' – she won!

## *January 1944. Grass Fire Endangers Us*

That night soon after we had gone to bed, I smelt smoke. 'Can you smell smoke?' I asked Tom. 'No,' he replied sleepily. I too fell asleep. Presently the smell of fire came through my dreams and woke me up.

A red glow lit up our room.

Running to the window I saw clouds of smoke rolling up towards us against a background of crimson sky.

Tom was already up and, slipping on a coat, raced out to the garage. 'Get what you can out of the house,' he called, and a few seconds later was driving down the hill to the camp to fetch the labour up.

The fire was about a mile away, sweeping straight down towards us with a raging wind behind it. Slipping into a pair of slacks which were lying on a chair, I went out to rouse the house servants. Together we lit a couple of hurricane lamps and collected some sacks which we dipped into a tub full of water. Then we filled every basin and saucepan with water and carried out two tin baths of water on to the front lawn. The gardeners ran for some ladders (always at hand to patch our thatched roof) and climbed up with wet sacks and waited for the sparks to begin falling.

Jenny was fast asleep, so the Seychelles nanny and I decided to let her sleep until the last minute, meanwhile propping open the doors so that we could run in and fetch her. Mammy was quite a sight, her ample figure tightly swathed in a pink satin dressing gown and her hair tied up in rag curlers. We walked to the edge of the grass terrace together to look at the fire. It was a fearful sight. Tree after tree caught fire and sparks flew up in the air. 'When it reaches our boundary, Mammy, we take Jenny out,' I said. Meanwhile we set about clearing the cupboards of linen and silver and the more precious pieces of furniture, piling them on the centre of the large vegetable garden behind the house. There seemed little hope of saving the house as sparks were already being carried ahead by the wind and descending on the roof where the boys beat them out with the wet sacks. While this was going on all the labour force arrived up with sticks and branches to beat.

Tom shouted some orders and we saw them light a counter fire across the line they expected the fire to take. Mammy and I helped to pass up wet sacks to the boys on the roof, now about twenty of them, and I wondered where we would go if the house did catch fire.

The flames came in a fiery pattern nearer and nearer to the boundary. 'The bébé, the bébé,' called Mammy, 'you live her to burn?' 'No, she's all right yet,' I said, and hoped she would not have to be carried out.

The Cranswicks from next door turned up dressed in extraordinary pyjamas, with old Burberry macs on top. Chas went to join the beaters while Marjorie stayed with me. 'Chas has sent for all our boys to come and help,' she said. 'It was lucky I happened to look out of the window and saw your wireless pole silhouetted against the flames. "Chas," I called, "the Bank's are on fire, we must go to the rescue." Then I told the servants to prepare beds and Ovaltine for you all, including Mammy, and here we are.'

I was very touched and thanked her profusely. The fire had reached our road leading up to the house and had also swept round in a half circle towards the back of us. Shouts mingled with the crackles of flames as smoke swirled over our heads blown by the wind. Just then a large limousine drove straight through the flames and up the drive. Horace, another neighbour, tumbled out dressed in a dinner jacket, having dined out. 'My dear,' he said, slightly swaying on his feet, 'I wash jush on may way home and saw your fire worksh. Tha's Tom and Peggy goin up in shmoke I thought, and jush shtepped on the juish. Now don't be anxious – I'm going to hep put-it ous.' He stumbled off, and disappeared into the ground. We ran to his rescue and found him struggling to get out of an ant bear hole. 'Naughty girl – give us a hand up – not fair to bring a fella to his knees thish way – where's the fire?'

Meanwhile, more and more sparks were falling on the roof – Pedro our head man said we would not be able to put them out much longer – it was getting too hot. 'In five minutes we must take Jenny out and try to save a few more things before it all goes up,' I warned Marjorie. Then quite suddenly the wind dropped. 'Mees Banks, chère Madame,' called out Mammy, 'the flame has stop.' The flames had not quite stopped but were no longer advancing, thank God. Another half an hour and the beaters went off singing triumphantly to their camps, and all that remained of the fire was a black stain on the hillside. Mammy wept and said 'eet is a miracle, a miracle' as she went to bed. The kind Cranswicks returned home and only Horace remained sipping hot coffee on our verandah by the light of a hurricane lamp. 'What a party,' he remarked. 'Mush say – I'm disappointed not to take you all home with me – five lil'l beds – so shweet – one for you and one for Tom and one for me and one for baby – how many – ish-tha-lets shtart all over again.'

My father, who had been in hospital during the fire, returned to us with an Italian P.O.W. orderly to help nurse him. He liked sitting under the thorn trees trying to learn Italian when he was well. He spent a whole morning sorting out a basketful of old padlocks for me as these were unprocurable any more and were always being stolen or broken.

*

The weather grew hotter and drier. The weekly shopping expeditions to Nakuru were rather a trial. The garden boy who accompanied me would look greyish white and I the colour of an Indian Babu by the time we reached town, dust off the road having completely smothered us during the 12-mile drive. The garden boy had recently arrived from his native reserve and had to be taught everything – the other good Kikuyu gardener had left 'because his mother had died,' he told me. Tom informed me that Pedro had told him that the gardener had gone straight from us to Mombasa and not to his dead mother at all, as all wages in Mombasa had risen enormously since the influx of troops from overseas. He predicted that all the labour would depart for Mombasa and Nairobi if the war did not end soon.

One morning Pedro brought up his wife before breakfast and said she was not well. She was lying on the lawn groaning, obviously about to have a baby. Pedro strenuously denied this, saying it was much too early. When Tom came in for breakfast he agreed with me that Pedro was wrong. We bundled the woman into the back of the landrover and made the unwilling Pedro get in also. Tom drove off. Apparently he had only gone a few miles when Pedro begged him to drive faster. After another couple of bumpy miles the plea came to 'go slower, slower.' Almost immediately after that he was told 'she has given birth'. Tom trod on the accelerator until they reached Nakuru Native Hospital where he jumped out and told the orderly on duty to see to everything and to clean and disinfect the car. A few days later the mother brought up the baby for me to see. Its huge black eyes looked out from a funny little frilled bonnet. 'What are you going to call it?' I asked. 'Adika motorcar,' she replied. Of course.

Jenny had now learnt to talk and dropped her H's all over the place, greeting everyone cheerfully with 'allo, allo'. Where she got her cockney accent from no one knew.

All materials and clothing had become very scarce, especially shoes. Many mornings were spent making up old dresses into clothes for the children. Jenny enjoyed these days muddling up everything in the sewing baskets, draping herself in bits of silk or underclothes and trailing round the garden in them. We had food coupons for some things but there was no shortage of fresh vegetables or fruit. Sugar was rationed although it was grown in East Africa, but was needed by the Forces.

Rose had gone to a new school at Turi with four little friends, all of them children of old friends of mine from the days before any of us were married. She wrote to us long letters and sent me her doll's measurements asking me to make a school uniform for it like hers!

Of all our animals Ginger, the cat, was Tom's favourite. Jenny would give it a saucer of milk and then lie down full length beside it to see how it drank. The day dawned when Ginger did not bring his mouse up to the house as he invariably did. Tom made it clear that Ginger had to be found and we all searched high and low. Eventually Ginger was found in a corner of the stables with a litter of kittens.

After a month of restricting ourselves to the one weekly visit to Nakuru which was all the petrol we were allowed, we reckoned that we had saved enough juice to visit the Frank Baillies, who lived about three miles down the valley. Jenny and I and 'Tedbo', my old teddy bear, squeezed into the bench beside Tom while Minty the spaniel jumped into the back from where she could lick my neck and shove her face between us.

It was very hot and we arrived all stuck together like a bag of melted boiled sweets.

The Baillies' garden was an oasis in our droughted valley. Acres of green lawns watered by sprinklers and shaded by jacaranda trees; lily pools, miles of rose hedges and herbaceous borders, all leading from one garden to another. Daubie and Frank always had tea on the long deep verandah where Daubie fed the birds with cake crumbs which they took from her hands. Some cheeky little nigger-minstrel birds used to fly on to her shoulder, run down her arm and take a crumb from her hand just as another small bird was on the way to pick it up. Another one perched on her shoulder and gently took a little piece of cake from between her lips.

Pink blossomed Cape chestnut trees cast their shade across the lawns as we walked down to a pool flashing with brilliant blue kingfishers and Cape starlings. We talked of her only son, Bunny, killed flying over Italy with the R.A.F. This hideous war was only the other side of the hedge.

My bedside book that night was H.V. Morton's *In Scotland Again*. Tom asked me if I could remember the name of the river below the Victoria Falls. My mind was on the Isle of Arran, and I suggested the Limpopo. 'No, I'm sure it was not *popo* anything', he replied. He left early for Nakuru next morning, saying he did not know when he would be back as he would have to wait for the spare part for our tractor.

### Father Has Another Stroke

Hardly had he left in the Chev. when the Italian orderly from the P.O.W. camp who helped us to look after Father called me. 'The Signor has had a stroke,' he said. Without a telephone or a car we had to wait all day until Tom returned before taking Father to a doctor in Nakuru. The servants had been wonderfully helpful and kind and lifted Father into the car with great gentleness.

The diagnosis showed that he had a haemorrhage behind the brain. He might partly recover or he might die. In any case if this was not a fatal stroke he would continue to have them fairly frequently until the end came. While Tom telegraphed to my mother, our head houseboy who had accompanied us said to me, 'It is bad for you, Memsahib, but God knows and God will take the old Bwana when the right time comes.' The sun set over Lake Nakuru in a golden haze, flamingoes silhouetted against a green sky made their evening flight to Lake Baringo.

Venetia came down from Bahati to enquire after my father, and finding us rather low, tried to cheer us up with amusing stories and risqué anecdotes. One rhyme stuck in my mind:

> *There was a young lady called Myrtle*
> *Who went for a swim with a turtle.*
> *In the cold hours of dawn*
> *She gave birth to a prawn*
> *Which proved that the turtle was fertle.'*

She succeeded in making us laugh, for which we all felt much better.

Two days later Mother arrived, our telegram having taken two days to reach her. It was after dark when she arrived, bringing a Kikuyu chauffeur and a servant and provisions, i.e. a joint of cold meat, a dozen eggs, cooking apples, a jar of peach chutney she had just made, bunches of sweet peas and two live cockerels in a crate. In addition she had her pillowcase full of embroidery wools and her embroidery frame, 4' x 4'. She seemed to think that as it was night time she should sleep on the sofa. It took us some time to make her believe that we had plenty of bedrooms and beds to spare. It was about 1 a.m. when the lamps were turned out. At daybreak we were wakened by raucous squawkings from the cockerels who had been left in the car, parked outside our bedroom.

Father remained in Nakuru Hospital and was not expected to live. This meant that one of us and a car had to be on call every day and all day. One of us stayed in Nakuru so that we could visit the hospital every hour or so. There were no telephone communications to our valley or up-country at all then, so that was the only way we could keep in touch with the hospital. The District Commissioner gave us some extra petrol coupons for this period, which was a great help.

## Turi School Burns to the Ground

On February 20th 1944 Venetia drove me to Turi School for Rose's half-term. Rose was in high spirits and showed us all round the school before we were joined by some little friends for a picnic in the grounds.

Mr and Mrs Lemesurier Lavers owned the school and had joined our conducted tour. Noticing that all the windows were protected by heavy chicken wire in the dormitories, I asked her what would happen if there were a fire? All the buildings were made of wooden offcuts and the roofs of corrugated iron, the inside walls whitewashed and the windows curtained with printed chintz. Replying to my question she said, 'Oh we have regular fire drills. In fact we shall be having one tomorrow. We have to cover the windows with wire netting as nowadays there is such a lot of thieving; something we never had to worry about when first we built the school ten years ago.'

Passing through Nakuru on our way home, we called in at the hospital. Father had taken a turn for the better and would be able to go home in a few days. This did not cheer me up as we knew that within a few days or weeks he would have another stroke.

Three days later, when Tom and I went to Nakuru to collect the mail and Father from hospital, we found a telegram which read 'School burnt down stop all children safe stop collect them immediately Lavers.' Hurriedly we transferred our weekly provisions into a kind neighbour's car, handed him the telegram after scribbling a note on it to Mother telling her that we had gone to Turi to fetch Rose, and drove off. Tom stopped at the only bakery and bought up all the buns he could find. 'Rose will be feeling hungry,' he remarked. I drove while Tom read a library book to keep himself from thinking, he said. Recklessly racing along forty miles of bumpy road, skidding in the dust several times, we arrived at a smoke-blackened hillside where St. Andrew's School had stood a few days before.

We got out and picked our way amongst sheets of corrugated iron and the end of a clothes line with pieces of burnt towels flapping in the breeze, a row of salvaged pets in their coops – desolation. We found Mr Lavers in a garden shed on the edge of the fire line. He was still in his pyjamas and dressing-gown with a toupée on his head and a muffler round his neck. All 109 pupils were safe and unharmed, he assured us. There had been no panic, as the previous day the school had done a fire drill, and when the fire broke out that night the children thought it was only another fire drill.

Not a single building remained. The only thing which stood up amongst the ashes was a row of children's lavatories. Mrs Lavers was sitting at an improvised desk under a pepper tree directing salvage work. She told us we would find Rose at a senior girls' school nearby, but would we first look through the few piles of clothes. We found one of Rose's vests and her school tunic. Later a school dormitory mistress told us that as the children were filing out of the dormitory Rose was seen to leave them and go back towards the building. She was stopped and hurried clear, protesting that she must get her beloved doll. At that moment the dormitory went up in flames and fell into the swimming pool. Subsequently the doll was seen floating amongst the wreckage.

With Rose we found three sobbing little French girls – the Richards from Bahati whose parents were in Tanganyika just then. So we took them all home with us, feeding them with current buns on the way which quickly revived their spirits. They were dressed in a strange assortment of garments but we soon found suitable clothes for them when we got home.

All went well until lighting up time. At the sight of the servant lighting a lamp, the youngest Richard became hysterical and the other two burst into tears again. Poor mites, they were still all terribly shocked. One of them said, 'I see my poupée fall into zee bars – and I zeem my room fall into zee bars – and we do not like to go to school.' Rose told her to 'shut up!'

*

In March, when tempers were stretched to breaking point by heat and wind and dust, the rains broke. The relief was instantaneous. Boxes of seedlings were carried outside and lessons on how to plant them with roots down and not up were given to the new garden boy.

Father came back from hospital. Tom became actively interested in political meetings and A.I. development, and we listened carefully to the news, wishing and hoping to hear of an invasion of France.

Rain thundered down every afternoon and poured through the nursery ceiling. One particularly wet day Leopoldo the P.O.W. hospital orderly was helping me to carry basins and buckets to the worst leaks when the maker-of-heavenly-pancakes came to the door for orders. Should he cook the leg of the buck which Bwana Cranswick had shot and left on our boundary? Had I remembered we were seven in the house to feed, and that the Seychelles woman ate a *lot?* He would make a special pudding for Memsahib Kidogo (Rose) as she had suffered much and his heart cried for her.

Venetia called in to enquire after my father who had been ill again and offered to have the children to stay with her. She wore a turquoise beach pyjama suit with a cerise top and large straw hat. She offered to teach the children Italian and reminded us she was called Venetia because her parents had spent their honeymoon in Venice. Catching sight of the garden boy, she ordered him to remove a basketful of tomatoes from her car and bring them on to the verandah. With a cheerful grin he obliged.

Another neighbour arrived just as the rain began to come down. Could she borrow some petrol? Her husband was on sick leave and in a highly excitable state. He had come in to the room the day before and announced that he had killed the cook. She rushed to the kitchen and found the cook stretched out on the floor. She revived him, but as soon as he was able to stand he had run out of the house and not been seen since. She needed petrol to go into Nakuru to consult the doctor about her husband. We gave it to the poor girl and hoped Captain J. was not going off his head.

Rose went back to Turi where Mrs Lavers carried on 'school' in three large houses nearby while an army of Italian P.O.W.s began building a new school of concrete blocks.

*

News that Rome had capitulated to General Alexander. No fighting in Rome.

At the beginning of June Gran came to stay again. We had been without our wireless for several weeks as our batteries had expired and we could not get any more. On 5th June a kind friend arrived with some spare batteries which he let us have and we were able to listen in. Glorious news! Rome had fallen to General Alexander's troops. A young district police-man called in to see us just as we switched on. He sat down to listen with us. We heard that it was the 5th Army which entered Rome first – that the Italians had gone quite mad with joy – that a B.B.C. reporter was nearly killed by adoring Italian women who would pull him out of his jeep to embrace him, that no fighting took place in the streets of Rome itself. Oh! wonderful, marvellous news. Tom said we must celebrate and opened our last bottle of whisky – 'I'm keeping the champagne for the invasion of Europe,' he said.

Granny was most indignant that the American (5th Army) should have entered Rome first. But the policeman argued that 'the British Tommy gets 2/- a day and the American 10/- a day, so he would expect to be in Rome first.' We toasted General Alexander. Then I proposed a toast for Monty. 'Why?' asked Father. 'Because I have a feeling the invasion of France is imminent,' I said. No one agreed, but we drank to Monty and many others before retiring very happily for the night.

## *June 6th 1944*

Granny gave me a pile of airgraphs and several cables to send off for her from the post office, and the gardener and I drove down to Nakuru once more.

While I was sending off a telegram, somebody behind me said, 'The invasion has begun.' Immediately everyone in the post office clamoured for more news. Icy chills ran up and down my spine again – Granny's cables were forgotten.

'There have been landings along the coast of Normandy and on the Cherbourg Peninsula. Everything is going according to plan,' we were informed. I did not like this as it reminded me of the days before Dunkirk. Thoughts were beating round my head – what did it mean? Desperate fighting now on land, sea and air – the end of the suspense – perhaps the beginning of the end of the war? Dear God I hoped so. Every one of us wished with all our hearts that we could have been in England, doing *something*, anything to help in this supreme effort.

Progress from the post office to the shops was slow. Everyone stopped to say 'Have you heard?' or 'It is not official – don't raise your hopes too much – it is only what the foreign agencies have given out.' But at the saddle shop Mrs M. leant over her counter and told us that on the B.B.C. nine o'clock news it was officially announced that 'there were beach landings between Cherbourg and Le Havre – airborne troops had landed – and fierce fighting was in progress.'

It was in truth the invasion. A hand gripped me by the arm. 'It can't be true – it can't be – after all these years – I can't believe it – Oh the awful fighting. May they win.' 'Excuse me Madam, it is true,' Mrs M. affirmed. 'The B.B.C. will be giving out special news flashes every half hour during the whole of today and keeping us informed.' Racing home in the car we nearly overturned in a dust skid at Lavender's Corner.

Tom met me at the top of our drive. 'Be quick, sweetheart, the news is just coming on.' Handing the Kikapu of meat and fish to the maker-of-heavenly-pancakes I joined Gran and Father, Mammy and Jennifer, Tom, Minty and Ginger by the wireless.

In a calm voice the announcer said 'The invasion of Europe began at 6 a.m. this morning . . . 4,000 ships of the Royal Navy took part as well as 7,000 other smaller craft . . . Air Force troops were dropped behind the enemy lines . . . landings all along the coast . . . gliders and heavy aircraft carried anti-tank guns and motor transport to our troops – severe fighting on beach heads and inland.'

We listened breathlessly until the news ended. 'Mzuri sana Bwana ayee, Mzuri sana Bwana,' said Alo in my ear. The infallible bush telegraph had told them of the invasion in its own mysterious fashion and all the servants had come silently into the room. They wanted to hear more.

## The King Speaks on the B.B.C.

After supper that night, Gran and I decided we would wait up for the King's speech which was to be broadcast at 10 p.m. East African time. For once the wireless reception was perfect – no 'atmospherics' nor 'canaries' trapped inside the box.

'His Majesty the King,' it was announced. Straining our ears lest we miss one syllable, we heard his calm, rather sad voice speaking. 'Only three years ago Britain stood alone, fighting for her existence.' (Was Gran's heart pounding like mine?) 'Once again we and our great allies with us, are at a crucial time in our history. But we are not, now, fighting for our existence, we are fighting for the good of the cause, for what we truly believe to be a better world where men may live in honour and freedom . . . It is not for us to ask God to do our will, but for us to be able to carry out *His* will . . . Surely there can be no one too busy, no one too young, no one too old, to join in the vigil of prayer for all those taking part now in this great battle.'

The National Anthem came over the air while we sat motionless, profoundly stirred. 'That man is a saint,' Gran said. 'Thank God for our King.' She them reminded me of the story told about him when he was visiting the bombed slums during the Blitz. A man in the crowd said to him, 'You are a great King.'

'And you are a great people,' he replied. But I was weeping and did not really attend.

While Granny was with us Tom took us up to visit Venetia. 'What a very charming person she is,' said Mother, 'but I don't agree with her about the Africans. She thinks the natives are completely trustworthy but of course you could never leave small children in their care.' When I asked Venetia if she left Sally in the charge of Africans she said she did. However, a few minutes later she told me that Mrs X's little girl of 12 had a baby fathered by the Kikuyu houseboy. Granny then asked, 'How can you say they are trustworthy?'

Tom was jubilant about the invasion forces and the astonishing rapidity with which they overcame the coastal defences in Normandy. Gran said what surprised her was that the Germans had not poured that inflammable spirit on to the River Seine to prevent us sailing up it. Liquid paraffin!

Grannypa was very much better and like his old self again. The day before my mother was due to leave he crumpled up with another stroke. Granny had not actually seen this happen before and could not believe her eyes. Leopoldo gave my father an injection of morphia and sat patiently at the foot of his bed until he should regain consciousness.

A welcome diversion came in the form of Marianne and John who called in to see us with four ratings who were on a week's leave with them. The sailors each drank three cups of tea and demolished our week's sugar ration, but Jenny aged two thought them gorgeous and made eyes at them. She was waiting for some little friends to come and spend the day with her – Diana and Susan Cranswick. They spent every Saturday with us and on Tuesdays and Thursdays Jenny visited them. I wrote a little song about them:

### Saturdays

*Cool in the shade of a green pepper tree,*
*Susan, Diana and Jennifer B*
*Played with their dollies contentedly.*

*'This one,' said Susan 'is mine if you please.'*
*'No,' said Jennifer. Then, just to tease,*
*She threw Susan's doll up, over the trees.*

*'Naughty,' screamed Di, and immediately went*
*To pick up the doll, whose poor legs were bent.*
*Then there began a most fearful lament.*

*Susan was crying and Jennifer too,*
*Di thought that she'd better join the boo-hoo*
*Never was there such a fuss or 'to-do'.*

*Just at that moment the orange juice came*
*Susan stopped crying and Di did the same.*
*Jenny had stopped, rather bored with the game.*

*Calm 'neath the boughs of that soft pepper tree,*
*Three little maidens, as good as can be,*
*Drank up their orange angelically.*

## 16th June 1944

Marianne and John had been to Nakuru to get their new ration books. The previous week they had been unable to get them as they had not taken their passports or Head Tax Receipts with them. 'This time we took our marriage lines as well, to make quite sure,' they told us.

'Will you be going to the coast this year?' they asked me. 'Well, it depends on whether we can park Jennifer and how my father is – life is so uncertain these days – but we have booked in at Diani for ourselves and Rose from the end of July'.

Granny remained with us for a few days more until Father recovered, as he always did, but never absolutely; sometimes he was unable to see for a week, at other times he lost all sense of direction or movement. We never knew how it would affect him nor when the next stroke would hit him.

We managed to engage a nurse to look after Jenny in July and began to prepare for our holiday at Diani.

The 16th of June 1944 was our tenth wedding anniversary. We took the day off and drove up to our plantation on the edge of Bahati Forest a thousand feet above the coffee farm. The sun shone in a cloudless blue sky over the great Rift Valley.

The track was full of ruts and potholes. While Tom and our head man Pedro were helping to push us out of these I walked on. Tall green delphiniums grew along the banks beside crimson gloriosa lilies and deep blue acanthus. In the forest everything dripped and we stuck several times in pools of water, until we reached the newly cleared land. Africans were busy planting up another shamba and we watched our new drier working for the first time. 'One day, my sweet, we shall retire here and you will be able to make a water garden beside the dam – come and see it.'

We carried our picnic baskets down to the river and ate our lunch beside the small dam which Tom had made. A troop of colobus monkeys swung through the trees overhead, one very large fellow sitting on a branch just above us, with his beautiful white tail hanging down. He peeped at us, first from one side of the branch, then from the other. Tom said 'peep bo' and threw him up a piece of banana. He took no notice but turned his back on us contemptuously as though we were too vulgar to be worthy of his notice. After lunch we fished the river and Tom caught a bagful of small rainbow trout.

The labour knocked off work at 2.30 p.m. After they had gone, peace fell upon the hillside, there were no sounds except bird calls and distant tinkling of goat bells and the sound of somebody chopping wood in the forest.

We fished the river for a couple of hours or so and then packed up and began the homeward drive. Tom broke the silence. 'Perhaps by next year the war will be over. Rose will be nine then and the following year we might be able to take the children to England and leave Rose at boarding school there?' My heart sank and I wanted to cry out 'No not yet.' Seeming to read my thoughts Tom said 'Don't worry – a lot can happen in two years.'

Halfway home we stopped to leave some trout with Marianne and John. They remembered it was our anniversary and persuaded us to stay and have a drink with them. 'To your next ten years,' toasted John. 'And may they be as happy as these ten years have been,' replied Tom. It had been a perfect day, utterly peaceful and happy. As we approached our little thatched house, Tom remarked 'How lovely it is ! If I should die tomorrow I would think I had had a darned good life.'

We were destined only to have another ten days together, not ten years.

*

# End of My World with Tom's Death

The 28th of June began like any other day on the farm. Morning tea arrived at 6 a.m. Tom was out on the coffee shamba by 6.15 a.m. and I took Jenny out into the garden with me before breakfast. Our Seychelles girl had left to get married and we had not yet replaced her.

Leopoldo, the Italian orderly who looked after Grannypa, came up to me while I was picking flowers. 'Your father is not so well this morning, Signora, and should rest today,' he told me. We agreed to keep him in bed and hope for the best. After breakfast Tom left for a political meeting up the valley which he was chairing. While Grannypa slept Leopoldo gave the cook a lesson in how to make ravioli.

When Tom came back for lunch a little later he said he did not feel like anything to eat as he had indigestion, he thought. Later that afternoon he walked down the hill to see our new Guernsey bull and I collected Jenny for tea from a neighbour's house. Before sundown our head man Pedro came up to the house as he always did for orders for the following day. Tom told him to bring five boys up to the house by 7 a.m. as he would drive them up to the Bahati (pyrethrum) farm to plant pyrethrum and fill the sacks with all the dried pyrethrum which would be ready for taking to Nakuru.

Father had spent all day sleeping and seemed better. So we cancelled our plan to take him to the doctor next day.

There were still no telephones in the Solai Valley and the two

116

doctors lived 12 miles away in Nakuru over a deeply rutted earth road. The patients had to get themselves to the doctors and not the doctors to the patients.

During the night I was wakened by stifled sounds of pain coming from Tom. The hurricane lamp on the bedside table would not light. After a frantic search I found the torch and realised that Tom was very ill. Stumbling outside with the torch I knocked on Leopoldo's door and called him to come immediately. He took one look at Tom and diagnosed angina. 'He must be kept absolutely still, Signora. I will give him an injection of morphia which I have for the old signor.' He administered the morphia and for a while it worked. Meanwhile I found and lit two oil lamps. Leopoldo retired, telling me to call him at once should Tom wake. What was angina, I wondered? Surely it could not be anything really serious?

Just before sunrise Tom woke. The pain started again but not acutely apparently. Suddenly I felt that something terrible was happening. Jenny was woken up, dressed, and our head houseboy told to take her round to our neighbours the Cranswicks with a note asking one of them to please go for a doctor. As Jenny left the room Tom looked up at her and said, 'Goodbye, my darling.'

Leopoldo was roused again and said the only hope was to give Tom another injection. Right or wrong? I did not know. As Chas, our neighbour, came into the room Tom looked at me smiling and said, 'Give us a smile, darling,' and fell back on the pillow. There was nothing more anybody could do.

## *Widowed, June 1944*

The kindness and help given to me by neighbours and friends during that time of darkness stands out like a warm light in my memory. One South African neighbour insisted on loaning me £500 to keep me going until probate was obtained – a lot of money in those days. Another farmer recently released from the Army took over the running of the pyrethrum Bahati farm temporarily. Kind Mr Rothschild, who was managing Michael

Blundell's farm adjoining Banks Estate and was eventually to buy Michael's estate, helped me to run the coffee farm. Friends were indeed friends then and never to be forgotten, although time and distance have separated us.

My darling Rose had to be told of her beloved father's death. She already knew, so Mrs Lavers told me when Jack, my brother who got compassionate leave, and I went up to the school. Mrs Lavers explained that in the early hours of the morning when Tom died, Rose woke sobbing and saying, 'My mummy needs me, my mummy needs me.' She was inconsolable. Yet no one there even knew of Tom's death. She was eight years old. The first thing she said to me after being told about her father was 'How are you going to live without him?' From then on she seemed to have grown up and to take charge, poor lamb. Jenny was only two and a half and for some days kept on telling us that her Daddy had gone to 'Kuru' and would bring her back a doll's pram. Finally Rose could not stand this any more and told Jenny he was *not* coming back as he was dead. Jenny paused, then said 'What a shame!' Even I had to smile. Jenny had to come farming with me every day as I could not leave her. By a stroke of good luck an Army wife heard of my problems and offered to come and live with her small daughter on the farm for a few months until I found a manager.

# 1945 – End of the War

A t that time Kenya was swarming with soldiers of all kinds.
There were several large P.O.W. camps, mainly Italians or
Poles. The impact of these people and our own soldiers on the
Africans was to alter their whole outlook on life. Hitherto
relations between Africans and Europeans had been happy
ones. They had come to us from their native villages, first
slowly, then enthusiastically. On our farm we had built a
chapel for them, given them a football ground and taught them
the game. We all fed, housed and clothed them, dosed them
and helped them with their endless litigation. We shut our eyes
to their beer drinking and endeavoured to keep them from
brewing the lethal Nubian gin. We also put up a school house
and paid a Mission lad to come and teach them the three R's.

Much has been written and distorted about the so-called
exploitation of the African by the European, but until inevitable
progress overtook us all when the war broke out, the Europeans, Asians and Africans in Kenya were a happy breed of men.
Many years later I was to try to tell this to the Minister of State
of the Colonies, Ian McLeod, but he would not listen. A
nephew of Tom's on the adjoining farm to ours died of menin-
gitis by contracting it from an African he had been coaching at
rugger. He was just 18 years old and died a month after Tom.

Soon the labour learnt about strikes. There had been several
strikes on neighbouring farms run by wives whose husbands
were still in the Army, and it was becoming serious.

119

One evening when Pedro was taking orders from me for the following day's work, all our employees came shouting up on to the terrace waving their *pangas* and *jembies* and knives and brandishing them round me menacingly. Then they hurled them at my feet, narrowly missing both Pedro and myself. Pedro asked them what it was all about, whereupon they all shouted at once. He told one man only to speak or the Memsahib would not listen to them. An ugly-looking customer advanced towards me demanding more pay. Reminding him that every Saturday (the rest day) all complaints were dealt with, I ordered him and the others to pick up their implements and take them away. He refused, so Pedro and I gathered them up under their astonished eyes and impounded them in a locked store in the house. I told them that in the morning, Pedro would hand them back on payment of ten pence a tool to those who wished to return to work. The rest would be fired. All but a few asked for their tools back there and then, much to my secret relief, and the others were signed off. But that was not the end of it. Early the following morning the ringleader was waiting for me in the coffee shamba. Pedro immediately stood in front of me, arms outspread. The pruners collected round us and we began to talk.

All but three accepted our suggestion (it was a question of 'piece work' in relation to the seven-hour day which was worrying them). Those three which included the 'agitator' were signed off. It was the only occasion when there was ever any attempt at a strike on the Solai farm while I was running it.

*

At last the war came to an end. It was over and nothing would ever be the same again.

An R.A.F. pilot, released from the forces, came to help me with the farm, while he looked round for a farm for himself and his family. Although Banks Estate was small, it was a difficult one to manage without knowledge of coffee, cereals or machinery. Our coffee factory alone needed someone with technical experience to run it, which I did not have. Nobby Clark, my new assistant, had some knowledge of engines and during the four months he was with us, he galvanised the farm into action, mechanising it regardless of our overdrafts at two banks and in spite of total ignorance by the African and myself of any sort of machine. Two second-hand tractors appeared on the farm and ploughed up the land, in fits and starts, accompanied by whoops from the Africans and shouts of '*harambe*' when the machine broke down and they tried to get it going again. That year some of the new coffee, planted by Tom, started to come into bearing and the financial clouds began to lift.

*

In May 1944, in Cairo, a Lt. Col. George Frampton had met and married Deidre Jones. One of the guests was Archer Cust, who many years later was to become Jack's father-in-law.

*

Our darling Madrina died in 1944. She had moved to Anneslea in Haslemere. A 'doodle bug' exploded in her drive, the blast lifting her off the sofa where she was having her daily siesta with her small Griffon at her feet. Betty Bus, her devoted maid, found her lying on the floor perfectly well – but the little dog was knocked unconscious. After that Madrina slowly lost ground and died not having quite reached her hundredth birthday.

*

By 1945 most Kenya settlers had been released from the Army and came back to their farms. Meanwhile their wives had become accustomed to running the places and the labour to working for the memsahibs. Considerable adjustments had to be made and it was a difficult period for many married couples.

Both my trustees had been overseas with H.M. Forces in 1944 and had returned to Kenya in 1945. Michael Blundell was one of them.

Whether it was the feeling that all no longer depended upon me I do not know, but towards the middle of the year I had a complete collapse and was ordered home to England by the doctor.

An old couple took over the management of the Solai farm while a neighbour at Bahati acted as manager for the pyrethrum plantation. My nice airman had by then bought his own farm.

Rose was then nine years old and due to go to school in England according to our plans. Jenny was four and we were all to go on the first available boat to the U.K. We were told that a ship carrying P.O.W.s would be sailing from Mombasa in four weeks' time but that accommodation was very crowded. When my mother heard this she thought of a better plan. A flying boat service had just been started from Lake Naivasha to the U.K. and she suggested that Rose and I go by ship and that Jenny remain behind and fly home with her a few months later – and so it was decided.

*

# Post-war England

It was thirteen years since I had left England and in spite of the traumatic upheavels in the world I still thought of it as it used to be in 1931.

Mama knitted glorious jerseys for us all, first unravelling old jerseys and rewinding the wool which was still in very short supply. Even more difficult to find was any kind of thick tweed or cloth. One friend gave me an old blue blazer to make into a skirt and another gave Rose her daughter's fur coat, which had been in moth balls for ten years. Of warm underclothes we had none but managed to collect enough to go on with from generous friends who had marvellously kept their children's winter woollies for donkeys' years!

The voyage home was rather like a nightmare which lasted for four weeks. Rose and I were in a dormitory with 62 other females of all ages. Three days out to sea the first lumps appeared on our skins. 'Bugs,' said my neighbour in the next bunk. She was right. After breakfast we queued up for 20 minutes to see the ship's doctor, an ancient relic thrown up from the sea bed. He peered at the bites and told us they were mosquito bites. I determined to catch his 'mosquitoes'. That night Rose and I went to our bunks armed with empty matchboxes. We again queued up and showed the old relic his 'mosquitoes'. Bugs! It had the immediate effect of our bunks being turned inside out and soused with *Flit* and insecticide. Although those on the other side of our dormitory continued to be bitten throughout the voyage, we ourselves never suffered from them again.

The incident had a pleasant sequel to it when we were taken to Ascot that June. There was a horse running called *The Bug* on which I placed the entire contents of my slender purse for a 'win'. It came in first. This was the first time any money had come into my purse and not just gone out of it and I felt the tide had turned for the family fortunes – all thanks to the bugs on board ship!

Rose went to school at Moira House in Eastbourne and I went to Oxford to learn how to earn my living as a secretary, or so I thought. We survived an extraordinarily cold winter and learnt many things about life in England – how people had changed in thought since the war, how profoundly tired they were; how strained and sad and proud and under-nourished. There were scarcely any domestics left, all our friends and relations were doing their own 'chores'; great areas of London and of every town we went to were devastated by bomb damage. No one was interested in us and seemed to resent the fact that we had lived in safety in Kenya and had never known the uncertainty of air raids. It was in vain to point out that we could not get back, and had suffered losses of family and friends even as they had. They were still too shell-shocked to understand and the whole of their way of life lay in ruins around them.

Mother wrote that she was not coming home after all as she considered everything was too difficult at present for people living in England. I decided that under the circumstances it was not the right time to leave Rose behind at school and that she would benefit far more from her home life in Kenya than from being left to the mercy of overworked relations during the holidays in England. Having made this decision we had to find a ship to take us back to Kenya. Every week for six weeks I hammered on the doors of East Africa House in London begging them to find two berths for us on any ship likely to go to Kenya. I began to think I would never see Jenny again.

*

During the last six months I spent in England, waiting for a passage back to Kenya, I went to a secretarial college in Oxford and learn how to type and do shorthand. I was no good at either and my brain at the age of 37 creaked painfully when told to study again after so long. I worked with girls who were all between the ages of 17 and 22 and I felt like an old Queen Cow who has strayed into the heifer herd. But they were so sweet to me that it became rather a game and great fun and I managed to scrape through the slowest speed test before sailing for East Africa. During this time the weather was atrocious – the coldest, longest, fiercest winter in living memory – no heating – not enough food – everything ration-ed – transport difficult and often impossible because of the snow.

I had bought a bicycle and pedalled to college every day and it was so cold that I got a chilblain on the tip of my nose, which remained there for two months. At Christmas I fetched Rose from school in Eastbourne and went by train with her to Battle where Joan had an old, freezingly cold cottage. Rose's toes froze in her shoes on the train so we took the shoes off and I rubbed and smacked her feet back to life during the railway journey. We comforted ourselves by saying we would soon be back in sunny Kenya.

After the holidays, we still had no news of a passage home. Rose went back to her school and I to mine. Then an epidemic of measles swept through Oxford. One morning when I was trying to type without looking at my hands, I looked across to a girl opposite me and I noticed she had very red eyes and a rash on her face. 'Measles,' I thought, and so it was. The poor child felt ill and left before the end of the morning. Next day a girl who had 'digs' in the same house that I was living in also developed measles. Our landlady came to me and said she could not look after the girl and had no intention of going into her room or allowing the maids to go in, either to take her food or anything else and that the doctor said the hospitals were full. In vain I expostulated and said the girl must be fed and washed and that I would take her food in and nurse her myself.

This girl Angela's parents were in India and she lived temporarily with her grandparents, General X in Gloucestershire. I nursed her for a week and then the doctor said she could go home if a car could be sent for her. Would I make arrangements? So the old General was contacted. A pre-war model of a Daimler arrived with a pre-war model chauffeur at the wheel. The doctor and I wrapped Angela up in a cocoon of blankets, first bandaging her eyes against the light from the snow, and off she went. Subsequently the grandmother wrote saying Angela was better but had developed ear trouble, and finally Angela wrote an ecstatic letter saying she was going to her parents in India and hoped never to see Oxford or a snowflake again.

One day when we were seriously contemplating driving out to East Africa in a jeep, the girl behind the desk in East Africa House told me we had got berths on a ship sailing in a week's time. Both Rose and I were bursting with joy when we stuffed our luggage into the tiny cabin we shared on the *Edinburgh Castle*.

On board was a friend of ours taking a 21 year old girl out to Kenya on a visit – Jemima Cust – who was to become my sister-in-law. She was engaged to a young naval officer who had given her a very beautiful diamond and sapphire ring.

On our arrival at Nairobi, Jack was there to meet us and was introduced to Jemima. Jack and Jemima fell in love at first glance. He stared and stammered, unaware of Rose tugging his arm and asking which car we should put our luggage into. Jemima seemed equally unaware of anyone but Jack. When we all said goodbye Jack told me he had arranged for Jemima to spend the following weekend up at the Naivasha farm.

Within a few weeks they were engaged. But there was quite a struggle on Jemima's part when it came to giving up the really beautiful ring she already wore on her engagement finger. 'Do you think X would mind if I kept this?' she asked me. 'Yes,' I replied firmly, 'I do – so would Jack, so you better make up your mind – Jack or the ring.' She plumped for Jack. Telegrams were sent to inform Jemima's bewildered parents. A telegram came back from Jemima's father which read: 'Who is Jack stop is he black?'

They were married in London in December 1947.

*

# Return to Kenya

T he return journey to Kenya was uneventful.
    Jenny, aged six, was at Mombasa Loreto Convent. I longed to see her after eleven months' absence. As soon as the ship berthed, a little figure came running down the deck towards us and flung herself into my arms. We all cried and laughed and talked and hugged one another, so wonderfully glad to be together again under the shining African sun.

## Disaster

After arriving in Kenya I went up to the Solai farm. First I rented a small house in Nairobi so that I could be near the children and get a job and not interfere with the running of the farm. On arrival at the farm I could not believe my eyes. The coffee shambas were full of weeds and choked with couch, that deadly grass which spells disaster to coffee plantations. Worse still, I found that instead of the 40 tons of clean coffee which we had expected to pick, we only got four and a half tons. All the rest had been left to go to M'buni. The coffee berries were piled in heaps round the outside of the shambas. All this I saw while driving myself through the coffee on my way to the manager's house. Halfway there I met Pedro the head man. He told me that in my absence the old Bwana had spent his whole time drinking in Nakuru, that no orders were given, no boys paid, no work done.

I sat in the old Chev. and wept.

That day I paid off the old manager and gave him an extra month's wages as well as telling him I never wanted to see him or hear of him again.

Pedro and I stayed up half the night planning the work for the next 12 months. Labour had to be recruited immediately to fork out the couch grass by hand, root by root, from the coffee trees. Tractors, tractor drivers, oxen and ploughs, all had to be put on to weeding and cleaning the coffee, and a gang of skilled pruners put in to cut back fiercely in order to resuscitate the trees.

One ray of light in the appalling darkness came from the pyrethrum farm. Ham Holmes had continued to run that independently of the other farm and it was yielding large crops of flowers and paying very well indeed.

During these awful days I stayed with Venetia Irving in her enchanting home and received much help and encouragement from her and from John and Marianne Price.

By the grace of *le bon Dieu*, I heard of a Danish manager with experience in coffee and in handling labour, and engaged him. He took charge of the Solai farm at once and moved into what used to be Tom's and my house with his wife and small daughter.

The N.B.I. bank manager in Nakuru agreed with the Land Bank to carry me, and I went down to Nairobi and began my first job with the European Settlement Board. I was private secretary to the Secretary of the Board. The director was an old friend, Stewart Gilbert, who had been for many years on the coffee board. But although I was amongst friends, my feet turned cold and panic filled me when I walked into the office for the first time.

I only lasted three months in that pleasant community. But those few months were the last straw on the back of the poor old General Secretary to the Board – one morning he quietly went into the garden and shot himself.

A year later the Solai farm was back in running order and we picked 45 tons of first class coffee berries off it. My trustees considered two farms uneconomical for me, so our little pyrethrum plantation was sold at a very good price. With the proceeds I bought a house and six acres of freehold land on the outskirts of Nairobi, near the racecourse.

After leaving the E.C.S. I took a part-time job in the East African Information Office and was in charge of their photographic library. The library contained negatives and photographs on every subject and activity that went on in East Africa from lizards to lions, canned asparagus to big game safaris – child welfare, H.M. prisons, fisheries, farmer settlers, ticks, postal services, natives, hospitals and housing projects. It was indeed an information centre and I learnt more about Kenya during the months I spent in that office than in all the thirty years I lived up country.

Europeans flocked to Kenya from the U.K. and India. The great days of the British Raj were over. The British Empire was out of fashion. European immigrants from India were known in Kenya as 'the Black Invasion'. They bought land and small holdings all over the highlands and built splendid houses. Trade boomed, the price of land soared and coffee rose from £45 a ton to £300 a ton and was to rise still higher. Overnight my fortunes took an upward turn and anxiety for the children's future melted away.

Jenny was at the convent in Nairobi and Rose at the Kenya High School so that I was able to visit them every week. We spent the holidays with Granny who had bought a house and 25 acres in a clearing in the Karati forest five miles north of Naivasha and on the way up to Jack's farm.

When we arrived up there invariably we were met with a crisis of some sort to deal with. Either Granny would greet us with the news that one of the dogs had tick fever so we must 'about turn' and take it immediately to the vet in Naivasha for injections – or there would be no cook as Gran had found him stealing something, or worse, had accused him of stealing something which she subsequently found she had put away; or one of the dogs was missing, having been taken from the verandah by a leopard.

Then there were the baboons. These little blue-bottomed pets would swing through the Karati forest, then jump from a tree on to the corrugated iron roof of Granny's house and slide down until they fell off the edge on to the lawn, their toenails making a horrid squeaking noise on the tin roof like a pencil squeaking on a slate. This was a favourite game of theirs, especially when they infuriated Granny into coming out after them and firing her revolver into the air. This revolver was a relic from her Argentine forebears – a beautiful thing inlaid with mother-of-pearl and silver. She would fill the barrel with dried peas and then shoot. The baboons would then take to the prickly pear bushes and pelt her with fruit.

Rose joined the Naivasha Pony Club which was just starting up in Kenya. Jack loaned her one of his horses. We had to find a suitable pony at Naivasha. When the Nairobi house was bought I found a Somali pony for the children, only 14 hands big, he was called Colonel Stuffy. But the municipality would not let me keep it in the stable behind our garage, so we kept it at Jack's farm at Naivasha. Rose was one of the founder members of the Pony Club. Colonel Stuffy won most of the gymkhana events which took place.

### 'Theatre' on the Lawn

The 'Colonel' also took part in amateur theatricals produced by Rose and Jenny. Sometimes he was a circus pony while Rose did trick riding or balancing on him, and sometimes he was the ass that the Virgin Mary rode on the flight from Egypt – or the donkey in the manger on Christmas night – that part he liked best as he could eat the hay. Jenny's parts were full of variety also; sometimes she was a fairy; at others the Madonna, and then a water-nymph clad in a green bathing suit with paper seaweed sewn on to it. These plays were acted out of doors on the croquet lawn. Chairs were arranged in rows, programmes made out and sold for two boiled sweets each (bags of sweets available at the entrance gate) and friends and family invited. Granny made the most enormous and heavenly cakes for re-

freshments afterwards and Argentine jam out of milk and sugar
called *dulce de leche*. The day before a play Granny would
cook the *dulce* in a very large saucepan over a charcoal brazier
set up under a pepper tree. It would take hours and hours of
slow stirring before it reached the light pale caramel colour and
the proper consistency – and then it was the most delicious
'jam' ever made, whether spread on bread and butter or in
sandwich cakes or simply eaten by the spoonful or licked off
the end of a finger!

Another member of our family was Balloon, a yellow bull
terrier pup. Jenny game him his name after his first meal when
his pink tummy swelled up as fast and as dangerously as a
tightly stretched balloon. He was a born clown and could flop
up and down and slide on puddles just like the famous Co-Co.
But after the first attempt to include him in the cast of their
play, Rose decided to sack him as he stole the limelight just
behaving naturally.

*

Soon after we were settled in Nairobi Jack had a serious
accident. He was out on the farm harvesting wheat when he
bent forward to adjust a bag. His trouser leg caught on the
caterpillar tractor wheel and his leg was torn off. He was
rushed to Nairobi hospital where he was successfully operated
on, but his leg was gone. That he survived at all was a miracle
as he and the African tractor driver were alone on the
Kinangop Plateau, ten miles from the house and without a car
as Jack had ridden up. When Jack was thrown to the ground
beside the wheel the African ran away in terror – leaving Jack
lying in spreading blood. The African ran to the road with the
intention of running on down to the house. By the grace of
God a solitary car was passing and the African waved to flag
the driver down. At the first the European drove on, thinking it
was only a greeting – but suddenly he felt he must turn and go
back, which he did, thereby saving Jack's life. This man had
come by chance from a different part of Kenya altogether and

had only decided to go up to the Kinangop on the spur of the moment to see about some timber. Whole days could pass without any vehicle traversing the plateau. Had it not been for this passing stranger Jack would have bled to death before any help could have reached him.

The new main road, made by the Italian P.O.W.s, had reached Gilgil and was slowly creeping on towards Nakuru. This meant that the drive to Nairobi from Naivasha was no longer the exciting adventure it used to be when you plunged through The Splash at the bottom of the Kidong Valley and crawled laboriously up the steep boulder-strewn escarpment to the township of Kikuyu, stopping several times on the way up to unscrew the radiator cap and let out the boiling steam, but first placing a couple of stones under the back wheels to prevent the car from running down the hill. The journey now only took a couple of hours or so instead of all day.

Not only the character of the road surface changed in those few years, but also the character of the African, particularly of the Kikuyu. In the old days if you saw an African walking along the road and had an inch of space left in the car you would stop and greet him and offer him a lift. But after the war, numerous unpleasant incidents occurred and no lone woman could risk giving a lift to a stranger. Thieving and house-breaking were rapidly increasing, in and around the townships, firearms and cash seeming to be the main objectives.

Hitherto, the *lingua franca* had been Swahili, or up-country Ki-Swahili, which had served admirably to confuse most of us, black and white alike, yet somehow managed to convey what we meant to one another. Now the smart 'collar and tie' Africans spoke slang English and discarded their simple attire for European clothes. Wages rose as prosperity grew. Trade Unions began to form, talk of rights and wrongs were loudly argued in the market place, and beneath all this, like the first earth tremblings before an earthquake, rose a murmur of dis-content. There was a subtle change in the relationship between the races, rather felt than realised, and the good humour of the African seemed soured.

One night in Nairobi I was woken by the sound of crashing glass. The only weapon I had was my shooting stick which was leaning against the cupboard. Our old bull terrier bitch who slept in her basket on the back verandah had not barked. Rawayo, my faithful ex-garden boy from the Solai farm and now head houseboy, slept on a camp bed on the front verandah. I sat up and listened: another crash and bump from the back of the house roused me furiously to my feet. Switching on the lights and grabbing the shooting stick I rushed through the house and found the spare bedroom window swinging open, the floor strewn with glass and all the bedclothes missing from the bed, also a large unpacked trunk. The bull terrier was lying drugged and half dead in his basket. Rawayo was so sound asleep that he had heard nothing, and in the pitch dark no trace of thieves could be seen.

Early next morning when the police arrived they found the contents of the trunk strewn over some waste land beyond the garden. This trunk had contained family christening robes, baby clothes and cot trappings, and therefore was of no use to anybody! After this the police made me put expanding metal over all the windows and verandahs. I felt like a caged bird. The thieves soon learnt to 'pole fish' through the mesh. They used a bamboo stick with a piece of string dangling from the end, attached to which was a large hook. They became very proficient at this, removing quite large objects from tables.

### Mau Mau Rebellion

Towards the end of 1948 or early in 1949 a movement had started amongst the Kikuyu tribe which was to become the notorious Mau Mau rebellion. Many books have been written about this period and how it started and why. It affected everyone of us who lived in Kenya and altered the course of our lives in a manner never dreamt of or suspected until the avalanche of change was upon us.

In his book *So Rough a Wind* Michael Blundell, now Sir Michael, says: 'At the end of the war the Kenya Government in conjunction with the Government of Great Britain announced an Agricultural Settlement scheme for European ex-soldiers in Kenya as part of the general rehabilitation plans for ex-soldiers from the armed forces.

'At every stage the Colonial Office was consulted on the main principles of the scheme and these had the support and full backing of the British Cabinet.

'. . . All of us were made to believe that Kenya would be administered as a British Colony for a period of forty-four years and that the areas of land in which the farms earmarked for settlement lay would be reserved for farming by Europeans for the foreseeable future.'

It was this scheme which attracted so many newcomers to Kenya and injected the economy with fresh capital and fresh ideas. Meanwhile, the Kikuyus, ever vengeful for the land which they considered had been taken from them by the first white settlers and had continued to be stolen from them ever since, began stirring up the passions of the younger generation. Prof. Leaky in his book *Mau Mau* tells very clearly of the breakdown of law and order within the tribe and of the growing dissatisfaction of the youths against the Chiefs, arbitrarily appointed by the British administration.

To the average European settler little of this was apparent, though a few who took an interest in politics and studied the causes of unrest, not just the effects of our way of life on the natives, became seriously concerned.

*

The coffee crop in 1948-49 was the biggest we'd ever picked. Our Danish manager had done extremely well and best of all, the price of coffee had risen beyond all expectations. Against the advice of my trustees and agents, I paid off the Land Bank Debt and found I was still relatively rich for the first time in my life. This is to say that there was some cash in my account, all bills paid up and lots of ideas in my head. Just before the coffee season I had sold one of our six acres of land in Nairobi for £1,000. With this I decided to take the children on a six-month holiday to Europe – our first! The kind Mother Superior at the Convent was all for it, and the Headmistress at the Kenya High School (Miss Stott) considered it would broaden Rose's education. So in August 1949, we packed and weighed our air luggage and flew up into the sky, our hearts as light as air, en route for Switzerland and the U.K.

The day before our departure Michael Blundell, one of my trustees, invited us to lunch and tried to dissuade me from spending all my money in one 'splash'. 'You should invest it wisely,' he advised. 'But don't you see, Michael, that if I do that the interest might be £40 a year whereas the interest on this adventure will be priceless and last forever.' He gave up trying and wished us good luck instead.

*

# Extracts from My Diary

*July 20th, 1948*

This has been one of those days which begin gloomily and end joyously – when the time passes all too quickly. Put on my pink jumper and cardigan which makes Jemima say 'she wears pink to make the boys wink' and add my green bead necklace in the hopes that May Mukle, the world renowned cellist, will remember the beads even if she doesn't remember me! She gave me the bead necklace when we were ashore together at Port Said, and bought it at Simon Artz in 1931.

Leave the office at 12.30 and walk into the New Stanley Hotel, Nairobi behind a grey-haired couple. The lady has legs which I recognise as being May Mukle's – the same width all the way down. Her companion, Dr. R.A.R. Scott, rather spare and charming, with whom May is staying, presses me to visit him and then leaves us to brave the crossroads. May takes a dive straight in front of a car while I remain on the kerb.

At the club we meet Jack and Jemima – very thrilled at the thought of Jack getting his new wooden leg tomorrow. Whole place crowded and gay and May remarks on the excellence of the food and abundance of it. All English visitors do the same and no wonder. Down the whole centre of the dining room is a long cold buffet from which we help ourselves – hams, tongues, French salads, Kenya salads, Russian salads, cold turkey, cheeses, meringues, avocado pear salads, black olives, French bread by the yard and so on. A whole week's English ration of food goes on one plateful. May tells us that she came by cargo ship in luxury as she was not allowed to fly out with her cello – it was made in Vienna in 1730 and is worth £3,000 or more. She is now the Chairman of the M.M. Musician's Club in London, has a flat in town and a cottage in the country and plays divinely.

We drive to Dr Scott's who is delighted to see us and shows us into his music room. The far end is curved and has a raised dais on which stand twin grand pianos – even knowing that I shall torture May, cannot resist Dr Scott's invitation to sit down and play. I at least enjoy myself. We drink sherry and begin to talk comfortably together when a strange little dark man appears round the screen carrying what looks like a bundle of giant asparagus. They turn out to be reeds, especially suitable for the making of flutes, but will have to be kept in a dry place for four years before they can be used.

The conversation is on a strata well above my head and I silently pray to be allowed to listen and not be obliged to talk. They discuss orchestration, instruments, conductors, so that I realise how little I ever knew about music and how much of that little I have forgotten since I studied at the R.A.M. 20 years ago. May asks if I ever compose things now. I say no, the only things I have composed in the last 15 years are my two daughters. She says daughters are more important than music.

Dr Scott gives me a large bunch of arum lilies and another bouquet of marigolds and tells me if I come back I may play his piano again!

Bless him. And so to bed.

## *July 1948 – Tea Party at Madge Shaw's*

Go to old-fashioned tea party at old Madge Shaw's. What a buzz! Youngest thing there is a charming young bride, Mrs Joan Parker, wearing the New Length dress. Dear old Sir Percy Glancy from India comes up to me and talks of Tom whom he knew well out there. Another guest is a remarkable elderly lady wearing a grey felt hat crammed down on her head and grey felt shoes. She begins to talk about birds most interestingly when we are interrupted by an ex District Commissioner. Madge Shaw's brother, Dacre Shaw, joins the party clad in a beautiful tweed suit and fishing hat. He complains of the heat. At teatime we juggle with plates and cups and delicious little sticky cakes. An old and distinguished-looking Russian gentleman tells me about Russia in the Tsar's days, the good vodka and manners and how well controlled everything was then, finally remarking that Russia and England would never go to war against each other as the British workmen would go on strike. The youngest person sits down beside me. She has been living in Rhodesia and Kenya but loves England where they are about to live. She has a 100% English husband, is in love with him and very newly married, so would love living in the North Pole with him equally well I think.

Somebody asks what is the name of a tree shading the lawn. No one knows except the African butler who gives it the native name. We all repeat this and immediately forget it. Time we left!

That evening Pat Fisher (later Bowles) arrives for supper with her current boyfriend, a most attractive man called Oliver Bonham-Carter. He discusses the government, the new National Health bill in the U.K. and Lawrence Olivier's film production of *Hamlet*, which we all agree is superb. He then takes Pat and me out to dinner. Am not surprised at Pat being *épris* with him. Pat is the last of the obsolete Happy Valley crowd and herself quite a girl.

### August 8th 1948 – Naivasha

Woken in pitch dark hours before dawn by yowling cat, wonder how Joan, with whom I am staying, has not drowned the nauseating animal, and make boo-ing noises at it. It goes away and returns making still worse growls and I retaliate. This performance is repeated three times, after which I go to sleep again. Come out of my sleep to find Joan standing by my bed, fully dressed, wearing dark glasses, check shirt, pullover, long trousers and tartan plaid slung across her shoulders. The sun is shining outside but cannot penetrate the house at any time or at any point, as Father, who built the house, understood (mistakenly) that we are living on the equator here (correct), and therefore we must shut the sun out and not let it in. We do live on the equator, but at an altitude of 7,400 feet, an exceedingly cold altitude, where we grow chilblains and wear woollies and have huge log fires and hot water bottles – or freeze.

Joan enquires if I am ready for breakfast, I say 'of course' and rub the sleep out of my eyes. As we are finishing the hot coffee, cream, eggs and bacon, toast and marmalade, Joan is sent for to speak to a Seychelles from a neighbouring farm. They talk just outside the window on the verandah and to my horror I hear him ask Joan if she will stand bail for a Seychelles mechanic in the village to the tune of £150. Joan replies that she would like to help the man but 'just what does going bail mean?' I call out that it would be as well to know what the man is charged with, as it is a large amount, and point out also that she has not got £150 anyway. Mercifully the man goes off before Joan commits herself. Joan says she feels she really would like to do a Christian act for once, with which I sympathise, but feel relieved when she decides to go up and discuss the question with Jack before doing anything. We both know in our hearts that Jack will say 'have nothing to do with such a thing.' We are quite right.

Later Joan and I go down into the forest where Mother lives, some five miles away. Rose and Jenny, who are visiting her, come out to meet us with the two dogs – Selou the Alsatian and Dickie the wire-haired terrier. They all, with Mother, have coughs and colds, as do Joan and myself. We stroll up to Mother's house, and sit on the property where she is building a two-storey cottage with an English builder and mason.

Mr Cope, the mason, appears. He is extremely smart in collar and tie and shirt and sits down at a steep angle in Mother's winged chair with his long legs corkscrewed round one another. The Persian kitten, Forever Amber, rubs against his feet which starts him off on the subject of his love of animals – all animals, particularly a pet monkey he bought for a gold half sovereign piece in Santiago during World War I.

We are all taken with him and his monkey on a magic carpet to Peru, Cape Town, Buenos Aires, Canada, the Falkland Islands and so on. R. and J. are enthralled and vastly entertained. He tells us that his monkey was a most faithful friend and how, when he played cards with the sailors on deck, Jacko would steal the cigarettes from behind the men's ears and give them to him, and how at San Paolo when the fat old Portuguese women came aboard to sell fruit and lace etc. he and Jacko would watch from the upper deck of the ship until Jacko would be told to 'go'. Whereupon he would leap down among the scared women, collect an armful of their wares and tear up to his master with them. Mr Cope, strange to relate, did not return these trophies but stowed them away under the canvas of a lifeboat!

Later, while cruising beyond the Falklands, Mr Cope went on expeditions over the ice fields and 'had words' with seals on several occasions, when trying to kill young seals for food. He says the mother seals would stand up and beat up the ice with their flippers until their opponent became smothered by flying ice.

The penguins! How they marched up and down in hundreds, drilled by their commander-in-chief; and how, underwater, they moved as swiftly as lightning; and the firmness of the mothers who pushed all the babies into the sea off the edge of the rock to teach them how to swim, regardless of pleas and excuses and promises to go in tomorrow instead of today. We listen entranced until visitors break the spell.

Later Jack and Jemima call in and have drinks on the verandah with Joan and me. *Why* on the verandah I cannot imagine as we all sit wrapped up in overcoats and mufflers and watch as cold-coloured sunset merges into an ever-colder night. Jack tells us he has just been making a round of calls on his boys in their huts to see what and who they have there. Approaching one hut, he asked the owner who else lived with him. After a little hesitation the reply was 'My mother.' Jack went into the hut and surprised two dirty but young girls, very obviously not the owner's mother. On him turning to make further enquiries of the owner, one girl bolted through the door and locked herself into the adjacent store and the other fled through the window. Jack, who is still on crutches, jokingly said he would chase them off the place, which produced instant panic and pandemonium.

I remind Jack that neither he nor his manager, Mr Berger, believed me when I told them I had encountered a lioness on my way down the escarpment the previous night. Jack apologises and says that he knows (now!) that it was a real lioness (really!) as his herd boy had a goat stolen last night and there was a large and deeply imprinted pad mark of a lion left in the ground. Now, it appears, the guns are being polished in readiness for a lion hunt. I shall insist upon being given the skin!

### *August – Summer Holiday*
Try to finish packing for the Coast. Jenny coughing and choking, poor pet, with what the doctor diagnosed as tonsillitis and croup but which Joan and Granny diagnose as whooping cough. Have to leave Jenny behind in their care as I have promised to take Rose and small boy Richard aged 11 to Diani for two weeks.

While carrying hairbrush across to suitcase Jenny says, 'Mummy, I hear that cat in the ceiling again – I'm sure he's going to do something.' I say, 'Yes, I wouldn't be surprised,' and continue to collect forgotten belongings. Suddenly receive unspeakable shower from ceiling on my bent back. The cat *has* done something.

Rose and I get into the baby Austin known as *Duckie* and drive to Nairobi to catch the train for Mombassa. We fall asleep to the sound of the wheels saying 'Agatha-Agatha-Agatha'. Rose remarked upon this when she was four years old. Since then Agatha has accompanied me on every train journey in Kenya.

At Mombasa Rose and I disdain all the numerous offers of help from black faces and proceed to behave as if arriving at a station in England. She goes on to the platform and I pass the baggage through the window to her!

We drive in a taxi at breakneck speed through Mombasa to the famous Manor Hotel, swerving violently to avoid three boys on one bicycle and again to miss an old Arab walking in a dignified unhurried manner across the main thoroughfare.

Eat large breakfast in a huge, cool dining room and then walk through the back garden to the Loreto Convent. It appears to be deserted but Rose takes me up to the front door where we ring the bell and wait. We wait a long time. Just as I stretch out my hand to ring again soft footsteps are heard and the Very Revd. Mother Superior Mother Borgia opens the door to us. She is delighted to see Rose, now 12 years old, and makes us sit down and talk with her. We discuss the excellent colour film shown at the Loreto Convent in Nairobi. I enquire what the origin of the *Corpus Christi* ceremony is, as we were shown this piece of pageantry in the film. Mother Borgia tells us: 'Corpus Christi, as you know my dears, means the body of Christ. Well, about the fourteenth century a girl called Juliana had a vision. You know, *always* it is to the very simple people that visions come, never to the clever people, their intellect seems to blind their spiritual vision. Well, Juliana saw the Christ who told her that he was a little sad because although there were feasts and celebrations for all things spiritual in connection with Him, there was no thanksgiving for his body. He showed Juliana the Church in the symbol of a full moon, with a small dark spot in it. This patch, he said, represented his body which had been forgotten. So Juliana went and told the bishops and priests what she had seen and they, so worldly and pompous, would not believe her. However, she persisted in all sincerity and finally made them realise that she had indeed seen this vision. So thereafter and now, the Corpus Christi is the feast held to celebrate the blessing of Christ's body. The priests carry the host in a gold casket shaped like a moon with a small glass section in it representing Christ's body. With it they bless all the people who, before the procession, carpet the path with flowers and pictures made of flowers, for the priests to walk upon.'

Mother Borgia, who is a very great lady, talks a long time to Rose whom she loves and makes me think hard. Wish I could spend many more hours in conversation with her – we touch on divorce and the effects on the children – on 'auras' round people – on present day tendencies and habits – all too soon we have to leave the peace and quiet of the cloistered walls and emerge into the glare and hustle of the outside world.

Back in the Manor Hotel Garden, we are entertained by the tortoise family – Mr Tortoise and his wife, who are reputed to be 400 years old and look like it, also their charming family of babies (surely this proves they cannot be 400 years old!) – half a dozen of them ranging from three months to four years old and varying in size from a teacup to a teapot. While we are watching them, a stout elderly Brittanic-looking lady comes up to us and sits down heavily on the arm of the iron garden seat. 'I think we human beings could learn many lessons from these creatures,' she says, leaning on her walking stick. 'Fancy, they eat practically nothing and have lived for hundreds of years – what must they know and what must they think of us, straining at gnats and learning only to destroy ourselves.' I suggest that perhaps we don't all wish to live for hundreds of years! 'Oh! but you would if you were like them, they are perfectly happy and they don't know worry or unhappiness; they eat a little blue flower in the morning and another kind of leaf in the afternoon and that is all. But all the same, the old man is boss – he wears the trousers.' (Take a look at my tortoise and remark to Brittania that the trousers seem to be falling off in wrinkles round his ankles). 'This morning,' she continues, 'they were at the bottom of the garden where Mrs Tortoise was playing with her children. The old man insisted upon them coming up to the terrace.'

At last Richard arrives, Rose's young friend. We say goodbye to Brittania and set off for Jadini and Diani, some 22 miles south of Mombasa, in a native bus.

*October 29th 1948*
Wake up, and without moving my head, look out through green shadows and waving palm trees to gently rolling breakers beyond. The sun is shining on the long golden curve of the

beach. The ever changing colours of the sea beckon me to the shore and I run down and plunge into the sea for an early morning dip. Oh how delicious! Richard and Rose scamper after me and from sheer joy we laugh and shout until hunger drives us in for a delicious breakfast.

There can be few if any more beautiful beaches than this one at Diani. A coral reef about half a mile out to sea runs parallel to the shore, keeping out all sharks, and at low tide this reef is a thing of beauty in itself. The smooth golden sand slopes gently to the near reef with barely a rock to be seen.

Hours and days are spent looking for sea treasures on the reefs and goggling with a snorkel. The magic of that beautiful silent world as described by Cousteau never fails.

Jadini is owned and was built by Nellie and Maxwell le Poer Trench some ten years ago and is unique in conception. All buildings are made of coral blocks. The guest houses apart from the main house have two bedrooms and bathroom and spacious verandah. We all eat in the large dining room in the main building. The wide verandah and grass terrace shaded by all kinds of indigenous trees are used as a 'lounge'. Some of the guest houses are two storied and others single storied, all kept cool and well aired by the top of the walls being honey-combed. All furniture is made on the premises by Maxwell himself, mostly of dark local wood and highly polished – very beautiful.

Maxwell's daughter-in-law told me one day of a young South African with radioactive eyes. He divines water with his eyes, not with sticks or instruments. He had done this from the age of six years and can apparently 'see' water no matter how deep down in the earth. He had found water all over Africa for individuals as well as for the South African Government. Nancy said that he had two completely different sides to his face, even the nose being another shape on one side to the other. Now he has had to give up divining as it is killing him.

The Peatlings and Joan Wolsey-Lewis joined us at Jadini and all of us were very sorry when they had to leave – Rose and I suffering from the 'I've got nothing to do now' feeling. Rose goes off and commandeers a native to take us out to the far reef in his canoe. This craft is made out of a hollowed tree trunk but is water-tight. I sit on the only cross-bench over a pile of fish and what looks like a pink octopus. Rose risks capsizing the boat as she stands up, refusing to sit amongst 'that stinking muck' on the floor.

Richard is wearing my straw hat trimmed with raffia flowers. Asked 'why', he says that he has lost his school hat somewhere on the beach but that his mother won't mind and can buy him another. Hope he is right.

Look over the side of the canoe down through clear green water to the bottom of the sea. It is unbelievingly beautiful. Weird forests of seaweed and whole worlds of coral glide soundlessly beneath us. Brilliant flashes of light explode as fishes chase one another through the waving weeds. Huge starfish, black and gold, orange, purple, scarlet, drift leisurely along. Jellyfish of translucent beauty and rainbow-coloured angel fish move amongst the towers and turrets of the watery world.

We grind to a halt on a sandbank and step out on to the Great Reef, the ocean stretching into infinity on one side and the lagoon on the other. The reef is only two to fifteen yards wide when the tide is out, and is entirely covered by sea when the tide is in. Anxiously tell the boatman not to forget to collect us before the tide turns. He merely grins, white teeth gleaming, and pushes himself off in his canoe.

Hours pass while we collect giant cowrie shells and treasures off the reef. Richard treads on a sea cow which squirts a yellow liquid over his shoe. (The sea cow is only about 4" by 10".) Come across a deep pool where some little seahorses are playing about amongst electric blue and orange fish. Never having seen anything like this before, we are all enchanted and forget about the time. Suddenly I notice water round my ankles and see that there are very few dry patches of reef left. Shout to the children who seem to have developed instant deafness and continued to poke things as they amble further and further away. Trying not to panic I shout to some other children who are putting out to sea in their own dinghy and ask them please to send someone to take us off the reef. When the children come within talking distance they seem quite unworried and Richard assures me that the taxi will soon turn up long before we drown. Just then the boatman does turn up. Feel a little foolish.

Rose and Richard are loaded with creepy crawlies collected from the reef which wave feelers out of the buckets. 'Where is the aquarium going to be?' I ask. The answers are vague. In the evening, coming in to rinse out the sand from my hair and eyes, I find a horrible little black hairy octopus looking at me from the basin.

Soon the last day of the holiday dawns. None of us is too sorry to leave. Three weeks was too long to laze about in the sun.

Back at home in Nairobi we return to normal. Darling Jenny is now out of quarantine and with us again. Schools begin and also my job at the African Information Office where I look after the Photographic Library.

## Nakuru Agricultural Show

Jenny and I set off in Duckie, my baby Austin, with camp beds, food, tickets, suitcases etc. to stay for the four days of the Royal Agricultural Show with old friends near Nakuru. Do not wish to stay on the farm as my manager and his Burmese wife already have her sister staying with them. The heat is excessive and the dust blinding.

Arrive at the showground and am most appreciative of the straw which has been laid down everywhere to counteract the dust. We find the Solai stall and I am thrilled to see a sample of my wheat No. 291 graded A1. Also find that our coffee samples and sunflower seed have won first prizes. Feel unreasonably proud and recollect that it is the result of my manager's sowing, not mine.

Hearing the band strike up I pin my agricultural and horticultural badges to my bosom and join lots of farming friends in the grandstand: Jack (my brother), Cecily Kingsford, Venetia Irvine, with whom we are staying, and many others. Later we visit the prize pedigree Guernseys, amongst them one from our Solai farm which is very exciting as we have only recently bred from the Guernsey bull which Tom imported just before he died.

A friend insists we should have a look at the original sheep of Kenya. 'Are they not goats?' I ask. 'No, not like anything else.' These animals do look like very brown goats or muddy sheep and are bred and reared by the Masai. Reflect that they have much in common with their owners: same colour, same matted hair, same thin legs and same expression. Pass on to the pedigree Romney rams, large beasts panting in the heat under their thick woolly hair, 6" to 8" long. Walk along the cattle stalls and get a little bored with the rows and rows of back ends only. After drinking lemonade at our stall we return to the ring in time to see Lady Claud Hamilton's pedigree Jersey bull win the award for the best animal in the show. Join Jack who is talking to a vaguely familiar-looking face. Suddenly Jack leans towards me and asks 'Who is this woman?' Neither of us remembers her name but we think she is something to do with Magadi Soda. It remains an unsolved mystery.

My manager persuades us after all to stay with them on my Solai farm, as their visitors are not coming. Early in the morning I wake up in our own house for the first time since Tom died. I go out on to the terrace and look at the farm stretched out below me. The view is beautiful beyond words.

Memories overwhelm me. Get into the farm box-body car and drive to the wheat plantation, passing through the coffee shambas on the way and stopping to pick up Pedro, the head man. He tells me that we are taking off 13 bags to the acre of wheat, a very good crop for that part of the world and most encouraging to hear.

Next morning Jenny and I leave the Solai farm (Banks Estate) early to have breakfast with Venetia at Stream Cottage. We find her in the water garden. A table is laid beside her spread with pawpaws and freshly picked strawberries. Queenie brings down fried eggs and bacon and we stuff ourselves with all these scrumptious things.

After bidding her farewell we return to the showground in Nakuru and join Jack and Jemima. There is an exhibition of miniature model farms. Above it is a notice which says 'Which is your farm?' Jack points to the one where they are playing polo. 'That is my farm,' he says with a twinkle in his eye. We take our seats in the grandstand and watch the Grand Parade of prize-winners walking round the arena in ever-smaller circles, a magnificent stallion in the centre called Senior. In the U.K. or anywhere else in the civilised world, this would be quite an ordinary sight. In Kenya it is the best agricultural show ever seen before and we are proud of it.

## *October Garden Party*

Terribly hot day. Rather wish I were not going to G.H. but look forward to meeting my old up-country friends again. Rebecca and George Fane call for me in George's large limousine and we join the queue of vehicles passing through the Gates of Government House. Every kind and sort of car, ancient and modern, grinds slowly up the drive. We get hotter and hotter and sprinkled with dust.

We wander about the grounds looking for His Excellency and Lady Mitchell, but do not find them. Under the trees are small tables with plates of dried-up sandwiches and small cakes upon them. We sit at one of these and drink tepid tea. Soon we are joined by friends, among them the fish warden, Archie Ritchie, and his regal-looking wife, aptly named Queenie. The Jex-Blakes bring a distinguished-looking man with them and introduce him as Mr Clinton-Wells. George whispers to me that 'he is better known as Wormy Wells.' He does not tell me why!

People keep stopping and asking 'Have you seen the Mitchells yet?' It reminds me of the Rabbit in *Alice in Wonderland* saying 'I shall be late for the Duchess.'

Am introduced to a beautiful Contessa, wife of the Italian Ambassador. She is the most elegant lady in sight. Astonishingly she tells me she has just walked all the 11 miles up and 11 miles down Kilimanjaro and that it is so easy and very beautiful.

Elizabeth Erskine appears under an enchanting feather hat. At last Lady Mitchell is located and we all make our curtseys. Lady M. is hideous and atrociously dressed but looks highly intelligent.

George Fane and Rebecca, formerly Ward, return home with me and we spend a happy evening discussing Stalin, world affairs, Lady Mitchell's ineptitude and Switzerland. George suggest that Silva Plana above St. Moritz might be the place for me to take Rose and Jenny on my proposed holiday next year. Rebecca is, as ever, a staunch and true friend to me in every situation and always ready to help and give useful information when asked. George Fane (her second husband as Hugh Ward died some years ago) reminds me greatly of Tom; he has that old-fashioned charm born of good manners and the same quiet sense of humour. He takes my *Goodbye Mr Chips* off with him and I know will return it!

And so to bed to the welcome sound of rain.

*

# Six Months in Europe

*August 1st 1949*
Having sold one of my six acres of land in Nairobi for one thousand pounds, I take the children away from school for one term to visit Europe and England.

Our plane begins to come down over a neat green valley and we collect our innumerable pieces of hand luggage while fields of stooked corn glide past the windows. We have arrived in Switzerland! Impossible to believe that 24 hours ago we were in East Africa! We have flown slowly over Egypt, Crete, Greece and Italy at an altitude of 16,000 feet, the Captain has informed us at intervals. We have dined at Athens, circled round the Acropolis, and spent a night in Rome. There it was very hot and we did not arrive at our hotel until after 8 p.m. Shown into a palatial apartment with marble floors and baths, Jenny and Rose asked which was the hot water and which the cold; the one labelled C. was scalding hot. *Calde* for hot I found in my dictionary and not for cold. Jenny hung out of the window, looking down into a crowded street where whole families seemed to be taking a stroll. 'Why are those tiny children up so late?' she asked.

We ate and enjoyed a delicious dinner and for the first time Rose and Jenny sampled water melons. Early next morning we were collected by the Airways bus and driven back to the airport through crowded streets full of colour and ruins and smells. All most exciting for colonial children, Jenny never before having been out of Kenya. We flew up the Po Valley, over Florence and the scorched plains of Tuscany. Lastly we passed over the Alps, a breathtaking sight. Looking down into their crevasses and valleys, spellbound by the sheer grandeur and size of them, I thought how *le Bon Dieu* must have enjoyed making the world.

At Silva Plana we were met by Hans and Berthe Erny in their Pontiac and driven to a place of enchantment – mountains, valleys, cows with tinkling bells round their necks, blue skies, excursions to Italy with the Ernys, long treks up into the Alps carrying our picnic lunches on our backs. Rose took photos of us up in the mountains from where we could look down upon the four little Lacs, Silva Plana, Sils, Complier and St. Moritz. Unfortunately she forgot to turn the spool round so none of them came out!

In our hotel were a very elegant Dutch couple who admired the children as being very well brought up. On their plates at breakfast one morning Rose and Jenny found a packet of delicious Swiss sweets. The Dutchman had put them there as a little surprise. They invited us all to visit them at the Hague before returning to Kenya. Sadly we were not able to do this, a missed opportunity. Another day an old blind gentleman in a wheelchair told his nurse to give the two little English children a box of Suchard chocolates each. The whole atmosphere for us was one of joy and happiness.

After three weeks, on the day we were leaving for Zurich, snow fell early in the morning. Jenny had never seen snow, and was leaning out of the window, pigtails swinging, trying to catch some of 'this stuff' and asking what it was.

A few days before that, we all drove up to Majoja. We went via the Fourcla Alps and on our way discovered a tiny Lac where trout leaped out of the water as though dancing a ballet. We felt like dancing too. A party of young Swiss students overtook us singing what seemed to be a rondelle in praise of the mountains. Certainly they were justified, the dazzling white mountains stretched endlessly above and around us, sharply cutting into the clear blue sky. Suddenly Jenny jumped into the air 'like one of the little trout in the Lac,' as Rose remarked. On either side a peasant was collecting cowpats and sheep drop-pings and scattering them over the grassy slopes with a large hand shovel. He stopped whistling to smile at the children as we passed and Rose greeted him with *Greutze*, which she has now learnt to say. Another day we took the Poste up to a mountain village where there was an exhibition of marvellous stained glass windows in an old chateau. We were fascinated by the glorious colours, the sunlight illuminating them, and by the landscapes depicted in coloured glass. We all felt sad at having to leave the mountains and return to earth when the time came to go back to Zurich.

### *September 2nd*

The Ernys knocked on our door to ask if we were ready. We were astonished to see Hans all dressed up in black tailcoat and carrying a hat box in his hand! They were going to a cousin's funeral at Freiberg and promised to put us down in Berne and to collect us again in the afternoon.

Hans drove us through the fertile valley of the Aar river which surrounds Berne. Most people today will have been to Berne or know of it, but to us it was Fairy Town straight out of *Grimm's Fairy Tales*. Left to ourselves, we explored the town, intrigued by the cobbled main street with its wonderful shops and fountains. Of course we watched the clock strike 12 and the procession of animals and people who emerged from the clock tower and paraded round the turret! And the *sweet* shops! And the patisseries! To this day my favourite little cakes are the ones that look like potatoes, made of delicious marzipan and fluffy filling, but the children liked the ones like mice and castles etc.

On the return journey Hans pointed out the enormous eaves overhanging the houses here and the pictures painted on the walls – hunting scenes, the vintage and country scenes such as the milking of cows etc. Then the bears! Big bears, middle-sized bears, teeny weeny bears, all in a huge well shaded by trees. The papas are separated from the mamas and the mamas from the older children by walls. They played all sorts of games, and we threw carrots down to them, and wasted lots of time enjoying their antics. The town of Berne dates from the twelfth century, as you may know, and still looks like a medieval city.

The Ernys took us along the valley to spend a weekend at their farm, run by a peasant farmer and his wife. 'Voilà, mes enfants, nous y sommes,' announces Hans as we draw up in front of a big chalet overlooking the village of Rutihoff. It is all too adorable as the children keep telling me.

The weather is still very hot, and after a cool drink Rose, Jenny and I are invited by Berthe to go out and shake the large plum tree on the overgrown lawn. We do this and a shower of large black plums falls upon us. Delicious.

The Ernys' chalet is quite perfect: light pinewood parquet floors, pinewood cupboards and wall panelling and ceiling to match. Shutters with heart-shaped 'peepholes' carved in them. Beautiful carved chairs and trestle table of the same wood and deep window seats. Curtains and cushions of oatmeal rough linen, and russet sisal rugs on the floor. Someone had arranged a bowl of wild flowers on an antique work-table to welcome us. This is the living room on the first floor and has a large balcony leading off it.

We get out a Swiss flag and fix it in place on the end of the balcony. 'What fun!' exclaims Rose.

We take a little walk after gorging on the *prunos* and as the afternoon gets hotter and hotter we sit down under a wild cherry tree and admire the view. Presently a haycart comes along, the horse led by a peasant. Both horse and peasant seem to be wearing the same hats, except that the horse's ears protrude through his. A young girl and a boy rake up hay with very wide wooden rakes and toss it into the cart. When the cart was full the peasant invited Rose and Jenny to join the boy and girl on the top of the hay and ride back to the village on the haycart. They were thrilled to do so.

Ding dong, ding dong, the church bells ring through the peace of the evening. A full moon climbs the sky and Jenny sits with feet up and chin on her knees on the balcony railing. Hans calls her 'Hartze-Pussy'. Pfeffell's rosy-cheeked face appears behind a tray-load of steaming soup and we sit down to supper. Unfortunately the next course is pink sausage! Pfeffell proudly says that they are a *specialité de la maison* and that her father made the horrid things. We try to eat them but Jenny after one mouthful asks to be excused, saying she is tired and is going to bed. Rose and I feel obliged to finish our helpings!

*September 12th*
Our packing is done and our nine pieces of luggage stacked up in the hall. Berthe pours out the coffee and we eat our rye bread in silence. We cannot really be leaving this happy toyland where life is a game and the sun shines every day and there is always the sound of bells. '*Pardon, mesdames.*' We are interrupted by the arrival of the taxi and a whole hour too early at the Erny's house in Zollikon Zurich. Berthe accompanies us to the airport, and as we drive through Zurich the flags are out again and banners flying for yet another public holiday.

I feel so glad that we see the last of Switzerland in this gala mood . . . the sun shines on the Lac, little boats chug up and down; far away a white-topped mountain reaches up into the sky: 'Goodbye adorable Switzerland.'

*

# Holiday in England

*September 13th – London*
Buckingham Palace with the Guards looking like tin soldiers in their scarlet and gold uniforms and busbies. St James Park, with its trees bending to the autumn wind – yellow leaves swirling, children's hair flying.

Hamleys, filled with little people, exhausted parents sitting on chairs while their children live a dream in toy world. Shiny red buses and twopence halfpenny tickets. Westminster Abbey as evening begins to fall. The great rose window and Unknown Warrior's tomb. The high altar gleaming, golden beyond the first altar. Ancient archways fanning out and above our heads. Beauty and peace, and gentleness flow through me. We kneel in the empty cathedral. Big Ben chiming the half hour, the Houses of Parliament etched in black against a pale grey sky. Good night to Uncle Jack Banks and Aunt Nessie with whom we are staying at the Grosvenor Hotel. Pink eiderdowns, pink lampshades and two little pink noses on their pillows beside me.

London belongs to us all.

*September 28th – Cornwall Kiln Quay*
We are staying with my godmother, Mrs Ethel Beresford-Riley. Jenny, who is sitting on the end of my bed like a cat watching a mouse, pounces upon me as I open my eyes. We might be living in the sixteenth century. Aunt Ethel's house is a replica

of a Tudor manor, modernised but furnished with priceless period furniture. Stuffed with treasures, glorious paintings, tapestries, a treasure house rather than a home. We should be wearing ruffs round our necks! Below the windows the gardens descend in terraces to the old Quay, Kiln Quay. On the right is a rather overgrown rose garden, tennis court, vegetable garden and orchard. Surely that is Sir Walter Raleigh walking towards me? 'What are you staring at Mum?' asks Rose, leaning out of the window still clad in her pyjamas. I stop dreaming.

Breakfast in a dark dining room hung with dark green velvet and tapestry. We sit at a long refectory table on uncomfortable King Charles chairs. Tierny, the butler, dressed in white coat, brings in platefuls of bacon, eggs, toast, everything I thought would never appear on an English breakfast table again. Aunt Ethel is already at the head of the table and begins to tell us about birds and animals she has befriended here. The story the children liked best was about a jackdaw which she found in France and carried across the country in a basket covered with a wire net to give to her professor of art, the great Brangwyn. Also she told of a parrot who could answer people, not just say things. She had to leave it for several months and on her return the parrot greeted her with 'Zou Zou. Ah! Zou Zou,' and died!

We bathed off the Quay in freezing water. I dressed in one of Aunt Ethel's ancient bathing dresses and the children in their pants. After the first shock the water was refreshing and the children adored it.

Aunt Ethel had two old friends staying at Kiln Quay as well as ourselves – Lady Allardyce and a fictitious aunt, old Boo. After lunch they would all dispose themselves on long chairs in various parts of the garden to have a siesta, while we discovered Falmouth and climbed the steep cliffs.

\*

Chug, chug, we move out to sea in the Falmouth ferry, quite a large boat and quite a rough sea. Aunt Ethel says she feels extremely ill but remains standing firmly on deck, her cloak flying out behind her. She tells us the history of St. Mawes castle, built in the reign of Henry VIII for his honeymoon with Nan Bullen. It stands on the top of the cliff – firm, round, strong and invincible like King Hal himself. We sail round St. Just in Roseland and enter the bay. Enchanting little St. Mawes! Its ancient water-front is the same today as it was some three hundred years ago or more. Most of the little houses are painted blue, white, pink, or covered with creeping roses. The tide is so low that we have to be rowed ashore in little dinghies. Aunt Ethel's friend, an artist, lives in a minute cottage on the summit of a hill. It has a superb view of the sea and St. Mawes Bay where small sailing boats weave across the smooth blue water.

After a Cornish tea with cream and jam buns we are gathered up by Aunt Ethel who does not want to miss the ferry and rushes off at great speed, cloak wound round her and hair loosening. Poor Lady Allardyce cannot keep up so we politely stay beside her, and are picked up by a kind old Admiral friend of hers who drives us down to the port in his old Lancia. On the other side, we meet up with more old friends of A.E.'s who take us on to their small yacht. The children bathe off this before we all eat another meal and finally get back to Kiln Quay in time for supper laid out for us by Tierny! All this is England as I used to think of it nostalgically in Kenya, with the difference that nowadays it always seems to be the Servants' Day Out!

Aunt Ethel has a terrible old Lanchester limousine which completely blocks the narrow winding roads of Cornwall. Tierny loathes it. One day, en route for Perranporth, the machine refuses to move from a filling station miles from everywhere. Stupidly I have a go at it when Tierny is approaching apoplexy! The engine turns over and we proceed. Ever after I am asked by Aunt Ethel to drive the car on our outings, and come to hate the heavy cumbersome vehicle quite as much as Tierny did.

Lady A. takes us to tea at Helford Passage. We drink it outside in the garden of the Ferry Inn so that we can watch the children while they have a swim. Lady A. orders tea plus 'a saucer of jam for the wasps, please'. The reason is made apparent when the cakes arrive and the wasps with them. Thanks to Lady A's foresight the wasps converge on the saucer of jam and leave us alone!

On the beach a shaggy dog joins us and refuses to leave. Then a portly old gentleman emerges from the sea, catches up a towel and walks towards us drying his white hair. 'Good dog, good old fellow, that's enough now,' and smiling a greeting to us, he and the dog go off, and almost immediately the old gentleman re-appears in sight, alone on the top of a flat roofed bungalow, still drying his hair and giving us a friendly wave with the towel.

Shopping in Falmouth is quite an education. The three old ladies wear hats, gloves and each take a basket. The shops are still rationed for most commodities. Asking for a film for my Brownie camera the answer is 'Sorry, Madam, we haven't any.' 'Will you be getting any soon?' 'I can't say at all.' 'But isn't Brownie an English make?' 'I expect so, Madam.' 'Well?' 'Most of the material comes from America, Madam. Sorry.'

This is the response to a lot of items on my shopping list. Aunt Ethel is also having problems as the only cheese she can get is rat-trap Gorgonzola. In a leather shop we try to find a suitcase as one of ours has burst at the seams. We find one but are told that it has already been put aside for an earlier customer. 'Will you be getting in any more?' 'I really cannot say, Madam, it all depends on the Board of Trade.' I have a vision of a monstrous creature sitting guarding all the necessities of life while life itself starves. The children go on ahead while I wait for the old ladies, who are still carrying their baskets and wearing gloves.

*October 2nd*

While playing tennis with Aunt Ethel on her dandelion-covered tennis court we are interrupted by the sudden appearance of a neighbour. 'Come quickly. The *Pamir* is sailing into Falmouth and you can watch her from the cliff.' We follow her as fast as we can run. Below us, moving slowly across the water, is the most beautiful sailing ship, the last of the tea clippers on her last voyage home. The sea is as calm as a millpond, the sun sinking below the horizon, hundreds of little sailing boats and small craft escort The *Pamir* into safe harbour. Church bells peel, the sky turns from pale blue to gold, there is barely enough breeze to move the lovely ship. We are watching the end of an era, something beautiful is passing out of history and our lives. No one speaks until The *Pamir* disappears round the end of the cliff. Rose slips her arm through mine. 'Did Queen Elizabeth's ships look like that?' she asks. 'Well, rather like that,' I reply. We go back to the overgrown tennis court, pick up our tennis rackets and play.

### Hampshire. Hampton Hill House

Hope and Freddie St. Maur give us a warm welcome with 'Jambo' and big hugs. This is the first time I have seen them since the war and they have bought a large red brick Victorian house in Swanmore. One half of it is divided by a far from soundproof wall from the other half, which is let to retired Indian Army people called Partiger or Pargiter. Early on our first morning we are woken by cries of 'Hope! Freddie!' Thuds and muffled curses are heard and Freddie's voice yells 'I'm doing all I can but the electricity has gone mad, and being Saturday no one is likely to come and put it right.' Mrs Partiger's contribution is to wail that 'I want to go home to Botley Grange as I *cannot* live without a *hot bath*.' After long and expensive telephone enquiries Freddie succeeds in persuading a pre-war electrician to come and fix things up.

Meanwhile Hope and the rest of us prepare for a large cocktail party to be held that evening, around 6 p.m. Hope becomes convinced that nobody is coming, but Freddie says nobody ever does before at least half an hour after they have been invited. Rose and Jenny do a highland fling in the drawing room and the Partigers/Pargiters enter and admire the colourful arrangement of refreshments.

The party is a success. Jenny and Rose help to pass round the stuffed eggs and sandwiches etc. and endless ancient admirals, generals and hons. circulate and eventually leave. Soon after the last guest leaves, while Hope and I slip off our shoes and get down to 'clearing up', the telephone rings. Hope answers it and returns in fits of laughter. 'Jenny darling, you did wonderfully. Admiral X has just rung to ask me to give his love to the little girl who was in the hall holding a plate of sandwiches when he left. She offered him one and when he declined she said "Well, why don't you take some home in your pocket!"'

*November*
38 Brompton Square! The very name enchants me. We ring the bell and the door is opened by Daisy (Cust) who welcomes us to London. We last saw her in Kenya five months ago. Since then she had flown home with her first grandson Sam under one arm and a large ham under the other. He is temporarily being looked after by Daisy until his parents arrive on Leave in the spring.

Jenny counts the stairs as we climb up to our 'flat' put at our disposal for the next ten days. It is quite delightful and the children are thrilled with it. We unpack and settle down to making out our programme for the next week: The Tower of London; Madame Tussauds; the Victoria and Albert Museum; Kensington Gardens; the Royal Ballet; Christmas shopping. So much to do and so few days left.

In Madame Tussauds I tell Rose to go over to the Commissionaire and ask him where we would find the wax Royal Family. She comes back rather cross. 'Honestly Mum, that is a wax figure, not a Commissionaire.' We look at Kitchener, Attlee, Madame Tussaud herself, Danny Kaye and the Sleeping Beauty, the latter apparently breathing regularly. Jenny is sure she is alive. We all agreed we did not want to visit the Chamber of Horrors.

The Circus at Olympia. Daisy's husband (Jack's father-in-law and one of the guests at Major George Frampton's wedding in Cairo in 1944) takes us to the circus in his old pre-war car. Jemima's sister, Tiny, and her new fiancé Oliver Ziegler come too. In the condensation on the back window of the car Tiny writes 'I love Oliver' in large letters. We all spend lots of time on the giant switchback railway and roundabouts as well as enjoying the circus – something Jenny has never seen before. On our way back to the car along the road, Archer suddenly has an attack of *joie de vivre* and proceeds to dance from side to side along the pavement to the astonishment of other pedestrians.

The Ballet – *Les Sylphides*. Rose and Jenny are spellbound by the magical dancing. Jenny says she does not understand how anyone can stand on one toe for so long as the ballerina did. Archer tells her 'That's easy,' and gives a disastrous demonstration in the gangway!

*November 30th*
Home again in Hampton Hill House with our toes held out to the log fire and dear Hope and Freddie pleased to listen to our endless accounts of what we did in London. We retire to bed late but completely satisfied. Scrambled memories float into our dreams of Aunt Ethel and her insistence upon painting a portrait of us. Guy Fawkes bonfires, Henry VIIIth's armour, Lady Jane Grey's head rolling off the block, lunch at the Victoria League House, Churchill in Madame Tussauds, catching the wrong bus home, toy fare at Harrods, delicious burnt mixed grill in the flat at Brompton Square, fog at night, sun during the day, leaves madly dancing, St Paul's and Nelson's statue. We sleep.

*December 18th*
As we are leaving before Christmas, Freddie and Hope give us a traditional Christmas party at Hampton Hill – turkey, plum pudding, mince pies, brandy butter, crackers and presents round the fir tree.

After lunch the Padre's daughter and Anne-from-next-door play endless games of Donkey and Old Maid with us until it is time to clear up. We only have a little supper as we are already completely full up with Christmas fare and retire to bed early. Looking down upon the moonlit fields from my window, the peace of an English countryside enters deep inside me. How lovely England is and how wonderful that it is still here and has survived the Battle of Britain and the horrors of World War II.

We shall leave in the morning but I know that I shall return someday. '*Kwaheri*, Hampton Hill House, *Kwaheri sana* to all who live in your domain, and thank you.'

\*

## Christmas 1949

### *Aunt Edie's, December 24th*
'Come and see the ham', calls Eva the cook. She must be one of the last of her kind and is a vast lady. She lifts the lid off an enormous pan saying, 'It is a tin bath which I borrowed from the school down the road. Nothing else was big enough for that Kenya ham you brought us.' She added that in England the size of the kitchen utensils corresponded with the size of the rations. She opens the oven door to show us a goose, something my children have never dreamt of. In the evening Angela and Kate Michell with Rose, Jenny and myself wrap ourselves in thick woollies and go out into the road to sing carols. We walk down the road singing at the top of our voices unheard by anyone but enjoying the fun of it.

### *December 25th*
Christmas Day has really arrived. Grown-ups as well as children find bulging stockings at the ends of their beds.

Bacon for breakfast, gloves for church, goose for lunch, Christmas cake for tea and presents all day long. Telegrams arrive from Overseas and are read out loud. Aunt Doll collects all the Christmas papers and folds them up neatly for next year. We listen to the King's Speech; he only hesitates once. 'Goodwill to all men'.

One more treat. We go to Covent Garden to see Margot Fonteyn in *Cinderella*. Liquid beauty flows over the stage. Colour, romance, pathos, humour, enchantment move in silent beauty before our eyes. How lucky we are to be finishing our holiday in England on such a magical note, after so many years in Kenya.

### *Brief Interlude*

On our way back to Kenya we arranged to join Mervyn Kemmis-Betty and his two nephews in Switzerland for ten days. Our flight was a little nerve-wracking. Owing to dense fog we were unable to land at Zurich. The Captain tried to land at Basle only to find that the fog was even worse there. 'We will try to land at Berne,' the voice announced. No luck there either. Finally we returned to Zurich, and with great skill the Captain brought us safely down in dense fog and no visibility at all. The train journey from Zurich to Grindelwald was long, cold and tiring.

In spite of this Mervyn thought we should all go tobogganing that night after supper. The moon was glaring bright, the twisting mountain road frozen solid, and the climb to the top of the hill almost too much for us. On the hair-raising rush downhill both Rose and Mervyn's nephew failed to turn the corner and disappeared over the side of a cliff. Mercifully they both fell into a large snowdrift and, apart from shock, seemed none the worse. In front of the hotel I trod on the end of my toboggan, feet flying up in the air, and broke my arm falling on the road. After that all ski-ing for me had to be done with care not to fall on that arm. Neither Jenny nor Rose enjoyed those ten days as the nephews knew very well how to ski and went off with their uncle all day while we struggled on the nursery slopes. Definitely *that* part of our holiday was *not a success!*

It was a holiday never to be forgotten, not only for its variety, but because it was the last time I ever spent a holiday alone with my two adored daughters.

*

# Back in Kenya

I t was bliss to be back in Kenya again a few days later, to feel
warm in the sun and to be welcomed by faithful Rawayo,
our old head man with his wonderful smile and greeting
'Jambo Memsahib, Jambo Memsahib Kidogo.'

## Marriage to William Bucknall

In 1950 we moved from Nairobi to Limuru where we rented
Tiny Kingsford's house, formerly occupied by his parents. We
were all very happy there – Jenny at Limuru School where Miss
Fisher, the Archbishop's niece, was headmistress, and Rose at
the Kenya High. Our closest friends lived on either side of us
and their daughters all went to the Kenya High with Rose.

At the end of that year I met and married William Bucknall, a
retired Lt. Col. of the Black Watch Regiment. He had divorced
his first wife (who was a first cousin of his) some ten years
previously, and had two grown-up daughters. Just why I married him I shall never know. Perhaps we both were tired of
living alone; we agreed that we were not in love but thought at
our age (I was 41 and he fifteen years older) that did not
matter. We were so wrong. Never mind. We made a good job of
it, as time was to show.

The beginning was inauspicious. I forgot that we were getting married that particular day and was in my gardening slacks
when the bridegroom-to-be arrived to take me to the Registrar's

Office in Nairobi. The honeymoon was plagued with misadventures. We reached the fishing inn up country covered with dust and feeling tired and cross. The electricity in the pub gave out so we groped about by candlelight until lamps were found. Then William stormed off on his own to the bar and picked up two very obvious ladies and informed me that he had asked them to join us for dinner! Not on your life! He had to decide between me and them.

The first day out fishing I caught several fish while he tangled with his line and hook. Eventually he cast the line and fell into the river. He emerged soaking and furious. In order to dry his clothes he had to strip down to his pants. Unknown to me he suffered from sunburn acutely. After an hour some wild bees attacked us and we had to move fast. By then he was bright red and could not bear anything to touch him. He did not fish again, and managed to get sciatica as well as sunburn and was in a frantic state of mind and body. Honeymoons are in any case rather overrated things, I always thought, unless both parties are totally besotted with each other.

Rose had been pleased when I told her that William and I were going to marry, but Jenny was not. While still at Limuru William was running a riding school at the Limuru School and we all became involved in the Pony Club which we ran.

### Move to Molo

About six months later a great friend of ours, Colonel Dick Sheppard, late of the 7th Hussars, asked us to join him up at Molo where George Alexander was selling off 25 acres of land suitable for growing pyrethrum. To Molo we went. Our caravanserai consisted of two cars, a hired lorry full of furniture and houseboys, four dogs, two kittens, eight horses and ourselves. The house was one of the very early settlers' type, wood, on stilts, iron roof which leaked at every pore and the Little House 30 yards down the garden path. There had been a hailstorm immediately before we arrived. The house stood on the top of a vertical-sided hill and was approached by a muddy and deeply rutted track which made the cars boil. The girls and I took an instant dislike to it. William said it was marvellous.

Immediately I decided that on no account would we live like the early settlers, and set about deciding where to build a stone house and how to do it. Rose and Jennifer went back to school and I tried to accustom myself to living at an altitude of 8,700 feet amongst a hunting community whom I did not as yet know. Jim Ryan was Master of the Molo Hounds and as mad as most Irishmen. The kennels were 9,000 feet up and we all really lived at Insanity Height. The forests behind our house and over much of the country there were quite beautiful – mostly olive and cedar trees of great height. Green parrots fed off the olives and laurie birds glided about amongst the tree trunks while colobus monkeys chattered and sunbathed on the tops of the trees. Every morning we went out riding at 7 a.m. with Dick and whoever was staying with us. The first time I went alone I found the perfect site for a house in a glade on the summit of the hill. Dismounting, I pulled out a wild green delphinium and planted it in the ground, swearing that that was where we would build our house. So *Kameko* was born!

With the help of John Crowther, my coffee estate manager, trained in architecture, the plans were drawn up and in no time the local *Sikh Fundis* and Africans built a charming stone house with a Makuti roof. It was called the Coffee House by Dick as it was paid for out of the coffee crop and also because we always had so many visitors. William was made Joint Master of the Molo Hounds and I was the President of the Ladies Hunt Committee and also became District Vice President of the East African Women's League and Hon. Secretary of the Molo Pony Club.

### Cressida's Visit

We led a busy and very active life and seemed to run every equestrian event in the area. A year after we were married, William announced that he had told his eldest daughter Cressida that she could come out and stay with us for as long as she liked. He also informed me that she was inclined to be promiscuous and he thought she had had more than one miscarriage and was still unmarried.

She arrived a few weeks later by air and we met her at Nairobi Airport. An elegant figure alighted from the gangway dressed very smartly in a black coat and skirt, red shoes with very high heels and her black hair done up in a bun on the top of her head. Cressida! Her large black eyes and delightful voice instantly appealed to me as did her sense of humour, and we have been the best of friends ever since. But it was tricky. She talked freely in front of Rose and her chums, all 16/18 year olds, of her beliefs in free love and one parent love children etc. However, as she soon gave signs of having a nervous breakdown because one of her free lovers had deserted her, I found it most useful to hold her up to the girls as an example of the results of the free love etc. which she tried vainly to follow. Cress was so attractive and such fun that everyone fell for her. Through my old friend Venetia she got a good job working for the Red Cross with another woman as advertiser for them over the three East African Territories.

Rose passed her exams brilliantly and the time came for her to go to England to be finished at Harcombe House in Dorset.

Before she left we went on safari to the Murchison Falls – Cress, Rose, William and I. We set off for Lake Victoria, some thousand and more miles from Molo, but were only about halfway when one of the few passing lorries threw up a stone which shattered our windscreen. Miles from everywhere, we had to knock out all the remaining glass and proceed. As soon as we accelerated to fifty miles an hour the back doors flew out and with them most of the suitcases. Some kind Africans came to our help and produced long pieces of copper wire, no doubt stolen from the telephone poles, and we wound the wire round the car to keep the doors shut. By the time we reached Kisumu Hotel on the Lake (known as Lake Kisumu to most people) we looked like a lot of Red Indians from the dust.

That evening we boarded our little launch called the *S.S. Livingstone* and sailed slowly out over the still waters. We were the only passengers, and the Goan cook served supper for us on deck by the light of a full moon, and one hurricane lamp. Romantic – a pity no handsome young men to entertain the girls, though Cress, then 24, 'got off' with the Goan Captain. Fortunately the voyage was short and taken up with looking at and listening to all the animals in the world coming down to the water's edge for their evening drink.

Next day we were woken before dawn so that we could watch the animal kingdom doing its morning toilet as the sun rose. It was like a living scene from *Genesis*. On every rock there was a crocodile, immobile as a replica in Madame Tussauds. On the banks were monkeys de-fleaing themselves or others, admiring themselves in the water's reflection, and generally capering about. Processions of pelicans sailed along, two by two. Buck of all kinds drank at the water's edge. Elephants splashed and rolled luxuriously in the mud, as did the hippos. Rhinos blundered blindly into objects they did not see. Fires were lit in front of us to make a path free of snakes to the Falls. I wondered what sort of a man Murchison had been and what became of him. What a marvellous sight the Falls were!

On the drive back to Kenya via Uganda we stopped for one night at Entebbe. While walking through the Arboretum that evening before darkness fell, something hissed and struck at my heel. A snake slithered away into the grass. It had hit my shoe and missed my heel.

## *Tree Tops*

Cressida's year with us ended and she returned to England. Far too soon the time came for Rose to leave for her finishing school. Before she left we spent a night up in the famous Tree Tops Lodge. Two weeks later the Tree was burnt to the ground. Now there is another Tree Tops there, bigger and more sophisticated. In our day, the Tree only accommodated ten people at a time. Our party consisted of my oldest friends, the Kingsfords, Dick Sheppard and Daphne James, a girl friend of his just arrived from England, and ourselves.

A few weeks prior to our visit there, Princess Elizabeth, Prince Philip and their entourage had occupied the Tree. While the Princess was watching two water buck fighting each other, an old African hunter was reputed to have told her that to see two male water buck fighting like that portended the death of a great chief. In the early hours of that morning news was given to her that her father King George VI had died. When she came down from the Tree she was Queen of England. Surely the only time in history that anyone became Queen up a tree!

## *Interlude in England*

Rose left for England and my heart felt as though it had been torn out. A few months later, Jenny, William and I flew to England for three months' holiday. We collected Rose from Harcombe House and drove up to Scotland, Mother with us. We booked in at the George Hotel in Perth where we planned to spend a few days. We had barely arrived and were still in the lobby when a tall, splendid-looking officer in the Black Watch uniform called at the office to enquire for Colonal Bucknall. He was Colonel David Rose. The Black Watch had arrived in Kenya from Korea as we were leaving for England. David and his wife, the Lady Jean Rose, were to become lifelong friends of mine.

After leaving Scotland and depositing Mother back in Eastbourne where she had a flat, Rose, Jenny, William and I embarked on the good launch *Sun Fish* on the River Thames, which we had hired for a month. We took it over at Bourne End. Rose went aboard first, and immediately announced that the gas stove was quite unsuitable. The boat agent went off and presently returned with another larger stove. As he stepped from the bank he accidentally dropped the stove into the Thames! 'Just a moment,' he said. Returning almost at once, he hung out a huge magnet over the place where the stove had disappeared. Up came the stove! Was it all part of the game? I wondered.

The adventures we had are too numerous to recount in full. One or two stand out. Oxford: we spent two days moored to the quayside while one of us took a bus back to where we had left the car. We went to a theatre, a horse show nearby and managed to get a bath in one of the pubs. This had been a bone of contention ever since we had started our exploration of the Thames: William always clamouring for a proper bath, and we all finding a bathe in the river all that was necessary. The weather was divine for four weeks, so all meals were had on deck. The little launch had four berths, a galley and privy thunderbox which had to be cleared daily.

At Wallingford we took on board two Kenya friends of ours, girls aged 10 and 17, the Fayles. After three days they left and Dinah Kingsford joined us. Every so often the propeller seized up, weeds becoming entangled in it. Usually one of the girls dived down and cleared it. One day they insisted that it was William's turn to do this. At Oxford we had to fill the drinking water tank and the petrol tank. Jenny was holding the drinking water hose over the inlet pipe when something distracted her, whereupon she let go and water shot everywhere. I was in the cabin and yelled to her, and in the excitement she pointed the hose straight through the cabin window, drenching me and flooding the cabin before realising what she was doing. Another day, while Jenny was washing her teeth over the side of the boat, she dropped her gold mouth plate which corrected her teeth into the river. Later when washing up breakfast Rose dropped a cup over the side. Jenny dived in and while groping for the cup, found her plate!

It was a gorgeously restful trip up to Lechlade and back to Henley, cows belly-deep in water, swishing their tails over their backs and drinking deeply. England's green and pleasant land bathed in sunshine all around us. At one of the locks, Rose jumped ashore to pull the boat into position before we moved off again. As the lock gates opened the gap between boat and land widened swiftly; Rose was left with hands gripping the boat while her feet remained on the bank, until she fell flat into the water, much to the delight of the horrid little lock boy who must have been waiting for years to see just this happen.

Again the day came all too quickly when we had to part from Rose and return to Kenya. Each time I hated it more.

## Back in Molo

Living at Molo was a totally different thing to living at a lower altitude in more civilised surroundings. It was all farm land and the estates were large, mostly sheep farming and wheat. Also good fruit orchards thrived there, apples and strawberries particularly. We grew all kinds of semi-tropical and European fruit. In the forest glade where we had built our house, Kameko, it was easy to make a garden and I really enjoyed laying out about three acres to lawns, flowers, vegetables and fruit. We were scarcely ever without visitors and never a day passed without riding through the forest and over the hills. Apart from working for the Pony Club we also organised the Hunt Dog Trials, the Hunt Balls, and the Molo Point-to-Point races – an annual event. The course was laid out by William and became quite famous throughout Kenya.

'Brora', my beloved grey horse, carried me everywhere safely. Dick Sheppard called it my 'Confidential Hack'. One morning while riding slowly through the forest a family of cerval cats met us on the path – a mother and five kittens. We stood quite still and after a few minutes the mother gave some invisible sign and shot off by herself, leaving her kittens to play round Brora's feet. Brora never moved except to look down at them occasionally. The mother cerval must have given another signal unheard by me, for in a flash all the kittens vanished.

Another morning we were all riding in the forest together with two African syces, to exercise the horses. A great crash sounded beside us, bringing us to a halt. 'Wild boar,' said a syce. Trossie, our little Aberdeen terrier, let out a bark and disappeared after the sound into a clump of bamboo. We called him back in vain and also dismounted and cut down some of the bamboo. No sign of Trossie. Very worried, we had to leave and return home, hoping he would turn up. For three days we searched for him without success. On the morning of the fourth day, not far from the house, I found him lying half dead on the ground. He was slashed across one side so that his leg was nearly off, his head was clotted with blood and he seemed to be lifeless. I carried him back to the house, forced brandy and hot milk down his throat and dressed his wounds with disinfectant, then laid him beside the fire to warm him up. Astonishingly he opened one eye and tried to move. Into the car and down to the vet, Charlie Thomson. He held out little hope of Trossie surviving, but told us to leave him at the surgery. Some weeks later we fetched him home with his leg in a splint and bandages over half his head, but as game as ever. When our golden retriever knocked him over, or the 'cur of low degree' made a dive for him, Trossie would attack in spite of falling over.

During one of Jenny's school holidays, Greta Kühle was staying with us while her mother was in Nairobi with her second husband who was dying of cancer. I had phlebitis and was unable to ride at the time, so drove the landrover to the meets and followed hounds in it. On the way to one meet William came with us in the landrover, having sent on the horses ahead. Greta and Jenny with another syce were in the back. William shouted that I was going the wrong way, and that to cut across country was far better. In vain did we tell him that if we went his way we would end up in a bog. 'No,' he insisted. In order to avoid an argument we did as he asked. The syce became very worried and gesticulated with his arms prior to leaping out of car. 'Go on, go on!' shouted William. So knowing what would happen, I did go on. A few yards further and the car sank down into the bog. William was so angry that he opened the door and jumped down straight into the water. The girls and I laughed and laughed, especially when William stomped off up to his knees in bog to Jim Ryan's house, just visible on top of the hill. Jim came to our rescue later, and much later sent a team of ten oxen to pull out the landrover. But that was not the end of the story.

Returning from the hunt in Jim's landrover, with William sitting beside him in front smoking a pipe and we three at the back, Jim turned a steep corner too fast and all but turned the landrover over. The door flew open and William fell out, half swallowing his pipe. Greta, Jenny and I thoroughly enjoyed the day, but not so William who remained in a grump for ages.

In 1951 William and I did a safari to the Congo.

*Lt. Col. W.R. Bucknall, 1954.*

# Fun in the Congo (Ruanda Arundi)

*October 24th 1951*

Long before dawn, I am woken by William who says 'It's time we started.' At 8.30 a.m. we have still not left the house as William is busy writing down last-minute instructions for Dick.

Cook, Kamau, Kingora, chicken-boy, gardener and hangers-on all pack, unpack and repack car before bidding us '*kwaheri*' and giving us a shove down the hill. The village is soon left behind in a cloud of dust, but at the next village we remember we have not sent a telegram to friends who were to have come with us in convoy and are to meet us in the Congo. We stop and do this before settling down to a 260-mile run to Jinja.

We drive through magnificent country, catching our first glimpse of Lake Victoria through a gap in the hills above Lumbwa. From there, we drop fairly steeply to take level, 3,726 feet, and into the midday heat of the valley.

All attempts on my part to interest William in the scenery are in vain. He sleeps soundly until I stop and ask him to take over the driver's seat. He explains that all moving vehicles have this soporific effect upon him. I ask him why he was so enthusiastic about coming on this motoring tour, to which he replies, 'Well, it's great fun, don't you think?'

At Kisumu, he mistakenly takes the tarmac road round the lake, which leads to the airport only. I ask William if he was asleep when this happened. 'No, were you?'

At Busia, on the Uganda-Kenya frontier, we are stopped by a barrier and asked to write a description of ourselves and our car in a large book. It is 1 p.m. and hot. William and I change places, I pick up a strange African who asks for a lift to Jinja, and we continue on our way. We go through eternal banana plantations and tropical-looking vegetation on an excellent earth road. The trees are tall and very beautiful. Amongst the few I recognise are the wild fig, yellow thorns, merenge, acacia thorns, nandi flames etc. Palm trees, elephant grass and monkey-ropes, many kinds of convolvulus, orchids and mauve black-eyed Susans grow luxuriantly on all sides, and the whole countryside is a vivid green after the recent rain.

We reach Jinja about tea-time and find the Ibis Hotel, Indian owned and delightfully situated by the lake. William sniffs disparagingly at our rather pink and blue distempered room and says there will undoubtedly be curry for dinner. Tell him I like curry. After a much needed wash and brush-up, walk along the lake to look at the Ripon Falls. A temporary dam is under construction here, but we are fascinated by the quantities of birds who apparently live on the many small islands dotted about the mouth of the river, especially the cormorants who dive right into the fury of the falls to catch fish. Flocks of ibis fly overhead and thousands of wagtails and sandpipers fish expertly for their supper. Leaving the source of the Nile, we walk round to the lake again and watch hippo floundering about below the cliffs. William says he has never before seen hippos at home and trains the binoculars on to them when they yawn, as the size of their mouths seems too huge to be true. Soon find myself yawning in sympathy, so we turn our backs on these strange animals and return, to curry dinner!

### October 25th

Next morning, we go in search of the new dam which is to provide Uganda with electricity and power. It is about two miles below the Ripon Falls and only in its preliminary stages. Passing through a gateway unhindered, we park the car alongside enormous piles of rubble. Great cranes swing perilously close to our heads as we pick our way across a temporary railway bridge to the edge of the main works. Dozens of European engineers work busily on the projecting dam head and take no notice of us. One man tells us not to get hurt as he passes us and I take a look round me. Water rushes by us, under us and around us. Wonder how on earth it will ever be controlled by a dam and am filled with admiration for those who conceived such a scheme.

After a short drive on a good earth road we arrive at Kampala, the capital of Uganda. William had difficulty in finding the right road to Entebbe as there are so many main thoroughfares, but once located we tear along at 60 miles an hour. We run into a rainstorm while driving through the forest, but this tends to enhance the primitive beauty of the scenery. Immensely tall trees rise out of dense undergrowth and William remarks on the almost insuperable difficulties this jungle must have presented to the famous explorers who blazed their way through here so short a while ago.

Plantations of coffee struggle against interplanted banana trees, presumably African owned. The bananas seem to be winning.

Suddenly we come upon the lake again, which seems to be higher than we are as we have to climb up to it. On our road we pass many pedestrians, all African and all seemingly busy. In addition to the pedestrians, we encounter hundreds of cyclists, thousands of pounds' worth pedalling by. The Buganda women look fat and prosperous. Of capacious build, they have a dignity and magnificence of carriage which is sadly lacking in their Kenya sisters. The women dress in brightly coloured materials swathed round them in layers, extra folds at the hips increasing the natural size of them considerably. All their bundles are carried on their heads even if it is only one stick of sugar cane. It is remarkable that one rarely sees a white face anywhere; this is an African country.

As we approach Entebbe, the scenery grows ever more beautiful but also more Europeanised. We drive up to the door of a large modern hotel which would do credit to any continental seaside resort. I feel slightly self-conscious of our dusty car and still dustier persons. After travelling for hundreds of miles, we are still on the shores of Lake Victoria which sparkles serenely in the afternoon sun.

In the Botanical Gardens we spend hours of enchantment looking at the wonderful trees and birds. Trees from all over the world grow here. All too soon the sun goes down and we walk back to the hotel along the fringe of the lake. It is more like a lagoon than a lake here, peaceful and inhabited by birds of all kinds. We watch flocks of ibis flying over the water to a nearby island where they all go to roost, falling like fruit blossom to the ground.

During the night a thunderstorm bursts over us, rolling round and round the lake. It wakes William who says he *must know* how the elections are going in England. Sympathise with him, but feel that 2 a.m. is not the hour to begin making enquiries. In the morning a large notice confronts us in the hall announcing that the wireless is not working, but it is reported that the Conservatives confidently expect a working majority of fifty. William says 'What is the good of that?' Am not sure if he means the wireless or the announcement so say nothing and order breakfast.

*October 27th*
The journey to Masaka is mostly through swamps and the road itself frequently submerges underwater owing to heavy rain the previous night. After driving for about ninety-five miles in this type of country, we climb up a hill and find ourselves overlooking vast tracts of Africa. Lake Victoria to the east of us stretches as far as the eye can see. After spending the night here, we descend into the marshes once more to continue on our way to Lake Bunyoni. In spite of the heavy thunderstorms the roads continue to be excellent. This is no doubt due to the gangs of boys repairing them every five miles or so. Where they all come from is a mystery, as the country appears to be devoid of human habitation.

We drive slowly in order to look at the many birds we see; on a bush alongside the road, a great spotted cuckoo alights, crest feathers erect; a little later we see two yellow-billed hornbills followed by four trumpeters. Shrikes, widow-birds, red-winged starlings, Wahrlberg's eagles, louries, Kenya robins, sunbirds are amongst those which fly past us. Almost imperceptibly the marshland changes to more open country. Conical shaped ant-heaps from four to ten feet high are scattered over the ground. Soon, small hillocks appear which in their turn change to hills and ranges of hills, one behind the other. As we wind in and out of these, tropical Africa disappears. Beyond Mbarara we come out into green moorland country where countless herds of sleek African cattle graze the pastures. They carry huge horns which curve vertically from their heads and remind me of ancient Egyptian pictures.

Climbing slowly, we approach Kabale and are greatly impressed by the hillside cultivation all round us. Every hill is terraced from top to bottom, however steep the slope, and every terrace is edged with Napier grass. In most of the valleys there are banana plantations but also coffee, sweet potatoes, beans, millet and various indigenous plants, growing prolifically. The peasant looks a well fed and prosperous individual and the land teems with busy people. I am impressed by their good looks and bearing, also their courteous manners.

While we are changing over the driving seat, a troupe of children come up and say in English 'Good morning, how are you?' and smile at us. Later, while we are trying to clean the windscreen outside a duka, an African removes the cloth from William's hand, produces a can of water and cleans the glass for us, beaming and saying, 'I will help you.' Yet no Mr Fenner Brockway has passed this way with his tea parties, nor have we donned the goatskin of brotherhood!

As the afternoon wears on we approach Kabale and the White Horse Inn where we are to spend a couple of days. Set on a hillside about six thousand feet above sea level, the inn affords all the comforts of European sophistication in the midst of primitive Africa. We are shown to our cottage, which is half hidden by rose creepers, and after dinner I sink into a gorgeous mattress and oblivion. I do like a comfortable bed!

Lake Bunyoni lies within a few miles of us, so we take our sandwiches and go off next morning armed with binoculars and the *First South African Bird Book*. Again the road climbs steeply uphill until we arrive at the summit and look down onto the charming little lake of Bunyoni, lying peacefully below us. A group of islands attracts the attention, one with a Catholic church on it, giving the impression that it is on the shores of Lake Lucerne or Maggiore that we are looking.

There is a leper colony on the largest of these islands. But what a beautiful place for these unfortunates to live in! In the reeds beside the lake we watch three young long-tailed cormorants waiting patiently for fish and swooping down when they see their prey below the surface of the water. A gorgeous little green and scarlet bird, a sunbird probably, though not in our book, preens himself on the top of a merenge tree, and pied kingfishers fly past.

After a quiet day without much driving we are ready to continue our journey to the frontier and to cross into *Territoire Belgique* the following day. We fill up everything we have in the way of containers as well as the petrol tank, as Essence is 5/- a gallon in the Congo, we are informed. The 75 mile drive from Kabale to Kisoro on the boundary between Uganda and the Congo must be one of the most magnificent in the world, and well worth the whole of the rest of the trip to see. At first, our road leads through a green valley with hills on either side. Then we come upon a notice warning us 'Go Slow, 33 miles of mountain road'. William promises not to go faster than fairly slow, and we begin the ascent into a world of splendid scenery to Kanaba Gap. Here we get out to look at the mountainous world spread out all round us. The view is breathtaking. The altitude given on a notice board is 8,170 feet but the impression of height is far greater than this owing to the precipitous character of the hills dropping beneath our feet. Several thousand feet below us we see Lake Bunyoni and other smaller lakes in the creases of the mountains. The sky is overcast and storms break on distant peaks, increasing the wild beauty of the scene.

As we drive down and down into the valleys we pass clusters of toadstool villages usually surrounded by hedges and with gardens round the huts. We leave the bracken and pines behind us and William begins practising his French in preparation for the Congo. We reach Kisoro as a thunderstorm bursts overhead and rush into the Customs Office while solid blocks of rain blot out the countryside. A Belgian traveller also having his papers examined talks to William in perfect English. We ask him if we should now drive on the right hand side of the road, to which he replies 'Yes,' adding with a smile at William, 'It's worth remembering.'

A few miles beyond the barriers the sun comes out and we stop for lunch at the foot of an extinct volcano, Muhuvulu. This is a gorilla sanctuary, or rather the forest on the steep slopes of the volcano is where they live. But they are shy creatures, and only appear when provoked and then in ferocious mood.

Taking another mountain road, we drive to Kesenyi, on the shores of Lake Kivu. The Belgian roads are excellent, well graded and with good surfaces. Double rows of gum trees line the road for miles and at every corner the safety of travellers is ensured by the road being divided by posts down the centre, not by a white line which is so often disregarded. Rounding a bend on the steeper part of the road, we are stopped by a barrier. An African leaps out of his small shelter, beats a sharp tattoo with two sticks on the tin roof of his hut, and lets us through. William, laughing loudly, asks what the devil that is for? We get the answer a couple of miles further up where another barrier is lifted at our approach. There is a notice beside the road which reads '*Sens Unique*'.

Nearing Kesenyi, on the shores of Lake Kivu, we drive through suburbs neatly kept, with pale pink or blue washed houses, geraniums bordering the pavements, and window boxes filled with flowers. All very continental and smart. But the Bugoyi Guest House where we are staying is surprisingly African. The Belgian Madame leads us down a path overgrown with bougainvillea, begonias, ferns and hibiscus to a round thatched hut. Inside, it is divided into a bedroom and bathroom, with electric light and running water. On the walls is a fine collection of African bows and arrows and shields. The windows are wide open and we are told that we may leave them so, as neither mosquitoes nor thieves will bother us. Later we drink tea on an enormously wide circular verandah and look across the luxuriant garden to the lake. It reminds me of Lac Leman with its mountains and villages and terraced hillsides, and also the air of continental finish there is about the place.

'My name is Money, Canadian, pleased to meet you,' says a stout middle-aged man sitting down beside us. He gives us a lot of interesting information about Ruanda-Arundi, which is the real name of the country we are in, being a Belgian Protectorate under the mandate of U.N.C. having been a German colony before the 1914 War. After a most excellent dinner, with salad tasting strongly of garlic served with every course (both William and I like garlic fortunately) Guy Money leads us out into the night to see the active volcano illuminating the sky. It is an extraordinary sight, rather awe-inspiring, contrasting strongly with the modern cars which swish past us. William is filled with a desire to climb up it and look down into the cauldron from the lip. The Madame, however, heads him off by telling him that it will require several days' preparation for such an excursion and the we would have to take porters, food, tents etc. and spend two or three nights at the summit or en route. Another time.

In the morning we are woken by a very black African bringing in a tray of very black coffee. Later at breakfast, we are offered cold spiced meat and cheese, all very delicious if unusual. The waiter tells us he has been scolding the hens for not laying any eggs!

Our Canadian friend accompanies us to the lava fields, now inactive. The last eruption took place in 1948. Prior to that, there was one in 1928 and another in 1918. It is easy to picture the scene of destruction, looking upon the now cold and solidified molten stream. Guy tells us it would not have travelled more than about two miles an hour, but we can imagine the slowly moving river of fire pouring down into Lake Kivu and the sizzling noise it must have made when contacting the water. After three years, no vegetation has appeared through the charred surface other than an occasional little fern; on the 1918 stream trees and plants of all kinds grow prolifically. On our return from the horrifying sight William expresses a wish to climb the volcano. Guy says to him: 'Well, I guess you won't meet with any gorillas, they got more sense than to go up there.' He then leaves us to go for a walk with a young Belgian and have a French lesson. Over his shoulder, he warns William, 'Now, don't you go climbing up that hill without telling any of us.'

*October 31st*
Early next morning we take our leave of the Belgian Madame and depart regretfully from this delightful African Riviera.

The drive to Ruindi Camp is an easy one. We drop down into the plains and through the National Park towards Lake Edward. William keeps his eyes glued to the road as he expects to see an elephant round every corner. Large droppings on the road indicate that he may have his hopes fulfilled. As we near the camp, he suddenly grips my arm, thereby causing me to swerve violently to the side of the road, saying 'Elephant!' And there they are, looming hugely on our left, about two hundred yards away. We stop and watch them and also two large buffalo grazing close by.

The camp is situated in the centre of a semi-circle of hills with wide plains in front of it, gradually falling down to Lake Edward. A flagpost flying the Belgian flag stands in the middle of the fort; one main dining hut, two rows of whitewashed rondavals with grass roofs and two or three uniformed game rangers lend the camp an air of military importance. It is surrounded by a barricade of thorn bushes, against the prowling animals presumably.

At 2.30 p.m. a ranger (African) comes up to our rondaval, salutes William and says he has come to escort us in to the

Game Reserve. We drive for a long way with the snow-capped Ruinzori Mountains lying ahead of us in the distance. For once they are uncovered and glisten against the pale blue sky. Impala buck, topies, buffalo, and somewhat distant elephant appear and disappear as we drive along; birds of all kinds and colours live down here and we pull up alongside a river bed to look at the flocks of water birds more closely. Egyptian geese walk sedately beside the water and hundreds of pelicans launch themselves into the stream as we approach them. They float slowly downstream, two by two, like a schoolgirls' crocodile. To mention but a few of the birds, we see marabous, kingfishers, sea eagles, bee eaters, cuckoos, egrets, duck and so on; a veritable heaven for bird fanciers.

At sunrise next day our ranger knocks at our door and soon we are driving through the animal world again. We come across a hippo in a pool all by himself enjoying his morning dip in the sun. He obligingly steps out a few yards from us and drips off into the bush. A little further on, our path is obstructed by an elephant standing directly in our road. We stop the car a few feet off his posterior. He looks round disdainfully and slowly, step by step, walks to one side to let us pass. Continuing on our way, we encounter herds of water buck, one family of Mr, Mrs and Miss Waterbuck standing quite still beside us in the grass. Then most unexpectedly, round a bend in the track a lion and lioness stalk across in front of the car. Again we stop beside them for several minutes and watch them lie down contentedly in the grass just off the road, the lioness full length on her belly and the old man sitting close to her. When we start up the car to go, he turns his head, gives us a haughty look, and takes no further interest in us.

The ranger directs us to *The great, grey-green, greasy Limpopo River, all set about with fever trees.* There we look upon a most enthralling and primeval sight. Scores of hippos loll and spout in the water, some remaining so still that William asks if they are dead. 'No, they are only in their dreams still,' the ranger says. Others are up and about. One baby trots along a mud bank to a couple of pelicans. But he gets a sharp peck on the nose and runs back squealing to his mama.

We walk down to the banks of the river, disturbing some grey monkeys from their toilet on the rocks. A troop of baboons swing along in the bushes and a shy elephant wanders towards us but retires silently when he sees us. On our way back to camp, we drive inadvertently through a large herd of buffalo, females and babies. Not unnaturally, they do not appreciate our intrusion, so this time we do not dally. The sun rises ever higher in a cloudless sky as we return to an omelette cooked by the hideous but capable Belgian concierge, if one can call her such. What better way to spend a morning than amongst these magnificent animals, unmolested because unmolesting, guests in the Animal Kingdom.

On the road once more, we drive up mountain after mountain for nearly 120 miles on wonderful tracks, the whole world seeming to unfold before our eyes. Here also, expert hillside cultivation covers the slopes from top to bottom. European farms and African farms run side by side apparently, all equally well cultivated. It is all the more remarkable when one considers that no railway runs through here. Yet every house and farm building is well built, usually of stone, and the grounds round about well laid out and maintained.

Coffee, pyrethrum, wheat, eucalyptus grown for oil, all flourish on the terraces. All looks prosperous.

By the time we arrive at Butembo, I have a streaming cold and get a jaundiced impression of the hotel and of the astonishing curtains in our guest house. They seem to be a nightmare sized pattern of brown roses with greenish yellow leaves. But perhaps they are not really like that when you haven't a cold. After a night there, we go on to Matwanga, at the foot of the Ruinzori Mountains.

On the way, we pass through the village of Beni, in pygmy country, hoping to see some of these curious little people. The forest here is tropical and steamy and we pass very ugly, smallish men on the road. Presently we meet a hideous little man, naked except for a loin cloth and carrying a bow and arrow. His skin is yellowish-black and his body very hairy and he closely resembles an ape. Following on his heels are a child and woman, completely naked and excessively ugly in form and face. It is this brutish, primitive appearance rather than their size which strikes one. William says he does not think much of them and is a little disappointed.

Our road takes us down into steep valleys and we wind through hills covered with giant ferns. They are most beautiful and their green tracery makes a lovely pattern against the darker shadows of the trees. Our destination is the Ruinzori Hotel, situated at the foot of the Mountains of the Moon, but they are hidden in thick mist. Later in the evening they emerge from the clouds and soar above us, shining white. A rushing river passes by the hotel and is diverted into the garden to make a small lake. It is a delightful place where we would like to remain for several days to climb up to the glaciers. But the Congo is a very expensive country for English people just now – £5 for bed and breakfast for the two of us, and everything else extra. So we leave the following morning for Uganda, heading for home for the first time.

Soon we reach the frontier and undergo a lengthy interrogation from the Belgian customs officer. He says that my passport is wrong and my papers right, and that William's passport is right and his papers wrong. At last we escape but come to a standstill three miles further on at the Uganda customs shed. Here we have a brief interview with a clean-looking Indian, in contrast to the extremely dirty Belgian officer just up the road. William asks the Indian if he lives all alone here, adding that if he had to do so he would take to drink. 'I do drink, sir,' he replies in a mild voice.

Once more we drive on the right side of the road until we come to a large river. We wait for a ferry to pull us across and look out hopefully for crocodiles, but are disappointed. About a hundred miles further on, before getting to Katwe, we see a notice to the effect that 'Elephants have right of way.' It also says that we are forbidden to frighten the elephants by blowing the hooter or waving our arms about or shouting. We do none of these things as we see no elephant. However, immediately before crossing on the Katwe Ferry we do sight a herd of mothers and babies, ten mamas and six children, all ambling along rooting up shrubs. Now and again a mother stops to scold a lagging infant.

The Kitchwamba Hotel is magnificently situated on top of a hill but indescribably dirty. The blazing afternoon sun keeps us indoors, much against my inclination, until about five o'clock when we take out the binoculars and examine the peaks of the Ruinzori Mountains again as they pierce the haze. From here we get a better view of them than from Matwango where we were immediately below them.

Early next morning we bid *kwaheri* to the Congo and head back to Uganda. The Fort Portal road in Uganda is not good and becomes bad as we progress. We cross the equator for the fourth time on our travels and certainly feel a bump. No longer do we bowl along on smooth surfaces, nor meet with repair gangs every few miles. Instead we are faced with pot-holes and quagmires. As we arrive at our destination, the Fort Portal Mountains of the Moon Hotel, a terrific thunderstorm bursts overhead. With one voice William and I thank *le Bon Dieu* that we are no longer on the road. From Fort Portal we look for the last time upon the lovely Mountains of the Moon or Ruinzori Mountains, but we only catch fleeting glimpses of them in between storms. And in cloud we leave them, to go back to Entebbe. For miles and miles we drive through blinding rain, but fortunately this road is well maintained and we experience no difficulty in reaching Entebbe, 225 miles away from Fort Portal, by 4 p.m. All along our route wild flowers, creepers and flowering trees grow in riotous profusion.

It is good to be in Entebbe again and we begin to long for our own home and our own fireside. For the first time the car lets us down and we are delayed by one day in starting for Kisumu. The rain continues to come down and we leave Uganda in typical English November weather. Everyone is wearing mackintoshes, carrying umbrellas or holding banana leaves over them in lieu of umbrellas. We are unable to see much of the country during the 220 miles run to Kisumu on account of the weather.

This is the hottest of all the ports we have stayed in on the great Lake Victoria. The morning is fine and the lake sparkles in the sun when we at last turn our backs on it and climb the hill to Lumbwa and the Kenya Highlands. The Peugeot seems to know that it is nearly home and races through the 95 miles of bad road to Molo.

William says that he feels sorry our safari is coming to an end but glad to be going home . . . so am I.

Soon horses appear on the scene and green hills with familiar contours come into view. We growl up the steepest and worst road of any encountered on our travels and arrive at our Hill Top Farm. The two Scotties dash down the verandah steps to greet us, Dick after them and the boys after him. The garden during our two weeks' absence has grown in all directions, over the borders and into the windows; flowers are blooming everywhere.

William discovers that the horses have not died, the hens are still laying eggs, and the electric light plant is working, in spite of all forebodings to the contrary. We have seen many sights and been in many beautiful countries. Volcanoes, great lakes, pygmies, enormous dams, gentle wild animals, exotic vegetation, majestic scenery, all this and much more will we remember with pleasure for the rest of our lives. 'And what's more,' says William over a drink by the fireside, 'when we hear people discussing Uganda or the Congo we shall know what they are talking about.'

# Second Safari to the Congo 1955

The second safari to the Congo in 1955 was more amusing. We went in convoy with the Furse family – David and Hilda and their two daughters and a nice *au pair* girl to look after them. The Furses' car (date unknown) arrived at the top of our hill boiling. After letting out the steam David refilled the radiator and also filled several empty cans with spare water for the long journey.

Off we set. There were innumerable stops on the way to Entebbe to cool down the Furses' car and the occupants.

On the road to Lake Kisumu we stopped beside a salt lake. It was full of hippos and a few elephants. Two younger teenager elephants were routling round with their trunks in the water when suddenly they lifted out a young hippo and tossed it into the air as though it were a sausage in a frying-pan! David tried to take a photo of it but was not quite quick enough.

The drive from Uganda to the Congo and into Ruanda Arundi was beautiful beyond words. Our goal and destination was a Belgian safari lodge in the Game Reserve. We reached it in roughly the time we had anticipated, catching sight of a little naked pygmy man who peeped out of the bamboos to look scornfully at us. We met a friend of ours at the lodge who was the river warden. He very kindly lent us his river launch with the skipper to navigate it. He warned that this individual, Joseph, as black as pitch, was likely to render the launch unsailable or completely impotent.

*On safari in the Congo 1955.*

We chugged slowly up the Kisinga Channel between Lake Victoria and Lake Albert, gazing at the wonderful birds and plants. Rounding a corner we were confronted by an enormous elephant at the water's edge. David Furse did a delightful crayon sketch of this encounter. At the time I tried to photograph the elephant, but it charged at us, screaming to his wives to run away up the hill with the babies. Fortunately our launch was drifting impotently on the far side of the channel, and after giving us fair warning, the elephant spun round and tore off screaming with rage after his harem.

The countryside seemed to be alive with elephant. We also had the luck to see a lioness teaching her cub how to hunt and kill a buck. She clearly told it first to sharpen its claws on a tree trunk, doing the same herself, then they fanned out, the young lion to one side, the lioness to the other. An unsuspecting Thomson's gazelle was grazing nearby and was the target. Every movement of the lioness was copied by the youngster, as they slid off tussock grass humps and streaked towards the gazelle. After a short chase they made their kill.

On another occasion we followed a wild dog bitch and her family of nine pups trotting through the forest. In a glade, all the puppies sat down together and mother shot off out of sight. We stopped the engine of the landrover and waited. Not long afterwards, one or two of the smaller pups began to play and leave the centre of the mob. Immediately the largest one snapped at them and they returned to their places. This happened again, but finally they all streaked after their mother, the leader in front, so she must have called them, though we did not hear her.

The Furses left us to return via Uganda to Kenya after two days in the Congo Reserve Camp. We continued on to Ruanda Arundi by ourselves, the aim being to see the still slightly erupting crater Muhuvulu. We stayed in the delightful Belgian/African Hotel again beside Lake Albert. Everything seemed very sophisticated after Kenya, the Africans speaking fluent French and large limousines being driven about in the shadow of the live volcano.

Our return journey through Uganda, taking a slightly different route, was just as enjoyable as our first safari into the Congo. The wonderful animals, beautiful scenery and awe-inspiring emptiness of Africa will remain forever in my memory.

*

### Mumbo – Dumbo

*Tinkly, winkly, dainty toe,*
*that's the way the elephants go.*

*In and out, and round about,*
*first a squeal and then a shout.*
*Softly tread upon the ground*
*When you move don't make a sound.*

*Tinkly, winkly, dainty toe,*
*that's the way the elephants go.*

*Some are big and some are small*
*some are hugely hugely tall,*
*some are young and some are old*
*over a hundred years I'm told.*

*Tinkly, winkly, dainty toe,*
*that's the way the elephants go.*

*Wrinkly, twinkly, Jolly Jo*
*now says 'stop' and then says 'go',*
*If you disobey him, 'Wow!'*
*He will make you pay, and how!*

*Mumbo-Dumbo, newly born,*
*munched a branch of prickly thorn,*
*Then he thought 'I'll have some fun*
*and take that other baby's bun.'*

*Tinkly, winkly, dainty toe,*
*that's the way the elephants go.*

*Whing, whack, oh! what a smack,*
*right in the small of his very small back.*
*Mumbo hid behind his ears*
*'case the others see his tears.*

*Tinkly, winkly, dainty toe,*
*that's the way the elephants go.*

*Rumbling tummy noises rise*
*from the ground up to the skies,*
*Jolly Jo says 'bring him back,*
*he can follow in my track.'*

*Silently they move away,*
*this is not the time for play.*

*Tinkly, winkly, dainty toe,*
*that's the way the elephants go.*

C.M.B.

*'Dumbo', Queen Elizabeth National Park,*
*1955. Sketch by David Furse.*

# Life at Kameko

On the Solai Farm, Banks Estate, John Crowther was doing a great job. We put down a bore hole in the middle of the farm and found an endless supply of water. This was wonderful. For the first time we no longer had to rely on water carts to carry water to the camp or the house. Immediately a 'pull and let go' was installed, and in the house a proper bathroom with running water from the taps. Also the kitchen was modernised and re-plumbed.

The Mau Mau was going on and one or two incidents occurred on the Solai Farm, but nothing really to worry about. Mechanical tractors replaced ox-wagons and a new coffee factory was built. John Crowther married our Joint Master's niece, Almary Ryan, and started a small tribe of little Crowthers – six in all! Almary's sister also married and was unable to have any children. So the problem was happily solved by John and Almary giving their sixth child to them for adoption! Typically Irish.

\*

At Kameko we not only built our lovely stone house with all mod cons, but also a cottage for Dick Sheppard at his request and our expense! This cottage was known as *Crookery Nook* as no two walls were parallel with each other and no angles square – in fact the original Crooked House.

194

The famous Ruck murders on the Kinangop aroused the fury of the settler community, and everyone learnt to shoot with revolvers, except me. I kept William's claymore within reach at home and hoped for the best. Only once did we have a little excitement at Kameko and that was when the Kingsfords came up to spend a 'quiet weekend' from Limuru. A small band of Mau Maus fired eight rounds behind our bedroom but were instantly attacked by some Kipsigi guards from the neighbouring estate. They were tied up and bundled into a lorry, looking extremely dirty, wild and dazed, probably the result of taking the filthy Mau Mau oaths.

As already described, I think the Mau Mau managed to disrupt one of the better hunt balls I had organised down at the Molo Club. Jean and David Rose were with us, Jean looking magnificent in gold lamé, and also in our party General 'Loony' Hinde and his wife Evelyn. Just as the party got going a policeman came in, jumped on to the platform beside the band and told us that a gang of Mau Mau were heading for Kameko! The gang was quickly routed and the ball continued. Evelyn Hinde, towards the end of the night, got on to the band platform and took a flying swallow dive off it, being deftly caught as she fell, by several young men who left their partners to catch her! More alarming than the Mau Mau!

## Witch Doctors

My old Kikuyu cook and Rawayo, my oldest long-serving servant and friend, who was a Jaluo from Lake Kisimu area, hated each other and were forever telling tales about each other. Finally one morning, when William went out on to the verandah of our old wooden house, a log hurtled past his head, meant for Rawayo and thrown by the cook. I was persuaded to sack the cook, much against my will. He was replaced by a strange Jaluo. At the end of a week our head man came up and whispered to me that I must go with him to the farthest boundary as he had something very serious to tell me. He informed me that the cook was a witch doctor; at night he daubed himself with luminous paint and frightened the wits out of all the younger members of the labour force. They would all leave unless the cook was dismissed! Exasperated, after verifying this, I had to tell the witch doctor to leave at once. However in the wings a really good cook was waiting to be signed on, much to my relief . . . his name was Joram, also a Luo, a lake tribe.

While on the subject of witch doctors: Jack made use of an old magician to find Jemima's jewellery which had been stolen while African workmen were doing alterations to their house on the Kinangop. The witch doctor was brought all the way from Kikuyu, the native reserve township where he had gone into retirement. Jack fetched him and his small boy (apprentice presumably) in the car. All the Fundis (carpenters etc.) nine of them, were told to line up while the old man and his boy lit a fire in the centre of one of the native huts. A brew of goodness knows what was stirred over the fire while the old man muttered incantations. This mixture was then put into a hole in the ashes and baked until it was the consistency of a cake. It was then cut into nine equal slices and given to each man in the line. They were told to eat it and that any guilty party would *not* be able to swallow their slice while the innocent ones would. After a few minutes, two men were seen to be struggling to eat while sweat poured down their faces and they turned pale. 'Those are the thieves,' said the witch doctor. He then ordered them to take him and Jack to the place where they had hidden the jewellery. Jemima got it all back!

My old and trusted Jaluo houseboy, Rawayo, had always wanted a bicycle, so on his 20th year of service with me I gave him one. It was his pride and joy. He came with us on a short visit to Nairobi and on our return jumped out of the car to carry in the luggage when he was informed by the cook that a cousin of his had borrowed Rawayo's bicycle and had fallen off it and was now in hospital. We were still getting ourselves out of the car when Rawayo leapt in again and told us to hurry to the hospital as fast as we could as he must see his sick cousin. We turned and drove all the way back to Molo. On arrival at the hospital, while the car was still moving, Rawayo hurled himself out, ran up the steps, pushing the orderly out of the way, and disappeared inside. At once there was a terrific noise of shouting and yells and Rawayo was precipitated down the hospital steps. The orderly told us to take him away, as he was a dangerous lunatic apparently. Holding Rawayo down on the way home I asked what it was all about. 'Oh,' he said, 'my cousin stole my bicycle so I tried to kill him.' The bicycle was a write-off, so I had to give him another before murder was done.

*

The Black Watch Regiment was out in Kenya then after serving in Korea. Several of the officers and their wives and families came up to spend their leave with us at Kameko, amongst others Jean and David Rose, Jean's sister, Ida (Lady Ida Johnston) and the Moirs, and Inneses.

The three Moir children were notoriously disobedient and unruly according to their parents. Indeed they were; building houses in the fork of the big olive tree on top of my beautiful red orchid; taking an old tin bath on to the lily pond and rowing it round and round until it and the occupants sank; removing our small Somali pony 'Colonel Stuffy' from the stable and trying to ride it bareback helter-skelter over the hillside; and giving some of their clothes to the African children, who immediately gambled them away. On one occasion the exhausted parents brought the children to visit us when they had impetigo! This was soon cured by giving them – aged three, five and six – constant baths in permanganate and scraping off the scabs. When the worst was over, Jean and Claud left the children behind with us (at our suggestion) and spent a few days up-country with friends. On their return, the little Moirs ran out to meet them with cries of 'We want to stay here. Go away and stay away for *nine days*.'

*

In 1956 Rose was in England. She was taken with another couple to a hunt ball in the Midlands by the current young man. William and I were leaving for a polo tournament at Machakos when we received a telegram. It read: 'Rose in hospital after motor accident, has hurt her back,' and signed by the young man. Instead of going to Machakos I stayed and telephoned to *Enquiries* in England to look up a map and to find out *which* hospitals took in accident cases. The operator was marvellous and finally located the one Rose was in. But at the hospital there seemed to be no one in charge and all the idiot nurse would tell me was 'Oh well, she won't be paralysed.' Daisy Cust was the next hope and I got on to her immediately. She was wonderfully helpful and went up to find Rose in a huge case of plaster. She organised an ambulance to drive Rose down to their house in Brompton Square, London and phoned me after Rose had arrived. Their specialist removed the plaster, put Rose into a light jacket, and at the end of that awful week Rose was back with me in Kenya. Meanwhile dear Dinah Kingsford visited Rose in the hospital and I had a letter from The Young Man asking for permission to marry Rose! Not b. . . likely! I wrote back telling him that all I knew of him so far was that he had upset Rose in his car and he could go to 'Hertford, Hereford and Hampshire.'

Poor Rose was miserable at having to leave all her friends in England, if only temporarily. The only time I ever found her in tears was one day when she sobbed 'All my life is over.' However, she soon found that, on the contrary, it had only just begun. She went to stay at Limuru with the Simpsons and got a job in a solicitor's office near all her old Kenya friends.

## Rose's Wedding, April 1957

A few months later Michael Oakshott came up for our point-to-point meeting with Robin Higgin. After the Ladies race in which Rose finished a close second, the day ended at Kameko (our house), where dozens of known and unknown race-goers came to drinks, some remaining to supper and going on to a dance.

That night, driving back to Kiambu where Michael managed a coffee estate for Robin Higgin, Robin said to Michael 'I've dated Rose Banks for lunch next week.' 'Oh no you haven't. I am going to marry Rose, so she will be lunching with me,' replied Michael.

The wedding was in Limuru where most of Rose's friends lived, and the reception was held in the Kingsford's lovely garden. Joan and Hendrie Oakshott had flown out for the occasion, the sun shone and Jenny looked beautiful as the principal bridesmaid. Sally Kühle was a bridesmaid also, and very soon became engaged to Michael's lifelong friend Robin Higgin – the best man. That year, 1957, was a year of wedding bells – first David Kingsford and Margaret, then Rose and Michael, then Sally and Robin, followed by Caroline Byge-Hall whose parents were friends of mine long before any of *us* were married. Caroline married a relation of William's, Vivian Bucknall. Cynthia Simpson also married. A lovely year for us all.

## *Jenny's Activities*

That was Jenny's last year at Limuru School where Miss Fisher, niece of the Archbishop, was headmistress. All too soon Jenny left to be finished in Europe and later in England.

Her brief sojourn in Lausanne was a fiasco. We flew over and collected her and her friend Juliana Ward, taking them to Germany where we picked up our Mercedes. From there we drove to Bruges, the town of chiming bells, and little humped bridges over narrow canals. I still have a lace-edged cloth given to me by the girls after they had watched an old woman making the lace sitting on the pavement in the glaring sun.

Jenny's last Christmas in Kenya was spent at Kiambu with Rose and Michael.

Out to dinner one night at the Higgins, Jenny met a young man called Robert Jocelyn. He was to pursue her and be a perfect pest for the next seven or eight years. An impoverished Irish Lord, he invited himself to stay with us at Kameko several times. The first time he never spoke at all until Jenny poured some cold water down the back of his neck while he was kindly damping out the drawing room fire for me. He leapt to his feet and chased Jenny all round the house and garden; even then he hardly spoke. From us he went to visit Genessie Hamilton (formerly Genessie Long of the Happy Valley crowd). When I met her in Nakuru she asked me if Robert Jocelyn had talked at all when with us, adding 'He only spoke on Tuesday and left on Friday.'

## Wind of Change

When Harold Macmillan made his famous speech in the Cape, *The Wind of Change*, it spread through Africa like a prairie fire, leaving chaos in its wake. One could say of Kenya:

> *'The Wind of Change blew,*
> *and in a trice,*
> *what was Harmony*
> *now is strife.'*

We had been a happy breed of men, no apartheid, and little social discrimination. Looking back I am immensely grateful for the wonderful 30 years I spent in that heavenly country and for all the real friends I made there. For the marvellous climate, the beauty abounding, the many opportunities to serve, for the happy faces of all colours and the fun we had. But the politicians far away came and told us that we were *not happy* and we had to alter our way of life. It was too much for a lot of us, who were getting old and unable to change our customs. I would have stayed, but Rose and Michael decided to leave and live in Scotland, and William would not stay on any account. One morning he came in and announced 'I have sold all the horses and we are off back home.' 'Not my horses, surely?' 'Yes, all of them,' and that was that.

### June 12th 1959
This was to be a memorable day. For the first time in 25 years I had a telephone installed in the house, Kameko, and on the Solai Farm.

Early on the morning of the 12th Michael rang up to tell me that Rose had gone into the nursing home as the baby was on the way. My desk where the telephone stood faced a large window. As I was speaking to Michael about Rose and the imminent arrival of my first grandchild the under-gardener, Kitui, appeared in front of the window. He was holding up his hand, thumb down, from which blood was pouring. As soon as Michael rang off, I ran out to enquire what on earth he was doing. He informed me that he had had a fight with his mad nephew who had bitten off the end of his thumb. 'Where is the end of your thumb now?' I asked, hoping that it could be stuck on to his hand temporarily until he could be driven to hospital. 'Oh, my nephew swallowed it,' was the reply.

After disinfecting the wound and binding it up, we ate breakfast and prepared for Nakuru and the Royal Agricultural Show. As we got into the car, Cook ran out to say the 'box' was ringing again. It was Michael to announce the birth of Tom, my first grandson.

The Solai Farm went on the market. I knew from past experience that never would I find another manager like John Crowther whom I could completely trust. One manager I had drank, another just neglected the place, and others were plain dishonest.

On December 21st the Hon. Secretary of State for the Colonies, Ian McLeod, paid a state visit to Banks Estate accompanied by H.E. the Governor, Rennison, and District Commissioners etc. About forty or fifty neighbouring settlers came to the Baraza to hear our fate. McLeod told us we would be able to remain under the British Raj in the foreseeable future. In fact we were, or rather Kenya was, handed over to the Kikuyus within a couple of years. My one and only appearance in History!

Before all this and after Dick and Daphne Sheppard had left Crookery Nook in Molo to live nearby in a house of their own, we let or lent the cottage to friends. A young policeman and his bride took it for a few months. When I called in to see if all was well she gave me coffee and told me about herself in a sweet naïve Scottish way. They came from Aberdeen, he told me.

*Visit of Colonial Secretary & H.E. Sir Patrick Rennison to Banks Estate, Solai.*

'And you?' I asked her. 'What is your name?' 'Just Joan,' she said. 'You see, I was a foster child and David's family (her husband) brought me up although they already had five children of their own. I always loved David. We had such a happy childhood, except . . . oh! I do wish I knew my mother!'

'You never knew who she was?' I asked. 'Oh no! You see I was found on the steps of the kirk, wrapped in a woollen shawl and in a wee white hat. Oh Mrs Bucknall, my mother did love me, didn't she? She must have loved me for I was wearing a wee white hat.' The idea of the baby wrapped in a shawl and half hidden under a 'wee white hat' nearly finished me and I had to turn away so that she would not see my tears.

## 1960

What a calamitous year for Kenya! Everyone wondering if they should leave and start again elsewhere – but where? and how? For me, illness most of the year except when Jenny came out for the summer holidays. With her, Rose, Mark Ryan and Mike Whittal we made a safari to Ngoro/Ngoro Crater and Lake Manyara. Sleeping accommodation was provided by the Safari Lodge in caves on the face of a cliff. They were makeshift rooms to accommodate the ever growing tide of tourists to Kenya. At this particular Lodge we did see every animal imaginable, but the heating of our 'cave' was done by wood fires and we were all black-faced in the mornings.

South Africa was now a Republic although still within the Commonwealth. Tanganyika had its first Minister. The Congo was going from bad to worse and on the brink of a bloody revolution. Belgians were pouring over the Kenya border between us. A Red Cross friend of ours helping the immigrants on their arrival was surprised to meet a Belgian walking hand in hand with a chimpanzee. 'Why do you have to bring that with you?' she asked. 'But Madame, I could not leave Coco behind. They might have made him Prime Minister!'

All our friends were ill with worry about the future. In spite of everything we had a lovely Christmas with the young Oakshotts at Kiambu. All the family were there including Jenny, out for four weeks which were to be her last in Kenya. Baby Tom was the star turn. Jack, Jemima and Philly stayed with mutual friends next door. Kameko was full for New Year. While the young danced we played Bridge and sat up to see in the New Year, praying that it would be a happier and more peaceful one for us all.

We prepared to leave the beloved country. Some months previously Rawayo, sensing change, gave notice, after 27 years of faithful service. I asked 'Why are you leaving me now?' I was told 'Memsahib, if I stay with you I might steal.' 'But you have never stolen anything at all in all these years. You will never steal, Rawayo.' 'Not from you, Memsahib. But all my friends are stealing and I would rather steal from a new Bwana.'

It was heartbreaking for me, but he was adamant and left. Soon he returned from his reserve covered in smiles to bring me a present. It was wrapped in a cloth and laid on the ground. He undid it and proudly showed me three delicious little native pineapples and a quantity of sweet potatoes. 'I grew them myself,' he said. Then after a sad farewell he went off to Nairobi to find work and presumably to steal! Whatever he did I shall always bless him, and hope that life has been good to him.

Our cook, Joram, came down to Nairobi for a few days with me. On the road was a discarded broken lorry. 'What will we do when you leave?' he enquired. 'We cannot mend things like that or get new ones. Also before you came to live here, when I passed my enemy on the road we fought until one of us was killed. Now we take it to court. When you have all gone, and I meet my enemy on the road, I will kill him as we always used to do.' I had no philosophical solution to give him so kept silent, and have often thought about it since.

Bidding farewell to the Solai Farm Banks Estate was heart-breaking. All the head men presented me with little gifts which they had either grown or their wives had made. Lastly came Arap Kipsoi, the magnificent Kipsigi Bull Boy. He took my hand gently in both of his huge ones and said 'Kwaheri (fare-well). If I do not see you again down here,' pointing to the ground, 'I shall see you up there,' pointing to the sky. I pray that he is right and that we shall indeed meet again, in either of those places.

Finally all was packed up, Kameko deserted, the garden looking quite at its best. Goodbyes and tears. The train pulling out of Nairobi station and our dearest friends waving through a blur of tears. A couple of nights in Mombasa with Jenny's friends the Wards, and then embarkation. On board a long letter was waiting for me from the dear old Tryons, Spencer quoting at length from Byron and saying we would not meet again. I can see him and Lillian now, as on that last visit to Vilima, the sun pouring down upon them as they stood amongst the glorious rose terraces with Duki the spaniel at their feet.

*Kwaheri.*

*

# Scotland – a Different World

S ome three months before leaving Kenya, unsure where our
next home would be, I had a vivid dream. I was walking
with two friends beside a river. We came down a narrow lane
ending in between two houses, one small, and the other a
larger one-storey house. We walked round the side of the
larger house which was L-shaped. A gravelled drive curved
round the inside of the L, with an expanse of green lawn
stretching to a river opposite the house. In the sky above us
was a flock of pigeons, wheeling round and round before they
came to rest on the grass all round us. On waking, I told
William that I had seen the house we would live in and that it
was in Scotland somewhere, and described the dream to him.
He was naturally sceptical. However, on the strength of the
dream we decided to send all our furniture and belongings to
Glasgow. Why Glasgow? I really did not know.

We sailed for the U.K. on 11th June 1961 on a banana boat,
one of the Elliman Line ships which used to be the Bucknall
Elliman Line before the family sold out. All very luxurious with
proper beds and state room and private bathroom.

The young Oakshotts had decided to leave Kenya also and
probably meant to live in Scotland. In May of 1961 their second
baby boy Charles was born. They left Kenya after us, in September.

On our arrival in England Cressida and Alistair (Col. A.
Rumbold), whom she had recently married, met us at Dover

and took us to stay with them for a few days in Warninglid,
Sussex. We had given the Inneses (Betty and Berowald of the
Black Watch) our address and date of arrival and had promised
to pay them a visit in the summer. Four days after our arrival at
Cressida's we had a telegram from Berowald Innes saying
'Come up and visit us *now* three properties on the market
might interest you.' We got on to the Perth sleeper train that
night and were in Perth early next morning. The Inneses drove
us to their house, Tulcan, in Glen Almond, where I froze in
spite of the sun shining every day. My clothes were quite
inadequate for a Scottish summer.

Dear Betty and Berowald took us to see two quite unsuitable
houses, one of them nearly falling to the ground, which William fancied as it had several disintegrating stables. I pointed
out that we no longer had any horses and I could not stand the
gloom of the place anyway. Next day we went to see a cottage
by the Tay belonging to Toby and Gwladys Campbell, which
they wanted to sell. It was charming but much too small. 'But
the other house is for sale I believe,' asked Berowald. 'Oh yes!
My cousins the Evans are selling that,' Gwladys agreed. Betty,
Berowald and I walked round the side of the other house and
there was the same picture I had seen in my dream with
pigeons circling round above the house, before coming down
all round us! Fortunately I had told the Inneses all about my
dream. We all looked at each other. 'This is the house,' I said.

A great deal had to be done to it. The roof was taken off and
a second storey built on to the foot of the L wing. The interior
was gutted and reorganised throughout. Jean and David Rose
put us on to a friend, Betty Maxwell, in Edinburgh who was the
top interior decorator at that time. Installing central heating
was priority No. 1. But it was not put in the right place, the
boiler against my protests set up in the garage and the pipes
going all round the house, so that any heat got lost long before
it reached the leg of the L.

While all this was being done, we rented Jean and David's
small flat at the end of their house 'Huntingtower'. The first
morning when we woke up, the silence came as a shock, and

with it the realisation that nothing would happen at all unless I got up and made it happen. After taking servants for granted for thirty years I was at a loss to know where to start! Hope St. Maur sent me Philip Harben's book *Cooking* which was a wonderful blessing and still is.

Darling Jenny was in London working for the Red Cross at their main office. I visited her for a few days. We went on a much needed shopping spree. She took me to Selfridge's and made me buy all the mechanical machines she insisted I *must* have to survive. We bought everything excepting a dishwasher, which at the time I considered a luxury. Jenny was sharing a flat with her second cousin Angela Michell. One of the young men to weave in and out of Jenny's life was Robert Jocelyn, the impecunious Irish Viscount.

The world was in chaos. The Queen visited Ghana against public approval as it was feared she might be in danger from the two-faced Nkrumah. Men went into space. Nehru annexed Goa. Attacks on Kuwait.

In Perthshire we disappeared under feet of snow, and endured the coldest winter since records began. The Tay froze over and everybody skated about or skidded. Mother was well but announced that she would have to come and live with us as she could no longer look after herself. We ourselves had sciatica, blood poisoning and influenza, but William still maintained that Scotland was the only country to live in. By the end of the year we were living in the Campbell's cottage, the only other house in sight from The Hatton, the village being Stanley seven miles, or Perth ten miles away. We might just as well have been in Kenya, only we did not have the glorious climate nor the servants!

## Events in 1962

There were a great many deaths in the family: Uncle Bill Benn, Aunt Joyce Benn, Harry and Madge Peet, Awrie Bucknall, Archer Cust, and so on.

We had a glorious month at The Hatton between August 15th and September 15th. Jenny and her many young friends, also the baby Oakshotts, Tom and Charlie with their Scottish nanny all stayed with us.

After one of the big balls, the house party were lazing off their late night when Tom and Charlie entered the kitchen doing the Twist. They were only about three and five years old and fairly chubby. They stopped twisting to inform me that 'The Bodies want a Dwink, Gwanny.'

Jenny and Sylvia Montgomery sailed for America on September 20th to New York.

Rose and Michael bought their own farm at Gelston in Kirkcudbrightshire, by Castle Douglas, and moved in at the end of September.

On 22nd October I flew back to Kenya to finalise the sale of the Solai Farm – one of the saddest days of my life. Kenya had changed sadly in the past two years. So many friends had left or were leaving and there was a general feeling of depression.

Also during that year Cressida and Alistair's only daughter Belinda was born.

William was persuaded to take up painting by Mick Lindsay. This was to provide William and me with great joy. It prevented him from doing some of the ghastly things he used to do and gave me a breather to get on with my own life. During the summer we went to Loch Awe with Jack Merriot's painting group. Joan (Lindsay) and I accompanied them and thoroughly enjoyed our holiday. It was to become an annual event for many years, sometimes taking us abroad. One year the artists group went to Mentone in April, which was *not* a success. We stayed in a very cold, very uncomfortable little hotel and the journey was appalling. As most of the students were travelling third class we thought it would be rather disparaging to travel in a sleeper. I had grave misgivings as had always travelled first on the continent. At the last minute Mick and Joan changed to first class very wisely, but William would not hear of it. We were like a lot of cattle, and I stood up in the corridor most of the journey which took 24 hours.

Another time we went to Uzes near Orange in Provence, during a very hot June. We stayed in a disused monks' hostel –

very bare and excessively hot. Joan and Mick slept in an attic under the roof. One evening they were in our room when Joan let out a shriek. A huge spider was walking across the floor. William let fly, hit it with his shoe and killed it.

The next day William painted rather a good watercolour of a cornfield, but to do so he sat on a stool amongst the hay. Next morning his leg was very swollen, red streaks running up to his thigh. We had great difficulty in procuring a doctor. Thanks to the Lindsays we got William to Marseilles and on to a plane within 24 hours and he spent the next two weeks in the King George VII Hospital in London.

1962/63 was the Year of the Great Freeze. 1963 began icy and continued to sub-zero temperatures until April. The Tay froze over. Snow up to ten feet and more marooned us and most others in the Perthshire countryside. When the thaw set in the Tay carried down sheep, cattle, horses, houses, trees and enormous blocks of ice which crashed and splintered like glass. The noise was indescribable, but what a dramatic sight.

Mother had come to live with us by then. She enjoyed the drama but she created problems also. Either she was not on speaking terms with William, or with me, or she ganged up with William against me! It became too much for everyone. Stomach ulcers for me and swearing from William.

Finally Mother went on hunger strike in her room (she got my dear daily to take food in to her). This broke the camel's back. I went to hospital to eat a Barium meal. She arrived in the car with William to take me home and greeted me with, 'Well darling, all is well and I have found a charming place in Perth called Rio and will be moving into it next week.' And so it was.

### Ambrose the Rabbit

Our kind next door neighbour, Gwladys Campbell, was having trouble with a rabbit who ate all her flowers. I called the rabbit Ambrose.

Ambrose was black, large, with pink linings to his ears, and apparently tame. He first came into our lives when Tom aged five and Charles three were staying with us in our house on the banks of the Tay.

We went for a little walk along the river the first afternoon of their visit. Tom asked me if Peter Rabbit lived here and his cousin Benjamin Bunny. I said I felt sure they did though I had not actually seen them – but perhaps Peter Rabbit would appear tomorrow.

Next morning, two excited little boys came into our bedroom *very* early. 'Granny, Granny, there's a *rabbit* on the lawn – we don't think it's Peter Rabbit, 'cause he's black!' I was dragged to the window; there, sure enough, was a rabbit, quite unlike any other one. He sat in the middle of the lawn, nibbling happily and occasionally lolloping to another sunny patch a few inches further on.

We gazed entranced. 'What shall we call him?' Tom asked. Charlie made some sort of noise which sounded like 'no nose'. 'Ambrose, did you say?' I asked. 'Yes, yes, let's call him Ambrose.' So Ambrose he was christened.

Tom and Charlie ran outside, going straight up to Ambrose and sitting down beside him, stroking him and talking to him. Ambrose allowed them to do as they liked and seemed pleased to see them.

Later, Tom and Charlie rummaged in the garage and found a wooden box. They stuffed it with hay and put it in the middle of the porch where William immediately bashed his shins upon it. It was removed and put in the greenhouse.

Ambrose, still wandering round the lawn in spite of being sniffed at by our Pekingese dog, was picked up by Tom and laid in the box. A saucer of water and a lettuce were placed beside him. After a while, the boys left him in peace.

Instead of straying or disappearing as we thought he would do, not at all. Ambrose took up residence in the greenhouse, coming and going as he pleased. He used to go off now and again to find food, but *never* ate any flowers in our garden. Unfortunately he wandered into the garden across the lane, and there he ate and ate, systematically devouring pansies, snapdragons, everything that our neighbour Gwladys had so carefully planted.

We had complaints, but whenever Gwladys arrived, Ambrose discreetly disappeared, returning after she had left. Ambrose however did not leave us. He transferred himself from the greenhouse to a hole under the coal shed behind the house. He continued to run about our lawn, and to nibble the flowers next door and to evade detection.

Winter came and went.

In the spring a horrid man with a gun came and looked over the fence between us and the field. 'Ye ken ye hae a rabbit in your shed?' he enquired. 'Oh, have I?' I asked innocently. 'Aye, ye have – and if I catch him in the field wi' the turnips I'll be shooting him.' 'Well, if you come into my garden it's not the rabbit that will be shot,' I retorted haughtily.

Ambrose continued to survive.

One sunny morning when I looked out of the window an extraordinary sight met my eyes. Across the lane, in Gwlady's garden, Ambrose was eating his breakfast. Round one corner of the house Gwladys crept up behind him with a butterfly net – on the other side, to cut off escape, the postman stood with a sack, and out of the door beside Ambrose came Toby, Gwlady's husband, clad in dressing gown and pyjamas and brandishing a stick.

Ambrose hopped away. As he did so Gwladys swiped at him with the net and missed. Ambrose moved on again, keeping just out of reach of Gwlady's net. But in the end they all closed in on him. Before I could open the window and shout 'Stop!' the postman had landed himself full length on top of Ambrose, smothering him in the sack. Kicking and struggling, Ambrose was tied up in the bag.

In vain I ran out and pleaded for him. 'No, he ate *all* the garden and must be knocked on the head,' they said. The postman picked up the bag and threw it into his van. Then he sorted the letters and brought us our mail.

'Please, please don't kill that rabbit,' I implored him, and told him the whole story, stressing how dreadfully upset the little boys would be to hear that Ambrose had been murdered by their friend 'the Posty man.'

'Och, dinna fasch yer sel – I'll no kill him till I'm awah over yon brae.' 'I know a better plan,' I said. 'Promise me, faithfully now, that you will take him alive in your van on your morning round and when you get to Scone over the other side of the river, let him go there – no one will be any the wiser.'

The postman looked at me, blue eyes twinkling. 'Aye, there's nae harm in that – tho' they'll no be best pleased,' he said.

End of Ambrose.

## Unfortunate Visit to Aunt Ethel, Cornwall

Most years Aunt Ethel Beresford-Riley, who was my godmother, expected me to spend two or three weeks with her in Cornwall. One year William came too. They disliked each other on sight. On being introduced to William, Aunt Ethel remarked, 'I have seen you before.'

It seemed that several years previously, while on her way to take tea with Lady Tuker, a farmer had stopped her car and asked Aunt Ethel if she would be so kind as to take a gentleman, who had fallen off his horse and hurt himself, to his sister who lived close by, Lady Tuker.

Aunt Ethel gave William a lift to his sister and greeted Lady Tuker with 'I have your brother in the car. Evidently he had an accident and fell off his horse, concussing himself. He is suffering from shock.' William's sister contradicted Aunt Ethel by saying 'My family *never* suffer from shock. Come along William, a hot bath and cup of tea and you will be all right.'

While we were at Aunt Ethel's that summer, William had invited his younger daughter, Felicity, with four small children, to come and join us in Cornwall, and had booked them in at a local bed-and-breakfast farm. They all came to tea. Aunt Ethel's sitting room was full of all kinds of *objets d'art* and small tables. The three eldest children aged four, three and two years sat nervously on the edge of a long stool while Felicity held the baby. This individual began to cry. Immediately Felicity opened her blouse and fed the infant. Aunt Ethel stared hard and all conversation dried up. James, the eldest, suddenly took fright and bolted from the room followed by the others, small tables of cakes flying in all directions. After the family had taken a hurried departure, Aunt Ethel said to me, 'Never bring those children here again.'

In addition, she wrote when we got home and told me that although she much enjoyed seeing me whenever I could spare the time, on my next visit she would not be able to have William. 'I do not like the way he eats a boiled egg,' she wrote, 'nor do I want to meet him every time I go to the little house!' William's reaction was 'She is quite mad anyway.'

The following summer, Jean Rose came to Kiln Quay with me, and as Aunt Ethel was a great snob, she was delighted to entertain the daughter of a Scottish Earl, and behaved charmingly.

## *The Cottage on Loch Fyne*

Soon after this visit Aunt Ethel became ill and told her companion to write to me, informing me that she had changed her mind and her will. She was *not* leaving Kiln Quay to me, having promised to do so at least twenty years ago. But she did leave me five thousand pounds, which was far better. With that legacy I bought a heavenly little derelict croft on Loch Fyne in Argyllshire. In those days five thousand pounds went a long way. It was the greatest fun rebuilding the croft and making it into a darling holiday cottage right on the shore of the loch. Many friends, relations and ourselves spent holidays there and I lent it to one or two members of the Black Watch who had served under William in World War I.

When Rose and her two elder little boys came over to see it the first time, they asked what it was called. As I had given that no thought, I asked them to choose a name. There were grey seals lying on the rocks below the cottage, and Charlie said, 'Let's call it Seal Cottage,' So Seal Cottage it was and still is, although circumstances made me sell it some years later.

In between our own visits I let Seal Cottage through a good agent in Edinburgh. I was lucky. Not one of my tenants (it was let for two weeks at a time only) ever left it other than in perfect order, and all of them wrote to say how much they enjoyed it. It made a lot of money for me and gave great pleasure to a lot of people, and it was a sadness to have to sell it when we came to live in Kirkcudbrightshire many years later.

## 1963

A year of assassinations and disasters in the world. President John Kennedy was assassinated. Jenny and Sylvia Montgomery were in Washington at that time and watched the funeral. Sir Alec Douglas Home became Prime Minister, a welcome relief from Macmillan, I thought.

In Kenya the monstrous Kenyatta of Mau Mau fame became Prime Minister.

William's old friend, Niel McMicking, died on the train at Perth shortly after attending the ball at Windsor Castle given for Princess Alexandra and Angus Ogilvie.

Jenny returned home from U.S.A. on 14th December. It was a great joy to have her back.

On Christmas morning poor old Toby Campbell died and I had to spend every available minute with Gwladys Campbell. As we were having a family Christmas lunch at the Hatton, I had to chance my arm and set the oven early in the morning to cook the turkey. It turned out all right!

For the first time my eldest grandson Tom came to visit us alone, aged four and a half. He was tremendous fun and no trouble except that he would poke about in the television and managed to disrupt it. We had a white Christmas but in two days the snow had all gone.

## 1964

After selling their Kenya farm, Jack sent all his household goods etc. down to South Africa to Somerset West, where he had bought a small vineyard with a house on it. Before going there they and their three small children came over to U.K. and spent New Year with us. They all arrived at the Hatton in sheepskin clothes, hats, gloves, coats, boots, looking like a flock of sheep!

Three of Jenny's friends in Kenya got married that year 1964: Greta Kühle, Juliana Ward and Cherry Waudby.

Henry Oakshott was made a Baron so Michael became The Hon!

One of Jenny's admirers spent a brief visit – Robert Jocelyn. He exasperated me for years, coming in and out of Jenny's life and upsetting everybody.

## 1965

Poor Hennie Oakshott had a coronary thrombosis and never really enjoyed life again. He missed the House where he had spent 25 years representing Bebington as Conservative Member. Berowald Innes also had a coronary in October.

During the summer William and I joined Jack Merriot's artist course at Polperro in Cornwall. I have a charming picture painted by J. Merriot of the Polperro harbour. While he was painting it, looking through his studio window his wife fell from the window above down into the water. She survived.

In November we visited Dodo Blair Oliphant who was temporarily in Windermere and had her mother staying with her. On arrival Dodo told us that her mother had been very ill and the doctor had prescribed an enormous pill the size of a horse pill for the old lady. The only way Dodo had managed to get it down her mother's throat was to administer a large whisky followed by another larger whisky. With the second whisky, her mother swallowed the pill without knowing anything about it.

At the end of our visit to Dodo we picked up a large water colour painted by Jack Merriot and drove to Ingleston where we had left Granny and our corgi Tika. We tied the picture on to the rack of the car with a spider, after covering it with rugs. Mother and Tika were in the back, William in front suffering from lumbago, and I driving. It was all most uncomfortable.

After halfway home, looking in my mirror I saw the picture sailing off into the air, missing an oncoming car by a fraction, and falling flat on the side of the road. Stopping and running back to collect it, I heard an ominous sound of shattered glass inside the rug.

We continued on our way. While getting Mother out of the car when we got home, and more difficult, William, who yelled with every movement, the picture was forgotten. Jenny arrived as we were unloading and took away the picture in its wrappings to the kitchen. She came to me shortly afterwards, smiling. 'Unbelievable, Mum, the picture is intact! It must have fallen on its face and all the glass fell outwards. No scratches so far as I can see!'

For the Black Watch ball before Christmas we had 14 to dinner. All the young disappeared and we did not see them until late the following day – in time for our cocktail party when a hundred people turned up!

Christmas Day we lunched with the Inneses and William was nearly driven mad with some violent itch. We had to rush home with him and call the doctor, who complained that he had tried to eat his Christmas Dinner three times already that day and still had not succeeded. William was given a morphine injection, an ambulance was sent to collect him and take him to the Dundee Infirmary. Jenny travelled with him in the ambulance while I followed in our car. The ambulance driver had evidently had a very liquid Christmas lunch so that the ambulance weaved from side to side of the road, but mercifully, no collisions. At that time everyone was enjoying their Christmas turkey except Dr. Hall!

The best news that Christmas was that Rose and Michael's third son had arrived without trouble, in time for Christmas Dinner – Angus Oakshott.

*

Pictures flash across my memory. Daisy coming to stay at the Hatton when we had a plague of mice. We bought dozens of mouse traps, set them all over the house and heard them popping off every few minutes. One mouse was found in the loo pan, drowned. A month later my electric toaster was jammed. A dehydrated mouse was found inside it. During Daisy's visit she made me go into Perth with her to buy a dishwasher. It was a blessing and I have never been without one since.

## *Water Rats*

The mice were not as bad as the water rats or water voles. A friend of ours, Beryl Critchley-Salmonson, who had come up to paint, and was staying with us for a fortnight, was sitting talking in the sitting-room one evening when I saw the drink cupboard under the window opening, by itself apparently! A *huge* water rat was sitting up beside a whisky bottle on the shelf. Yelling 'Rat' and grabbing a fire-arm, I jumped up while the creature cantered across the floor and went through the door and into the next room. We all ran after it but could not find it.

Our bedroom was on the ground floor. We searched everywhere for the rat, but in vain. At about midnight we gave up. William said he was off to bed. 'Well, I am not going to sleep in our bedroom downstairs until I know where that thing is lurking,' I said. But I had to go along to undress and collect some bedclothes for the upstairs bedroom. Looking round our bedroom for any signs of the rat, I saw a long tail protruding from behind William's bed. 'There it is.' 'Go and get my claymore,' ordered William. We were both in our nightclothes. William swiped at the rat's tail with his sword while I stood beside him with a walking stick. The rat's tail seemed to sink into the pile of the carpet, and it ran out and round the room until it got behind my tallboy which stood across a corner diagonally.

This tallboy had ten drawers and was about 5' x 2' high. William shouted at me to tip the tallboy up and hold it towards myself while he skewered the rat on his sword. Very nervously

I did this as I felt sure the animal would run up my nightdress. William stuck the rat with the end of the sword. But the rat was very game and strong and clawed its way along the blade. William swore and told me to fetch another stick. Meanwhile the tilt of the tallboy caused all ten drawers to fall out on to me, and there was no way I could move unless help came. It did, in the shape of Beryl, who had heard the commotion and came down in her nightwear to see if she could be of use. She has drawn a gorgeous picture of this scene.

The rat took advantage of her entry to shake itself off the sword and race round the room again, entrails half out. It vanished. We all searched again and again, so that the room looked as if a hurricane had hit it. But no sign of the rat. Hours later we all decided on bed. 'You had better come upstairs too, William' we suggested. 'No, I am sleeping in my own bed here.' So we left him.

Next morning when I went in to take him a cup of tea rather late, he was still asleep, and on the carpet beside the bed was the biggest rat I have ever seen. It was dead. Waking William and showing him the gruesome thing I enquired what had happened. 'Oh, I got into bed and read for a bit and must have fallen asleep. I was woken by a piercing pain at the end of my nose. The rat was on my bedside table and disappeared.' There was blood all over the bed and on William's face. Disbelieving, I said 'Don't tell me you went to sleep again without finding that creature?' 'Well, I heard a sort of kerfuffle and scuffling and then silence, so presumed it had either left or died.'

He was due to meet Mick Lindsay to join the painting tour on Loch Fyne that morning, so I dabbed him with Dettol and said I would take him to the doctor for an anti-tetanus injection. 'No, there isn't time.' The Rat it was that Died!

\*

In Central Africa atrocities were committed in the Congo where not long before we had enjoyed the most lovely safari in what had seemed to be a happy country.

## *1967 – We Revisit Africa*

From 1st January to 31st March we were in Africa again. First we paid a nostalgic visit to Kenya, staying with old friends for three weeks. I had almost forgotten how heavenly the climate was and how beautiful the country. I was very tempted to remain, but resisted the impulse. We flew down to South Africa and spent a few days with Jack and Jemima, then went by bus to friends of William's in Port Elizabeth.

The very first night William was stung by a spider in his bed. By morning he had red streaks right up to his groin. Our host called for an ambulance and William spent three weeks in hospital nursed by nuns. I loathed Port Elizabeth. Our hosts kindly gave me their Baby Austin to visit the hospital every day. That was all I saw of the place. They were a very strange couple anyway.

After spending a week with Jack and Jemima while William regained his strength, we flew back to Scotland.

*

In May of that year Jenny came back from her world tour looking as brown as an Indian. She remained with us and ran the house for me until September, bless her. After that I was fortunate enough to get an excellent daily, and felt more settled and less exhausted than I had for many years.

Tommy Oakshott went to Cargilfield prep school for his first term, poor little chap. He did not cry but grew as white as a sheet when we left him. At half term he bravely said he was quite enjoying it.

Gloomy world news. Wilson's policy disastrous. The pound devalued and the country bankrupt. So they say, but life seems to go on much the same. Ghastly air and rail accidents. Good news was that Francis Chichester successfully navigated the world solo in his little ship *Gypsy Moth*.

Resumé of 1968 says that it was a happy year personally with good health for a change, but a lot of our friends died, including Jack Merriot. A great loss to the art world. News at Christmas that three American astronauts had successfully circled the moon. For Jenny success meant romantically!

## *1969*

Reading through this it all seems very banal. After our life in Kenya it was bound to be. In this country life seems so trivial in comparison, possibly because everything is done for everyone by the State. Neighbours do not have the chance to help out in emergencies; there are always the fire brigades, the Health Service, the transport, telephones and so on. However, private lives are still varied and can provide amusement!

Old Sir James Duncan married Dodo Blair-Oliphant, the most attractive Irish widow who has a great sense of humour and obviously kissed the Blarney Stone at an early stage. She has enormous emerald green eyes and is a born mimic. Jim and Dodo paid us a yearly visit to pick elderberries which grew in profusion beside the Tay. They brought an old cousin of Jim's with them this year. As Jim climbed laboriously up our bank on to the lawn, his trousers fell down! 'What a wonderful stage entrance!' cried Dodo with peals of laughter. The old cousin was 'not amused'.

Another flash – driving with William at the wheel, always a dangerous affair, I suddenly remembered that I had left the cream behind which I had promised to take to the Hector Munro's where we were lunching. We were then driving up a very steep and winding hillside, with a railway line down below. Stupidly I told William I had forgotten the cream. He swerved violently to the right, hitting the side of the hill, ricocheted across the road to the left when the car mounted a parapet about two foot high and rested there, precariously balanced.

'Get out!' yelled William, beginning to struggle towards his door on the road side. 'If you move at all we shall drop down on to the railway miles below,' I yelled. He furiously stayed still long enough for me to slide inch by inch out on to the parapet and crawl along it to the safety of the road. The only casualty was Tika our corgi, who was knocked unconscious. The car was a write-off as the undercarriage was ripped to pieces.

*

In July, for my birthday, I went down to stay for a few days with Jenny who was sharing a little house in Kensington with Jemma Boyle and two other girls. The evening I arrived, Jenny said she hoped I would not mind if she went out to dinner, the other girls would look after me. She rushed upstairs to change and was actually ready when a charming young man called Garry Barnett arrived to collect her. It was so unlike Jenny to be punctual and ready for any of her young men when they called for her that I took special note of Garry. A charmer I thought.

Next day Jen said 'Mum, we are going out to dinner tonight as it is your birthday. Garry is calling for us at eight p.m.' After a happy day shopping we were duly called for and taken to a gorgeous restaurant and given the most delicious dinner. It became perfectly clear to me that at last Jenny had fallen in a big way and Garry was beaming joy from every pore!

'I do like your Young Man,' I ventured. 'Oh yes! You will be seeing a lot more of him, Mum. Have you got all you want for the night?' And with that she gave me a big hug and we went to bed.

Next day I took the train back to Scotland, none the wiser but dying with curiosity.

The following weekend Jenny said that she would be coming up and that a party of them would be going to spend the weekend at Ullapool. She would be getting a lift up with Garry. He deposited her at the Hatton and dashed off to his parents who lived on the other side of the Tay. Next morning he whizzed round the drive, Jenny flew down and into the car and with a wave off they drove.

Curiouser and curiouser!

The other two were Thomas and Belinda McMicking, newly marrieds and the son and daughter-in-law of friends of ours.

It stuck out a mile that Garry and Jenny were in *love*, but nothing was said. They all returned in high spirits, and just as Jenny was leaving to catch the London train I enquired (very bravely) 'Are you engaged or anything?' 'Oh Mum! Just a very good weekend, don't worry!' and off she went.

It was almost too much for me.

Next night Jenny rang up. 'Mum, can Garry and I come up again on Friday?' 'Yes of course. Delighted.' 'Okay, see you then.'

That was all.

Friday came. Garry immediately asked my formal permission to marry Jenny. His parents had approved and we were really pleased. If I had had to choose a husband for Jenny, Garry would have been the one.

## Jenny and Garry Get Married

Garry and Jenny were married on 13th September 1969 in Perth. The sun shone and the reception was held at Balhousie Castle. Over 400 guests came, a large proportion of them members or retired members of the Black Watch. Just before the family set off from the Hatton for the church Charlie Oakshott announced that he would *not* dress up in a silly shirt with a lace frill and would *not* be a page. It took some time and bribery to persuade him to co-operate.

At the reception, as it was very hot, we had organised drinks to be handed out to guests as they queued up to get into the marquée. One young man, Lord Wilmot, swallowed a large wasp which stung him in the throat. An ambulance was called and he was driven to hospital half dead. Mercifully we did not know of this until afterwards when Robbie Wilmot had recovered.

Charlie enjoyed himself by getting hold of a goblet of champagne. He weaved up to me saying 'G'anny . . . my nose is fizzing' and collapsed on the grass.

Finally the car which was to have driven the happy couple away did not arrive as scheduled owing to having had a

*Wedding at Balhousie.*

puncture! But the best man, James Arbuthnot, stepped in and drove them to the airport to catch a Kenya-bound plane.

The end of an era for me.

\*

# Spanish Holiday

## 1969

S ome friends offered to lend us their villa in Spain for three months from January 1st. It was situated near Marbella, outside the village of San Pedro de Alcantara. Living in Marbella at that time was our old friend and neighbour Gwladys Campbell.

The journey began in a heavy snowstorm when we disembarked at Bilbao in the north of Spain. I drove the Mercedes straight down through the peninsula, experiencing every kind of weather and negotiating mountains, gorges and eccentric Spanish drivers – great fun!

The Villa Tabraza was large and spacious and surrounded by orange groves. Our arrival there was inauspicious. No one had prepared anything for us. We were wet, tired and hungry. Fortunately a little Spanish maid turned up shortly after we did. She took me along to the village, introduced me to her family who owned the biggest little grocery in San Pedro, and realising I could not speak the language, she ordered everything she thought we would need. Her grandmother came into the shop, saw me still dripping wet from unloading the car during a rainstorm, ushered me into her living room and sat me down in her chair beside the wood-burning stove. This may bore anyone who reads as far as this, but the natural courtesy and kindness of these Spanish peasants is one of the delightful memories I have of Spain.

By the time Maria and I got back to the villa, the couple who should have prepared for us were there. He was a most sinister-looking man but his wife was a cheerful little round woman who did the cooking and cleaning.

For the first eighteen days tropical rain poured down. The earth roads turned into rivers, and we wondered why we had come!

On day nineteen, the sun came out and continued to shine upon us for the remainder of our three-month holiday.

We each had a huge bedroom and bathroom and upstairs there were two more similar rooms. I spent each morning having breakfast in bed and learning Spanish for an hour with the help of the cook and Maria. Delicious!

Amongst the visitors who came to stay with us were Margaret Rose and Jean Drummond-Moray from Perthshire. They spent a fortnight and we had lots of drama and much laughter during their visit.

Jean was interested in yoga at the time. She used to do exercises in the garden, such as standing on her head. She was doing this one day when the sinister gardener peered round a corner and glared at her. He rushed off and brought back his wife, the cook, with him. Both of them came up to me and remonstrated (or so it seemed) in Spanish, crossing themselves several times. Presumably they thought Jean came straight from the devil. They were a tiresome couple.

Another day I went to change some money at the bank. I found everything at a standstill while a noisy customer shouted at the bank clerk. The manager appeared and soon there were the makings of a first class row. Two policemen in theatrical clothes arrived on the scene and marched off with the offender between them. He was our gardener. It seemed that he was paid monthly by the bank while the Williamsons, who owned our villa, were away. The gardener demanded more money and became abusive, so was put into the local gaol.

Back at the villa, I was confronted by the rascal's wife, our cook, the news had travelled before me that her husband was in gaol. She threw down her duster, brush and pan, crossed her fat little arms across her stout bosom and marched off. Well! Obviously we would have to look after ourselves with the help of the little village girl Maria. Jean D.M. announced that she would go down to the village, buy some rubber gloves and cook some delicious dishes she knew of.

Margaret and I thought we should telephone the owners in England. We did this and they flew out by the first plane that afternoon and settled the whole business by next morning! It seemed that the cook and her 'Hombre' occupied the flat attached to the villa Tabraza (our villa) and would be turned out unless they behaved and did their work. Next day the gardener came into the house and hurled the gas stove at me! After that there were no more tantrums. Meanwhile the little village girl rounded up several cousins of hers in the village who trooped up to do the housework and cooking for us. But the cook, afraid of being sacked, saw them off and worked very well for the remainder of our visit.

We took a bus and drove up to Rhonda one day. It was most exciting as the mountain track climbed steeply up a narrow ledge cut out of the side of the mountain. The driver drove fast and recklessly, swerving out over the side of the cliff when an oncoming vehicle hurtled towards us. It was altogether too much for little Jean D.M. who clung to William crying 'Stop him, stop him. We shall all fall into the gorge and be killed.' William was too deaf to hear and did nothing, so Jean closed her eyes and stopped up her ears, and probably prayed for us all.

Rhonda itself is a wonderful old city and will surely already be known to most of you. Apart from the historical interest and marvellous ancient palaces still lived in, we enjoyed the colourful inhabitants and delicious sangria drink we were given at lunch-time.

Other visitors at Villa Tabraza were Jenny and Cressida with her small daughter Belinda. Jenny joined Garry in Gibraltar soon after coming to us. In order to get to Gibraltar, she had to take a hovercraft to Algiers and fly from there to Gibraltar. This nonsense because of some political disagreement between Spain and Britain.

A few weeks before we left for England, we met Henry Tiarks at a lunch party. He was sitting next to me asking politely about our visit and how we intended going home, by car? He then asked if I would be interested in driving his Mercedes back in convoy with ours when we went? I had told him Cressida would be taking it in turns with me to drive up the western side of Spain. I declined the offer. When I told Cressida about this she immediately said, 'Oh, I would love to do that.' So we went to lunch with the Tiarks and agreed to drive Henry Tiarks' Mercedes to England. We looked through his immense telescope at the firmament, took off our high-heeled shoes to walk across his croquet lawn and bade them farewell.

*Our Spanish guide through the winding streets of Zofré.*

In due course we set off on our return journey in convoy
with the two Mercedes. All went well apart from the inevitable
arguing about which was the right road to take and if we were
on it, and getting totally lost up in some mountain regions and
being rescued by an unlikely-looking city slicker turning up in
the village square. The city slicker knew a few words of English
and said he would guide us on our way. 'Uno momento,
Signoras.' He went off and returned immediately astride a
donkey. 'Follow me,' he shouted. He wore a pink silk shirt,
tight black trousers and pointed patent leather shoes. Encouraging the donkey with a smack on its backside, he rode ahead
followed by our two large Mercedes! He put us on the road for
Salamanca which we reached late in the afternoon and thank-
fully clocked in at the largish Spanish Castello, converted into a
hotel. It was still hot and the sun high in the sky, so Cressida,
Belinda and I explored the old town and bought beautiful
leather shoes. Belinda was always leaving her shoes behind
wherever we went as she would kick them off to jump-hop
over a loop on the end of a string attached to her ankle. It was
the fashion among children in England to do this and fascinated the street urchins in Spain.

The morning after our arrival in Salamanca when we were all
ready to depart, the Tiarks' car refused to spark. No one could
make any impression on the wretched thing. After an hour or
so had elapsed, an American emerged from the hotel, saw our
plight and offered help. He had a similar model and knew
about Mercedes, and in about another hour we were on our
way. Everywhere we stopped after that the Tiarks' car let us
down in some way or another. On our ship in which we
embarked for the U.K. poor William was seized with an acute
attack of arthritis while going up the short staircase to the
restaurant. He stuck sideways across the stairs, blocking the
way completely so that no one could go up or down. That I
think was the end of our Spanish Experience, though not of
course the full account.

While in Spain, I took up painting – water-colours. The
colours and scenery and contrasting sun and shadows were too

much to resist. Until then I had thought William should have his own field of interest without competition from me. But these resolutions faded in the Spanish sun. Painting has been a great source of pleasure to me ever since.

After leaving Tiarks' Mercedes with Alastair and Cressida who promised to deliver it next day to the agent in London, William and I entrained to Scotland. Three days later Cressida telephoned to tell us that she had *not* delivered the car as arranged, thinking she could for once drive a Mercedes down to Brighton to get her hair done! Halfway there, the Merc had finally broken down, the big end having collapsed. Very embarrassing to have to tell the Tiarks this!

*

# 1971–1976

S ome years stand out more clearly than others. 1971 was
one. The year started with us taking over Daisy
Templetown (Cust)'s cottage in Rockbourne for six weeks
while she went to South Africa. It was a most beguiling village.
A stream trickled past our front door where ducks floated down
or waddled along the winding road, reminding me of
*Jackanapes*, a story I loved. We made a lot of friends there and
might in fact have bought the cottage from Daisy had she not
asked a rather larger sum than we wanted to pay at that time.
Apart from one evening after we had given a small drinks party
to our neighbours and one of them had fallen into the stream
when he departed, time passed peacefully. The man who fell
into the water had a wife who bullied him unmercifully. On
this occasion she had left shortly before him. Hearing the
commotion, she rushed back and saw him struggling to get out,
holding up an umbrella. 'Just the sort of thing you would do,'
she screamed, 'and why hold the umbrella up *now?*' As far as I
know they are still happily married.

*29th March 1971*
Robert Barnett was born at Aldershot. Instead of looking like
mostly newly born babies do, like tree frogs, he looked like
one of Michelangelo's chubby cherubs looking down from the
ceiling of the Sistine Chapel – quite beautiful.

Meanwhile Mother fell and hurt her leg. She telegraphed to

me 'Return immediately stop have broken my leg.' Knowing her methods of attracting attention to herself when feeling 'left out' I telephoned her doctor to verify this. 'Oh no! She has not broken her leg. There is no need to hurry back. Your mother is an auld autocrat, she is living two hundred years out of her time.' Just so!

## Mother's 90th Birthday and Death

In August Mother celebrated her 90th birthday. She was then permanently at St. Johnson's private nursing home in Perth. With Matron's help, she was carried into the car and a collapsible wheelchair was stuffed into the boot. After the drive to the Hatton we managed to heave her out and sit her in a chair in the porch. Charlie and Tom were out from school and we all cut Granny's large birthday cake and drank her health. Jean Rose arrived with a brace of grouse she had shot for Mother and which were roasted and gobbled up with relish. After lunch Mother was very tired so I drove her back to the nursing home.

On the first of September Robert Barnett was christened at St. John's Church in Perth. He was dressed up in our family robes and was taken to see Mother on his way to the christening. This gave her a lot of pleasure although obviously she was very tired. A few days later, on 10th September, Mother died after having had a slight stroke. She left a great blank in our lives. Her forceful personality and unconventional outlook on life, though not always appreciated, could not be ignored, and her courage and humour and common sense made her many friends as well as enemies.

One of her talents was embroidery. She excelled at tapestry and while she was in Kenya she designed a vast quantity of tapestries for chairs, pictures, stools etc. She would pick flowers or fruit from the garden, or wild flowers, draw them with a pen and ink on her canvas, one at a time, first putting the flowers in a tumbler of water. Most of us have some of her work, hanging on the walls or on chairs and stools. Her last original tapestry she worked while at Rio in Perth and is on a footstool I have. She would have been about 86 years old then.

Unfortunately she had stated in her will that her ashes were to be scattered in the Garden of Remembrance at Eastbourne where Joan's ashes were. So I had to travel down to Eastbourne by train with Mother's ashes in my suitcase! Jenny joined me in London and came with me to the Garden of Remembrance. A gruesome occasion we did not enjoy, as there was a strong wind blowing and the urn lid stuck until it suddenly shot off and the contents of the urn were blown in all directions by the wind. Mother might have been amused by this!

*

Meanwhile in the world outside so to speak, all kinds of important events were taking place. In the United Kingdom, decimal currency was introduced, causing confusion amongst shoppers and sending the cost of living soaring up. Ireland continued to terrorise with murders, bombing, arson – *awful.* China was accepted as a Member of the United Nations.

India and Pakistan went to war with each other in the autumn. Russia supported India and China supported East Pakistan. India won that round!

### 1972

Early in the New Year dear Bill Broadhurst died unexpectedly while Moira was very ill with flu. They were very dear friends of ours and Bill was one of the funniest men I have ever known, in his quiet dignified way.

Jamie Drummond-Murray had died not long before this, leaving little Jean D.M. with three rather unhelpful but much loved sons to cope with.

What else happened that year? Oh yes! The liner *Queen Elizabeth* caught fire in Hong Kong harbour, thus ending the era of cruises, those blissful 'get-away-from-it-all' holidays.

The Barnetts flew to Hong Kong where Garry did a two and a half year staff job. Before Christmas their second son David Alexander was born out there.

King Hussein of Jordan divorced his English wife, Moona, and married an Israeli. Stupid man.

The most popular world trend seems to have been hi-jacking and kidnapping.

During the spring, William and I had joined the Lindsays on a painting course in Menton. The whole trip was disastrous and the journey a nightmare. We all had influenza and I followed that up with a frozen shoulder which lasted a painful six months.

We were always very social in Perthshire, and on New Year's Eve we gave a party for twelve at the Hatton and played bridge until two in the morning! Afterwards, Col. Rusk (known in the B.W. as Rusky) stayed on to spend the night with us. I left him and William and retired to bed, but was woken up soon after going to sleep by crashing noises outside. It transpired that both the old boys had decided to fill the rubbish bins and take them to the end of the lane, but Rusky fell head first into one of the bins while trying to move it.

## *1973*
### *Hong Kong*

Looking back, what do I remember of Hong Kong? First that in order to fly out there to visit Jenny and Garry I had to sell a beautiful little singing-bird box left to me by Madrina, our beloved great aunt. It raised enough money at Christies to pay for the air fare.

On getting to the airport, I went to the Ladies to change out of my winter clothes into lighter ones. The char looked nice, so I asked her if she would keep an eye on my luggage while I changed. She agreed willingly. 'Where are you going?' she asked. 'Ow! Hong Kong. Are you by yourself, dearie? Is no one going to see you off?' 'No, I am by myself,' I told her. On emerging from the changing closet, I thanked her for looking

after my luggage, and she said 'Ave you tiken your little pill
dearie? They sy that yer must do that or yer will be ever so
sick.' I reassured her that I had some. 'Well, there's a café
upstairs and you tike yer pill with yer coffee.'

As I walked through the Departure gangway where everyone
was waving goodbye to their friends, a voice cried 'Goodbye,
Ducks, 'ave a good 'olidy. You look ever so nice.' It was the
dear char, upset at my leaving without a send-off and waving to
me.

Then the excitement of flying to an unknown country. Looking out of the port window of the plane at dawn and seeing the
outline of the Himalayas etched against a pale pink sky. No one
else round me seemed to be remotely interested in the Himalayas, only in trying to get a little extra sleep.

Swooping down into a concrete jungle called Hong Kong and
coming to a halt just in time to avoid plunging into the sea.
Jenny and Garry there to meet me. Then being kept awake for
a while before dropping down into a sleep which lasted for
nearly 24 hours.

The joy of meeting Robert aged nearly two years, and of
seeing baby David for the first time.

We went sailing with James Arbuthnot, gliding through silver
mists and islands. What a fascinating world. Then a trip by
Hovercraft to Macao across the Yellow Sea, the very name
spelling romance to me. The junks, the teeming throngs of little
yellow people, the azaleas, the bamboo scaffolding of more
and more newly emerging buildings, the food, and last but not
least our Chinese art master. He came twice a week to give
Jenny and me painting lessons, Chinese style. It is a static art as
everyone knows, but so beautiful. Each movement made with
the brush is controlled, either from the wrist or the arm and the
brush held vertically point downwards.

Social life was great fun and the food an education to me.
When we went shopping it was difficult not to go berserk and
buy ridiculous things such as cabinets inlaid with mother-of-
pearl and priceless carvings in jade, which of course I could not
afford, or which would look idiotic in my house in Scotland.

As always, darling Jenny and Garry were the most loving and caring daughter and son-in-law imaginable, so that the whole visit was heaven itself.

On my return William was in a rage with me for going at all. So I left him with his daughter Cressida and went to visit my oldest and closest friends, Hope and Freddie St. Maur, in Hampshire. How glad I am that I did. Hope died a few months later.

While I was with the St. Maurs I spent one morning by myself walking round Winchester Cathedral. Looking at the tomb of William Wickham, which was enclosed, I noticed that there was a small bunch of roses placed at the head of the effigy. The door to the tomb was locked. Suddenly a monk appeared beside me.

'Would you like to come inside and look at the carvings round the tomb?' he asked. 'Oh yes please, I would very much,' I said.

We walked through the tiny arched door and admired the beautiful carvings on the tomb not seen from the outside. The monk, dressed in brown sackcloth tied round with rope, drew my attention to the roses. 'Today is William Wickham's birthday. I always put roses in here for him on his birthday,' he said. We then turned round and went out, I in front of him. On turning round to thank him he was not there. Looking up and down the long aisle there was no trace of him. An American couple came up and tried to get into the tomb, but it was locked. 'Did you see a monk?' I asked them. 'A monk? No, we saw nobody,' they said. So, who did I see?

\*

Just before Christmas, Jenny, Garry and their two little boys came up to visit us from Colchester where they had been posted after their two years in Hong Kong. Rose also came to stay at the same time, so for the first time I had the great joy of having them all under the same roof.

## *1975-76*

Life was becoming difficult at The Hatton with William's increasing illnesses, mostly arthritis and decreasing ability to move about. The domestic position grew worse as our sweet daily moved nine miles away to where her husband had another job offered to him. This meant I had to drive 36 miles three times a week in order to fetch Cathy and take her home. So, very reluctantly, we put The Hatton on the market and sold it very profitably far too quickly. The kind Frazers lent us their enormous house, Tulleybelton, to live in while we were looking for another smaller and more accessible house somewhere in Perthshire. We did not find anything at all in Perthshire then. Meanwhile Rose had been looking round for anything suitable in the Stewartry for us. In the end we bought Netherby, in Castle Douglas. William loved it and I hated it and it hated me! It was largish and in a good position but everything went wrong there that possibly could have done.

### *Goose v. Swan*

While still at Tulleybelton, I witnessed an interesting wild life incident. On the loch there, a swan had built its nest at the southern end and a Canada goose had built its nest on the bank at the opposite end. There were eight little Canada goslings in the nest to start with. One day, walking along the loch, I noticed that there were only four goslings left. Suspecting the swan, I sat down and waited to see if anything would happen. Soon, the swan flew up towards the Canada goose's nest and tried to dive down over it. Mrs Goose defended her brood vigorously while Mr Goose rose in the air and dive-bombed the swan, who flew back to his end of the loch. Very shortly afterwards the swan returned but was met head on by Mr Goose. There was a battle above the nest ending in the swan retiring once again to his own nest.

Mr Goose then took off down towards the swan's nest and was met by a furious counter-attack from the swan, sending the goose up the loch once more. Hardly had he reached his nest when the swan followed him and dived at Mrs Goose and her goslings. He was thwarted by a wonderful riposte from Mr Goose, who flew into the swan, striking it with his head on the side of the swan's head. It made a resounding crack.

There ensued a battle royal in the air, feathers flew and that the two birds clashed again and again until they were too exhausted to continue. After a short respite, Mrs Goose began to move, leading her brood almost invisibly through the rushes at the end of the loch towards the far bank. But the swan saw her and flew up to attack her. Mr Goose warded off the swan by dive-bombing him repeatedly while Mrs Goose crossed into the safety and shelter of the far shore. Mr Swan flew towards home but immediately swung round and rapidly returned to where Mrs Goose had disappeared. Our brave goose, obviously depleted, went into the attack for the last time, and the swan gave up the struggle. The Canada geese were seen no more on the loch.

*

# Loch Fyne Memories

L och Fyne memories will always give me pleasure and a sense of satisfaction. This is not an historic novel, so I can swing about as my recollections of past days flit through my mind.

One excursion to the croft on Loch Fyne was not quite the success we thought it would be. Rose and Michael were going on a short holiday to fish so they left the three boys, Tom, Charlie and Angus with us. We took them over to the croft with all the usual baskets of food, bedding, fishing rods and paraphernalia which accompanied us on these trips and also Tika, our corgi, and Ping, our peke.

We left very early in the morning and had a late picnic breakfast by Loch Fyne. The boys fought in the back of the car until I threatened to turn round and take them home again if they did not stop. On the surface of the loch we could see the fins of huge basking sharks. These creatures were quite harmless but could easily overturn a small craft such as we had if we got too close to them. They measured up to thirty or forty feet in length and were proportionately large.

Poor Charlie had terrible toothache all weekend and to add to his misery, Tom grabbed his fishing rod, cast into the waters of Loch Fyne and pulled out a fish! As Tom never fished and Charlie was mad keen on it, there was a lot of fighting between them over that rod, especially as Charlie did not catch any fish at all while we were there.

The day we left Seal Cottage, the boys were utterly fiendish. They chased each other round and in and out of the house, leaving all their belongings scattered everywhere, Tom teasing the others and upsetting their treasures such as creepy crawlies in jars and shells as he tore past. Finally he shut Angus up in the garage, locked all the cottage doors with me inside, and ran off. After being rescued by William who was throwing things into the car (his idea of loading it up) and liberating poor little Angus who was bawling his head off in the garage, and helping Charlie with his rod, I gave them ten minutes to pack themselves up and get into the car. By then Charlie and Angus were sitting in the car minus Tom.

'Granny, you *can't* go without Tom,' they said. 'Oh yes, I can!' was my reply, and let out the clutch. The boys looked really concerned and again told me not to leave. Knowing my Tom and that he would have heard all this from wherever he was hiding, we drove off slowly. Round the first corner Tom sprang out and jumped into the car. There was no sound from any of them for the whole of the two hour drive home!

Among our friends, Jean and David Rose visited us at the croft. The weather was perfect and all went well. Only one incident arose to disturb the peace. While enjoying our drink before lunch one day, we turned on the news and heard that the Queen was going to visit Ireland, at great risk to herself. William was leaning over the back of Jean's chair holding a mug of beer in his hand. The news gave him such a shock that he let go of the mug, spilling the contents all over Jean from head to toe. Very good-naturedly she laughed and asked me to get some shampoo from the village shop to wash the beer out of her hair. When I returned with shampoo, Jean was standing on top of our terrace, auburn hair streaming out in the wind, looking like Queen Boadicea, and a strange man was gazing at her from the road below. Apparently he was the electrician who had come to sort our electricity faults. He hurried away, saying he would come again another day, and looking as if he had seen fairies in the wood!

Jean Drummond-Murray spent a few days with us while I was still trying to furnish the croft. We went to Campbelltown together to a sale and bought a sofa and three very comfortable upholstered chairs for the large sum of £8. On the way down Loch Fyne we stopped to look at a big grey seal on a rock below the road. Jean told me that if you sang to seals they would also sing. She tried with *Annie's Song*. The seal looked up in astonishment and slipped off its rock into the loch.

During most of our time at The Hatton Tom and Charlie were at Gargilfield preparatory school in the outskirts of Edinburgh. Every alternative weekend they had an out Sunday, when I would drive over to fetch them out for the day. It meant leaving The Hatton at 7.30 a.m. as the Forth Bridge was still under construction then.

Tom's favourite meal was roast chicken with bread sauce etc. and Charlie's was roast beef. So we had these lunches time and time about. They were always waiting for me at 9.30 a.m., peering anxiously out of the windows amongst a lot of other little pale-faced boys, never quite sure of being fetched out on time or at all. They would leap into the car, take off their school kilts and get into jeans while I was still turning round in the school drive.

On arrival home Charlie would immediately grab a fishing rod and run down to the Tay while Tom gravitated to the piano. Sometimes they spent a whole weekend with us. On one of these occasions, Tom asked if I knew the Minister of Dunkeld Cathedral, as he would like to play the organ there. He was about ten years old then. We did know the minister, a charming man, and Tom rang him up and got permission to play that afternoon when there would be no service. We drove over and Tom climbed up into the organist's small gallery. He played by memory and extemporised for at least an hour. From my pew below, a tuft of Tom's hair could just be seen above the balcony. Presently, while he was playing, tourists came in and sat down to listen. One lady stayed for a long time listening with obvious pleasure. When she got up to leave she asked if 'that little boy is anything to do with you?' With great pride I told her that he was my grandson. 'Well, I have seldom enjoyed music in a church so much as I have listening to him today.'

Now, twenty years later, Tom is organist at Aysgarth School and plays at weddings and concerts all over the country. When he played that day in Dunkeld, his arms and legs could barely stretch out to the pedals!

## Ghosts at The Hatton

Some weird things happened at The Hatton. First, Toby and Gwladys Campbell gave a small cocktail party for us in their charming little house on the other side of the lane. Among the guests was a young Major from a Scottish regiment. He was talking about fishing on the Tay and told me that he had had an extraordinary experience while night fishing on the river just below The Hatton the previous night. It seemed that when he cast his line into the water he heard a tremendous noise, like the crashing of metal on metal and yells and shouts as though a battle was going on. He thought it might possibly be revellers but discounted this as there was no one in sight or anywhere near. Feeling a bit shaken he reeled in his line and went a little further down stream. On casting again the noise of battle was more pronounced than ever, and he distinctly heard men shouting. This was too much, and feeling slightly frightened by the strangeness of the battle cries, he left. He asked me if I could tell him anything about the history of Redgorton, our part of the Tay region. As we had only just come to live there I knew nothing about that area. Later I met an old acquaintance who had lived thereabouts for many years. He gave me a book to read recounting the history of Redgorton. There had been a great battle there several hundred years ago between the Danes and the Scots. The Danes had sailed up the river, burning and killing as they progressed. At Redgorton a farmer called Hay had rallied his countrymen and attacked the enemy, finally beating them in a bloody battle a few hundred yards down-stream from The Hatton. A huge Scottish stone still stands on the spot to commemorate this victory of the Scots over the Danes. Hay was honoured by the King (don't remember if it was David or Malcolm) and given all the land over which a falcon flew, let off at Redgorton, and landing at Kinnoul, Hay becoming the Earl (chief in those days?) of Kinnoul.

In The Hatton itself there was a ghost. Rose was staying with us for Mother's funeral in September, when it was still light most of the night. I woke up and saw a girl standing beside my bed, a strange girl dressed in a simple grey dress. She had straight black hair, large dark eyes and was slightly built. I felt icy cold and terrified and unable to speak. After a while she faded out of sight. Eventually sleep came to my rescue and when I woke the sun was shining.

At breakfast I told William and Rose about the visitor. They both discounted it as part of a dream. The next morning Rose looked pale. 'Are you feeling all right?' I asked. 'Oh yes, but in the middle of the night I woke to see a young girl with dark hair and dark eyes etc. standing beside my bed. At first I was frightened and then curious. So I asked her who she was. She said "My name is Myra, but they always call me Mary." Then she disappeared.' My ghost, in another room at another time!

In November, two months after this, we were going down south by car. On the morning of our departure, when I came downstairs to give William his morning tea, he said, 'I had a charming visitor last night.' He then described the same girl that both Rose and I had seen. 'Were you frightened?' I asked. 'Oh no! I wish she had stayed, but she melted away.' Ping, our Pekinese dog, obviously saw the ghost also. His hair stood on end like a ruff round his neck sometimes, as he stared at some invisible person, his eyes following it out of the door and down the passage. Nobody in the area could tell us anything about these visitations.

Other recollections while at The Hatton are of friends called Cherry and Humphrey Evans of Megginch. Cherry had six children and they lived in a tumbledown old castle amidst squalor and grandeur. On arrival to have lunch with them one day, we were greeted by a small boy in a King Charles outfit, complete with lace collar (not a ruff!) and velvet breeches. Cherry and Humphrey were sitting on the floor in the centre of the room surrounded by what looked like diamonds. 'Oh do come in, we are mending the chandelier and have to get the pattern right.'

Lady Anstice was also a guest and during lunch gazed at Cherry in amazement. No wonder, as something was wriggling about in Cherry's ample bosom. We were at the fish course and out popped a mongoose from Cherry's chest. In a flash it had taken a morsel of fish off the plate and popped back into Cherry's bosom, there to eat its meal in comfort.

Jenny came another day to lunch with the Evans (later Drummonds, as Cherry took her father's name when he un- earthed the title of Baron Strange, never more aptly bestowed!). We were taken upstairs to Cherry's bedroom to powder our noses and saw another mongoose frolicking on the huge dou- ble bed. On the post at the end of this bed sat a cowled Peregrine falcon. Pointing at the bird, I asked 'Does he live here in your bedroom?' 'Yes, he does, except when we take him out to find food. He was there during three of my accouchements, and we named one of the boys Peregrine after him.'

At this point a little boy turned up in tears, his face covered with blood. 'What have you been doing?' enquired his mother. 'I leant out of a window but the window wasn't there and I fell out.' Naturally!

They were a most attractive and colourful family and Perthshire would not be at all the same without them.

## The Edinburgh Tattoo

Then there was the memorable occasion when I became Queen for one evening. We were invited by William's niece and her husband, Brig. John Purser, to watch the Tattoo in Edinburgh Castle from the royal box. It was all pleasantly grand, our car being met and an A.D.C. taking it away and ushering us with the Pursers to the royal box where John was standing in for the

Queen. Dorothy pushed me in front of her and John made me go in beside him while Dorothy and William sat immediately behind us. In horror I tried to get up and change position but was ordered to sit where I was by John. 'You must stand up when you see the little red light come on in front of you on the balcony edge.'

The first time this happened all went well. The next time John and I were discussing the Tattoo and I did not immediately notice the red light until I felt a sharp dig in my back from Dorothy! It was rather nerve-wracking until I saw the funny side of it, when it became fun. We sprang up while *God Save the Queen* was played at the end of the performance, all eyes upon the bogus Queen I felt, and were at last ushered out in front of everyone else. So ended my only experience of being a Queen!

From the Tattoo we went to dine at a very smart restaurant in Edinburgh. No sooner had we sat down than an old friend in the Black Watch came across the room to our table. Bowing low over my hand he said, 'I hope you enjoyed the Tattoo, Your Majesty.'

### *Visit to Jenny and Garry in Colorado*

Soon after we settled into Netherby at Castle Douglas, the Barnetts, who had been posted to Colorado Springs in U.S.A., had a baby daughter, Joanna. Garry was in his seventh heaven of joy at having a little girl. I may say that before the event, when Jenny was heavily pregnant, they all went, with Sandra the nanny, on a motoring trip for thousands of miles across to the other side of America and to Disneyland. En route they camped far up on a cliff above a canyon. Down below there were hundreds of campers beside the river. Garry very wisely refused to pitch his tent there. That night there was a terrific thunderstorm. Their tent was blown down and they huddled into the large Volkswagen soaked to the skin. Sandra told me that she was terrified and thought Jenny would have a miscarriage. In the morning they saw that there was no trace of anyone or anything in the canyon below them, all having been swept away during the night!

In due course Jenny had her lovely little girl in Colorado. They invited me to go out to them for the christening about four months later, which I did. The Army camp was at the foot of the Rockies, a vast flat plain stretching in front of them and the mountains climbing up behind – like nothing I had ever seen before. Jenny and Garry took me on a weekend trip right up into the Rockies, the snow glistening against a clear blue sky. We spent the night in a chalet and drove up into the snow next day. The Rockies were a breathtaking sight, far grander than the Alps, spreading out as far as the eye could see in the most glorious white peaks and ranges, all shapes and with deep blue shadows marking the glaciers. On our way home to Colorado Springs, we picnicked beside the source of the Colorado River amongst pinewoods. I placed my camp chair and painting gear amongst the reeds at the water's edge and did a watercolour of the scene. 'There are rattlesnakes here, you know,' Jenny told me later. Ignorance is bliss!

Still in Colorado, the American army fascinated me. Watching a small contingent jogging along, I noticed that the last soldier was rather fat and definitely flagging. 'That one at the end seems weary. Will he make it?' I asked Garry. 'That one is a woman,' Garry replied.

Then the change-over of colonels which we witnessed from a stand erected for the occasion. To my surprise the outgoing colonel was white and had a black wife, and the incoming colonel was black and had a white wife!

But I cannot leave Colorado Springs without mentioning Tweetie Kimball. She dined with us and arrived in full evening dress carrying a gun in her hand. Large, jolly and full of life, she asked Garry to put the gun somewhere and to remind her not to leave it behind when she left, adding that it was loaded. She invited me to stay with her on her ranch, which I would have liked to do very much, but I had to fly back to the U.K. the next day. Jenny told me later that when she and Garry went over to see her the first time, they were met at the door by

Tweetie holding a glass of whisky in one hand and holding a gun in the other. She was clad in a leather jacket, sombrero, trousers with calf-length boots over the top. She was most interesting to listen to, having travelled all over the world with her husband, who was something to do with the Diplomatic Service. She also collected pictures and many treasures, ranched out in the blue and shot at any cattle rustlers she came across. One of the opportunities I really regret is of being unable to visit her.

Other memories of Colorado were of the little boys speaking broad American. The birds out there were not familiar to me. One in particular which was hopping round the verandah I could not place. 'What is that bird, Robert?' 'That is a Rah-bin, Granny,' he told me, in a strong nasal accent. 'And I suppose that your name is Rah-bert?' I remarked. He looked scornfully at me, but did not reply.

Another flashback was of David and his school mates attending an end-of-term presentation ceremony. All the children were from three to five years old and all were dressed up in sky-blue gowns with mortar-board hats, complete with tassels. They all sat on a bench and awaited their turn to go up and receive their scroll from the headmistress. When David's turn came, he marched up and then, clutching his scroll, burst into tears and rushed back to his seat at the end of the line.

On my last morning in Colorado Springs, David and two horrid little American boys set fire to the prairie behind our house. Mercifully it was at once spotted by Sandra, the Barnett's nurse, who dashed out and threw a cloth over the flames and bashed out all signs of smoking grass, with a nappy of Joanna's.

My visit had to end. But the vivid pictures of Colorado and the magnificent Rocky Mountains remain with me.

\*

# Netherby, Castle Douglas

W hen we moved to Castle Douglas, Kirkcudbrightshire, I continued to help with the RNLI in which I had been interested while we lived in Perthshire. Their stores were kept in the gunroom in our house, Netherby, where different district representatives would come to replenish their stock before any RNLI events took place. Also I was put onto the Committee of the Malcolm Sargent Cancer Research for Children Association which held an annual concert in Castle Douglas, and of which Mrs Bruce Fortune was Chairman. Sadly, these charitable activities did not last very long as William was losing ground, and it became a 24-hour job looking after him.

## William's Illness

At one time during these last few months, Sandra and Joanna paid us a visit. After doing some shopping and leaving them at Netherby, I returned to find the whole house smelling of smoke and bits of burnt paper floating about the hall. Sandra rushed up, carrying Joanna in her arms. 'Oh! The Colonel nearly burnt down the house. I smelt smoke and found him standing over the fireplace with the electric poker pushed right into the flames which were shooting out in all directions. Mrs Bucknall, I cannot remain alone in the house again with the poor Colonel as I shall never know what he will do next!'

Not long after this William nearly burnt the house down by accident. In the early hours of the morning I was woken by cries of 'Fire. I am on fire!' And there was William with his hair smoking, standing against a background of flames in the doorway of his bedroom. Reaching for the telephone by my bed I rang 999, told them to bring the fire brigade to Netherby and rang off just as William was trying to re-enter his room. I grabbed hold of him, beat out the burning material of his nightshirt and the sparks on his head and managed to shut the door. As I tried to put a shawl over him and put on a dressing-gown he wandered back to his room and opened the door again. Huge flames shot across both of us, singeing our faces and hair. But I pulled him away and somehow shut the door again before getting him downstairs. In a few minutes several fire engines and an ambulance arrived and took us to hospital.

The whole of the top floor was badly damaged and the wall of his room burnt out. But the ceiling held miraculously and did not fall down to the floor below. William had trailed his bedside lamp flex beneath his bed and put the lamp on the far side of his bed. The flex ignited, set the carpet and bed on fire and in no time set the room on fire. William did not notice it until he himself was alight.

My own health broke down and Dr Carmichael made arrangements for William to go into the Castle Douglas Infirmary for three weeks while I got away for a holiday. I went to Germany to visit Jenny and Garry and family which was always a joy for me.

It was April and we all drove into Holland to see the Bulb Festival – quite the most lovely thing imaginable. The only trouble was that on our first night in Holland an enormous spider leered at me from the middle of my bed. I shrieked and Garry ran in and promptly swatted the creature. This was a relief, but my superstitious Scottish instincts warned me that it would bring me bad luck!

We visited the famous Küchen Hoff gardens, originally planted as a vegetable garden for the Grand Duchess. The gardens were enchanting, the blossom from the tall wild plums falling lightly down over us while we strolled through acres of flowering bulbs, all colours of the rainbow. We continued on to Amsterdam and to the miniature town of Amsterdam where we felt like Gulliver amongst the Lillyputians. I began to feel very giddy and strange, hot and cold shudders running down my spine. With Jenny's help I returned to the car where I lay down in the back and can remember nothing more of that trip. It transpired that I had a violent attack of influenza. Jenny kept me in bed and rang up Dr Carmichael to enquire how William was and to tell the doctor that I was laid up with 'flu and would not be fit to travel next day. Dr Carmichael said that William was in great form surrounded by pretty nurses and visitors and that I was to stay where I was until quite recovered.

The following afternoon Jenny had an urgent phone call from the doctor to say that William had had a sudden attack, was unconscious and unlikely to live more than 24 hours. Dear Garry and Jenny set everything in motion but could not get me on to any plane until early the next morning. Jenny drove me to Dusseldorf Airport, where I collapsed. She managed to find me a wheelchair and not only came to the boarding exit with me, but also came on the plane with me. She had no passport, but showed her military wife's credentials and was allowed to accompany me. She never goes anywhere without her capacious embroidery bag, and I have hazy visions of her calmly doing her embroidery beside me during the flight!

## William's Death

My grandson Charlie met us in Edinburgh, raced back to Castle Douglas and the Infirmary, where my legs would not support me at all. William was unconscious but alive, and died that night.

After a private service and cremation we had a memorial service some two weeks later in Castle Douglas. For this the whole tribe of Penaliggons stayed at Netherby plus Cressida and Alastair. The whole county turned out and most of them came back afterwards to Netherby for the wake. Dear Jean and

David Rose came down from Perthshire and we all enjoyed a very happy party! Much later I stayed with the Roses and David and I went to Redgorton by The Hatton and scattered William's ashes on the banks of the Tay.

Five months later, as this was the Year of the Disabled, I collected all remaining pictures of William's and mine, had them mounted and framed at the cheapest cost, and had an exhibition and sale at Netherby to raise funds for the disabled. To my amazement all my friends as well as the public came, and although we only charged between £7 and £20 for a picture, we made £500 in less than two hours. Sam Benn was up for a few days and was a great help. We whitewashed the old fodder barn, hung all the 42 pictures in the best positions, and sat at the receipt of custom to take the picture money. The Fentons took the gate money and I provided the tea, and of course the cost of framing, as my contribution. Catherine Henderson (Sir Nigel's wife, Admiral) said it was like a happy garden party. So began my life as a widow.

We had been married for 31 years – incredible, as it was no secret that it was a difficult marriage. As already stated somewhere at the beginning of these memoirs, it was a loveless marriage, but we made a go of it. To pretend now that I was heartbroken would be totally hypocritical. In the series on television of *To the Manor Born*, Audrey is seen after her husband's funeral leaving the church and saying to her school friend 'Is anyone looking?' On being assured that no one was about, she throws her arms in the air and cries 'Whoopee!' Well, that was more or less what I felt, but a bit exaggerated and not realised fully at the time.

William was very popular with children who were always waiting for him to do something quite outrageous! Also he was much sought after by the ladies and always a success at dinner parties when he could be relied upon to tell rather risqué but amusing stories. Cressida, his eldest daughter, was and still is a great friend of mine. His younger daughter was a bit of a worry, as she married a penniless unqualified farmer when she was 19 and immediately started a family of six children. They were constantly having to be bailed out so to speak, as they regularly went bankrupt. However, they survived, but after 28 years of marriage and six children, St. John Penaliggon walked off with a major's wife and left Felicity, far happier without him!

## Last days at Netherby

Before selling Netherby, which was too big for me on my own, Cressida and Alastair spent a few days with me. We were clearing up autumn leaves and Alastair was stoking a bonfire behind the house when two small boys appeared on top of the garden wall. They perched there watching Alastair flinging grass on to the fire which flared up, the flames reaching almost to the wee boys' toes. Said Peter to Paul (let's call them that) 'Wha' a bonfire, Paul! Wha' would we feel like if we fell in?' 'Och!' replied Paul, 'we'd feel like Joarn of Arcc, but we' nae hair and nae balls.'

More recollections of Netherby were the days we went painting. On Mondays to Southwick to the beautiful house belonging to Charles Thomas, and on Tuesdays to the Findlays at Borgue. Isabella Findlay was a truly remarkable character. Her husband Bill was legless and dying slowly of cancer. But she still had us all for our weekly sessions painting in the studio over the stables, which was connected by telephone to Bill's room downstairs. Several times a morning she would have to go down in answer to his telephone calls and returned as though nothing had occurred to disturb her. Bill himself was very brave and up to the end used to give us all drinks in the sitting room before lunch, sitting in his wheelchair and being a marvellous host. Sadly he died and after that Isabella sold the farm at Borgue to live in Kirkcudbright and the painting mornings came to an end.

About two years after we came to live in Netherby at Castle Douglas the Oakshotts sold their farm and went to live at Twynholm at Barwhinnock. Thank goodness not too far from us.

The Queen celebrated her Silver Jubilee in 1977. It seemed to me that it was only yesterday that she became a Queen up a tree in Kenya!

What else do I remember of those days? Certainly I do not recollect things in chronological order, does anyone?

While still at Netherby and while Jenny and Garry were visiting us we gave a small dinner party with Sue and Bruce Fortune amongst the guests.

Just as our visitors arrived the telephone rang. It was Sam Benn in London, greatly agitated. 'Will you please find Gran (Daisy Templetown) and tell her that Christopher is dead?' After collecting my wits and finding out what had happened to Christopher (Daisy's son aged 50) and why I had to find Daisy, it transpired that a ghastly tragedy had taken place. Christopher, who lived in London, had married for the first time ten days previously and seemed blissfully happy. He disappeared early that morning saying he was going to fetch the papers. He did not return. By midday Sam was contacted by Christopher's wife and they then telephoned the police and hospitals. At 6 p.m. Christopher was found sitting in his car, having shot himself, and leaving a note on the seat to say, 'I am very sorry, but it is all too much. Christopher Cust.' As no one had been able to contact Daisy in Kirkcudbright, Sam rang me up as he did not want the police to tell his grandmother. It was one of the most dreadful things I ever had to do.

A happier memory is of the Oakshott boys arriving one evening, all dressed up in evening clothes and telling me they were on their way to a ball and had run out of petrol in Castle Douglas. Had I a spare can? I had not, so I lent them my own little car. Next morning, no sign of my car or the boys. Later they turned up. 'Sorry, Gran, your car is parked in a ditch unharmed about eight miles away. On our return from the ball about 3 a.m. your car ran out of petrol.' They had started to walk home when a police car picked them up. The policeman said, 'These are three likely-looking lads,' and drove them back to Barwhinnock. My car was retrieved in due course.

Going back some years, I remember what a quaint little boy Charlie Oakshott was. His grandfather, Lord Oakshott, took him to the House of Lords once. They walked up and down the terrace beside the Thames while Hennie told Charlie about historical events which he thought might interest his grandson, then about seven years old. 'Well, Charlie, what do you think of it all?' Hennie asked. Charlie's reaction was 'Are there any fish in that river?'

His passion for fishing increased over the years and he loved coming to The Hatton beside the Tay where he spent all his time by the river with his rod and landing net. Many years later, in 1989 when he had just become engaged to a girl in Australia, I wrote asking him to give particulars about her. His reply was to send me a photo of himself holding a large fish which he had caught while on a recent fishing holiday, giving me its weight, size etc. At the end of the notes on the back of the photograph he said 'Ann and I will be getting married on July 8th in Ireland.'

## *The Barnetts in Northern Ireland and Germany*

The Barnetts were posted to Ireland, Garry in a staff job. Jenny took up her singing again and joined the Belfast choir. As the I.R.A. were busy with their campaign of bombing and burning, I was always rather nervous of Jenny driving to choir practice once a week in Belfast, but she never took any notice of the I.R.A. I went over to Ireland to see them four times and always enjoyed it very much. The Irish are so charming to your face, but will shoot you without warning if they feel inclined to do so. The delicious soft colours and air over there are special and quite different from our Scottish climate.

One morning while breakfasting in the kitchen, Robert aged about seven years and David five and a half, and Joanna still in her high chair, rising four years, were talking about burglars. 'Mum, what would you do if you heard burglars in the house?' asked Robert. 'Oh, I would put my head under the bedclothes and hope that they would go away,' answered Jenny, untruthfully. 'Oh we wouldn't!' the boys said. 'We would bash them on the head and kick them in the balls!' Silence for a second. 'Oh yes, Robert,' piped up Joanna, 'and I would kick all the balls down the stairs!'

Their next posting was Germany, where I again visited them more than once. Travel was no problem to me then and it gave me great joy to be with the family as much as possible. At last they came back to England to Borden for six months, but that was after William had died and I was a merry widow!

## Move to the Bungalow

Rose, ever wise and helpful, looked for a smaller and more convenient house for me while Netherby went on the market. By November she had found No. 15 Bourtree Crescent and Netherby was sold at a good profit.

During that time I had to have an operation and the bungalow I had bought was completely renovated and redecorated. By Christmas I was into this miniature *paradiso* with its lovely garden secluded from neighbours and with a view out over the fields to distant woods.

Three years passed and I settled down to life in Kirkcudbright. It must be one of the most friendly places on earth. Everyone without exception, no matter what strata of the community, were helpful and kind. Social life became quite hectic. Dear old Bill Logan, now a widower, became a really good friend, and the garden grew ever more lovely. Old friends from Perthshire and Kenya visited me and Rose often popped in to leave a brace of pheasant or just to see how Ma was getting on, so that life became happy and untroubled. Joanna Barnett, my only granddaughter, came to stay with me for three weeks while her parents went off on holiday by themselves for once.

Joanna was a delight. Aged six, she went to the local Junior Academy in Kirkcudbright every morning. Immediately she made lots of little friends and appeared to be quite unconcerned that she had never been to so large or strange a school before. At lunchtime each day I brought her home and she played old-fashioned games such as grandmother's footsteps, hide-and-seek and snap. She taught me how to grill bacon until it was crisp and then to eat it in the fingers with toast. She would roll up her tiny sleeves, push a chair up to the sink, wear my apron by tying the waist strings round her neck and get to work. No visitor has ever given me greater pleasure.

Daisy Templeton was now a widow again and living in Kirkcudbright, as Twopenny (Lord Templetown) died six months after William. She and I had so many memories to share and our destinies had brought us together in a most unlikely fashion. She was so good, I remember, to Rose when Rose nearly broke her back in a car accident aged 18.

Shortly before Daisy left Kirkcudbright to live in a very nice and expensive sheltered cottage on an estate in Hampshire near Winchester, she asked me to go on a picnic with her. It was excessively hot that day. We drove to the coast near Borgue, climbed up a very steep hill carrying our picnic with us, as if we were children, not grannies. After lunch at the top of the hill Daisy thought we should go down alongside a fence and climb over a stile in order not to have so far to walk to the car. Alas, the stile was very high and wobbly. I scrambled over but Daisy could *not*, in spite of all attempts to pull or push her. That was our last picnic.

Daisy had stayed with me in every house except the Solai Farm. She never got over her son Christopher's death, but never moaned, and bravely battled on to the last.

A few years later she died. But before then she again came into my life at a crucial moment.

# Fate or Destiny – My Crock of Gold

After three operations and periods of convalescence at Barwhinnock and also with dear Betty Murray-Usher at Carstramon, Jack and Jemima invited me out to South Africa. It was an exciting time getting everything in order and clearing up before leaving.

The newspapers were hardly ever read by me, and the obituaries scarcely glanced at. However, one day I did read down the columns, and after finishing them it suddenly struck me that I had seen a familiar name. So I read the column again and found Frampton, Deirdre, wife of Colonel George Frampton of Smallridge Devon. Memories came flooding back of Burma, rides in the early mornings and evenings; pagodas, balls and dances; and always a very young charming subaltern, George Frampton, who had asked me to marry him so long ago. I cut out the notice, put it in a little drawer in my desk thinking it might be nice to look him up one day when visiting Bindy Kennard, my cousin in Devon, an annual event for me.

Two months later, a week before leaving for the Cape, it was necessary to clear up all my papers and files so that, should I fall out of the aeroplane, everything would be in order. While clearing the bureau out fell the obituary notice. Meanwhile Bindy had asked me to spend a week or two with her and Noel in Devon when I got back from South Africa. An old friend, Beryl Critchley Salmonson, had also invited me to spend a few days with her then in Exeter.

Looking at the obituary again, I felt a strange compulsion to write to George, as though it was something I must do. So, sitting down at my desk, I did so. The letter began 'If you are the young subaltern I knew in Burma in 1928-29' etc., for of course it might have been a complete stranger. The letter ended with the explanation 'My name was then Peggy Benn.'

There was a week to go before I flew to South Africa.

Three days later, a letter popped through the letter box on to the floor. It was from the young subaltern George Frampton I had known in Burmah. The right George! He said he remembered everything about those days and sent me a snapshot which he had taken of me, riding my little horse Rebecca outside the colonel's bungalow at Maymyo. Could we arrange to meet sometime soon?

Quickly scribbling a note on my way to the airport, I told him that I was on the point of leaving for a month's visit to a place he would not have heard of, Somerset West, Africa, where I would be staying with my brother Jack Benn. But it would be nice to meet on my return while visiting my cousins in Devon. To my amazement he wrote to me c/o Jack in South Africa saying that he knew Somerset West very well as his late wife's parents had lived there for many years.

After a glorious holiday with Jack and Jemima, which included a safari through the Karoo, I flew back and went straight to Jenny and Garry who were stationed temporarily at Borden. A letter from George awaited me there posted on from Kirkcudbright, suggesting that he would come up to me at Jenny's and spend a couple of nights at a pub nearby, and would ring me up to make a date. Another very old boy friend was also in England from Kenya at that time, Michael Blundell. First Michael telephoned but I could not fit in a meeting with him as he was leaving for Kenya two days later. Then George rang up. It was quite unnerving to hear him speak to me again on the telephone or any other way. He was ill with flu. A little disappointing and I wondered what old age had done to him! But he made a firm date to collect me from Beryl's house in Exeter two weeks later. Jenny was highly amused by all the telephone calls, and with a twinkle in her eye asked, 'Do I hear wedding bells?' From Borden I went to visit Bindy and then Beryl.

Well at last George and I did meet, at Beryl's house. She had provided coffee and when George brought my cup to me he shook like a leaf! When he stepped out of the car, he was wearing driving spectacles and was not immediately recognisable as the George I had known. He was stouter, having been as thin as a stick in his youth, but when he removed the glasses and came up and kissed me, it was as though 55 years fell away and we were back to 1928. As he told somebody a little later, 'we just went straight on where we left off.' Unlike me, who had been white-haired for years, he still had masses of wavy gold hair and a naughty twinkle in his blue eyes. He drove me to his cottage near Axminster where I spent two days before going on to stay with Daisy.

Back in Kirkcudbright correspondence between George and me by post and telephone became a regular habit. Bindy rang up about two weeks after my return to Scotland asking me to go down again as dear Noel had died of a heart attack. So back I went to the funeral and again spent a few days with George at Smallridge. This time I met a charming couple, Mary and Ken Mead. They obviously thought we would ultimately marry.

1983. Christmas that year was spent with Rose, Michael and the three boys, at Barwhinnock. A lovely Christmas, so happy, and after dinner that night Tom played old-fashioned tunes such as *I Want to Be Happy* and *Tea for Two* while Rose and I danced the Charleston. George telephoned to me after lunch by arrangement. Tom's comment was, 'Your chap rang and you must ring back.' When that was done and I returned to the sitting room Charlie said, without looking up, 'Is he rich?'

Rose had never met George until he came up to visit me in the spring, and was a bit concerned. A month later he came again to drive me south before I went to Germany to spend Easter with the Barnetts. The day after he arrived he proposed and I accepted him and he rushed out to buy a bottle of champagne. We rang Rose and said she should come round for a drink that evening and meet my fiancé!

A great friend and character, Betty Murray-Usher, telephoned that afternoon, informing me that she would be calling in to see me but would probably not get out of the car. She did call and I pressed her to come in for a little celebration drink. 'I know what you are going to tell me,' she said. 'You are engaged to George. I knew a week ago.' Well, a week ago I certainly did not know that. She drank half the bottle of champagne and left us with her blessing. Rose arrived as Betty was leaving and there was only just enough for the three of us to drink a toast!

And so that was how and when I found my Crock of Gold, at the end of the Rainbow which had stretched over nearly 54 years of my life.

We had not intended to marry until July or August, but time and age made us decide on an earlier date. So we got married very quietly in Honiton on May 11th 1984, and had a Blessing

*George & Peggy on their wedding day, 11 May 1984.*

Service afterwards given by dear old Canon Forster in Smallridge Church.

The grandchildren were furious with me for not having a proper wedding. But as a grandmother of 74 and getting married for the third time, that was really too much for me.

A few weeks later George and I flew out to Germany to stay with the Barnetts. It was lovely to be with them and to see how much they loved George and he them. To my amusement on our first morning there, a knock on our bedroom door was followed by Robert and David carrying in a tray of early morning tea! Their eyes were full of curiosity – Granny, in bed with George! Wow!

While in Germany, Jenny took us on a trip to Furstenberg. It was a most charming old town with an ancient castle in which the famous Furstenberg china was displayed. All laid out on tables as if for tea-parties or dinner-parties etc. and all for sale. Jenny asked us which of the many beautiful teasets we liked best. A difficult choice amongst so many exquisite pieces.

Some weeks later after we had returned to Bourtree Crescent a large parcel arrived. In it was the teaset we had liked the best. 'A wedding present to you both with love from Jenny and Garry and the children.' It was typical of Jenny and Garry.

There was a memorable visit to Bindy in Devon. Her cook, a Mrs Sweet, was so fascinated by the romance of our story, that she made a two-tier wedding cake for us! We all had a hilariously happy visit to dear Bindy who instantly fell in love with George.

We were still living in Devon and Scotland, driving up and down at least three or four times a year. This became too much for us and George sold the cottage at Smallridge to his daughter-in-law Yvonne Frampton, which turned out to be a very happy arrangement for all. We were and are blissfully happy together. But life is not like that. The Rainbow has every colour in it including black.

### Tragedy

On April 28th 1985 Rose and Michael came to dine. It was their wedding anniversary and for once the food turned out as hoped and we enjoyed a game of bridge afterwards. Rose looked radiantly happy and so did Michael: a joy to see them. It was the last time I was to see my adored daughter.

On May 18th Rose drove up to Edinburgh for a young cousin's wedding. Tom, her elder son, was playing the organ, so Rose waited while he finished the Voluntary at the end of the service. Tom came up to her and she said to him 'Oh darling, you have not got a buttonhole. We'd better take a carnation from this vase . . .' and dropped dead at Tom's feet.

The news was broken to me that evening. The agony of it and irreparable loss to us all is beyond words. Tom was marvellous. Charlie was in Ireland and due to leave for Australia the following week. Angus was in London. Jenny was in Germany. At a stroke, the core of our lives was torn out. George was a tower of strength and comfort. Jenny said afterwards she did not know what any of us would have done without him. Tom, that wonderful young man, played the organ at his mother's funeral. I can remember nothing about it but an agonising blur. Why? Why Rose? These are things we shall never understand. Poor Michael and the boys.

One unforgettable memory. Our dear daily help, deeply moved by Rose's death, went out and bought some orchids, the most expensive of flowers, and left them on the hall chest where I found them later. A kindness from the heart never to be forgotten.

*

Time passed. Garry Barnett was posted to Rome on a six month course for Brigadiers. George and I went out to stay with them for three magical weeks. Halcyon weather, wonderful buildings and ruins, works of art, delicious meals. The dominant dome of St. Peter's and a weekend in Siena. The three children were all there for the holidays. Heaven! Their flat, not the Army allocation, was huge and at the top of a six-storey building on the outskirts of Rome. It had a verandah 20 feet wide all round it.

On the road side, one could look down into the balconies of other flats opposite. The boys asked their father if they might borrow his field glasses one day. They were absent rather a long time. Presently Joanna asked Jenny if she could borrow her field glasses. Intrigued, Jenny followed Joanna to the balcony where the boys were gazing at a pair of lovers cavorting on a balcony across the street. Joanna, after looking through the binoculars, remarked 'rather bad luck on the girl!' She was ten years old then.

After their sojourn in Rome, the Barnetts were sent to Warminster where Garry was Commandant. Wonderful for me after so long a time when they were abroad. The boys went to Eton, and Joanna to Westheath School.

For my eightieth birthday on July 21st 1989, George and I were driven down to Warminster by Michael and Clare, his new wife. Jenny had all the Oakshotts and us staying in the house and they combined to give me the most wonderful birthday party I have ever had. The weather was scorching hot for a change, the luncheon party was held beneath the trees at the bottom of the garden, and the food, all made by the family, most *delicious.* The Kennards and husbands, the Rumbolds, the Benns and St. Maurs/Kemmis Bettys, and old Kenya friends rallied round contributing to one of the happiest days of my life. And of course George, darling George, ever loving and considerate, who was at the beginning and end of my life. God bless them all and everyone in my life, and thanks to *le bon Dieu*

*Kirkcudbright*
*21st July 1990*

# Epilogue

## *The Caravan Moves On*

Rose and Michael's sons have chosen their careers. Tom has never deviated from music and is at Aysgarth School in charge of all branches of music and choirs and plays. He has made a great name for himself in Yorkshire and goes all over the British Isles to play at weddings and takes his choir to sing and give concerts in aid of all the crumbling churches and buildings in the country. He has his own small but charming cottage near Richmond and appears to be completely happy.

Charlie is in Australia running a stud farm near Melbourne. He married an Irish R.C. girl from Newray last summer and they have a baby daughter, Roseanne, which makes me a great-grandmother!

Angus, who at the age of seven told me that he was going to be a millionaire, has worked hard, had many trials and works in a stockbrokers' on the Stock Exchange and lives in his flat for one in London.

Michael, after two years of dreadful unhappiness, met and married a Lincolnshire lass, Clare. After the initial family rows and storms, the boys have not only accepted her but have grown very fond of her. George and I liked her from the beginning. Totally different from anyone else, she showed courage in taking on the job of second wife and stepmother. Large, generous-hearted and honest, Clare is genuinely kind and very capable. Intelligent, hard-working and full of initiative and fun, she makes Michael very happy and is also most kind and affectionate to us old codgers!

My beloved Barnetts are coming to the end of their life in Warminster and about to take up a military job in Rhodesia. Oh dear! It is now called Zimbabwe. Jenny, ever-thoughtful for others, a wonderful daughter, stepdaughter, wife and mother, living a full life, still finds time to join and sing in choirs everywhere they go, as well as doing everything else as well.

George's nice married son, Jeremy, with his wife and daughter live in Devon and London. Judy, his daughter, seems happy with her life as a committed Christian and secretary to a firm of solicitors in Balcombe Sussex. George and I live so happily together, every day is a bonus.

We have many interests in common: birds, gardening, music, love of the countryside and also flashes of luxury, when we go off for a weekend to an expensive club in London and go to the theatre, or to a country hotel such as Knockinham, run by a young French couple who are perfectionists as well as the Premier Cuisiniers in Scotland. And bridge keeps our brains moving.

To all those I have loved throughout my long and varied life, to so many lovely people all round the world, I say *thank you* for making life so full of fun, interest, excitement, tragedy, romance, laughter and tears.

Life is a Rainbow!